Steven
Doctor
The Critical ...
Matt Smith's First Series
(Unauthorized)

G000134274

Steven Cooper
&
Kevin Mahoney

Punked Books

Published in 2011 by Punked Books
An Authortrek imprint

Punked Books
C/O Authortrek
PO Box 54168
London
W5 9EE

Steven Moffat's Doctor Who, the Critical Fan's Guide to
Matt Smith's First Series (Unauthorized)
Copyright © 2011 by Steven Cooper & Kevin Mahoney

Steven Cooper's reviews (Copyright © Steven Cooper 2010)
were originally published on *Slant Magazine*'s *House Next
Door* blog, whose editors have kindly granted permission for
them to be reprinted within this book.

Cover image © Rolffimages/Dreamstime.com

First Edition

Steven Cooper and Kevin Mahoney assert the moral right
under the Copyright, Designs and Patents Act 1988 to be
identified as the authors of this work.

All Rights reserved. No part of this publication may be
reproduced, stored in a retrieval system or transmitted, in
any form or by any means without the prior consent of the
author, nor be otherwise circulated in any form of binding or
cover other than that which it is published and without a
similar condition being imposed on the subsequent
purchaser.

Contents

Foreword

I first conceived this book in late 2010, as I had an inkling that Steven Moffat's first series of *Doctor Who* was complex enough to warrant an entire book devoted to it, and this has indeed proved to be the case. Since *Doctor Who* was revived in 2005, a lot of BBC books have been published about the series, which are very much derived from the production team's perspective. The advent of the internet during the long hiatus of the series has meant that you no longer see such a great abundance of printed fanzines, as most such commentary is now published online. Indeed, Steven Cooper's excellent reviews of the 5th series, which form an integral part of this book, were originally published online. So, I thought it would be a good idea to publish a book on the series from the fans' perspective.

Our aim in this book, as the title suggests, has been to provide constructive criticism of Matt Smith's first series. However, fear not: this does not mean that we endlessly complain, for we have not come to bury Caesar. No, we point out where we feel that there are inconsistencies in this series, and which aspects didn't work so well, but we also highlight the parts that we feel have been superbly executed.

Steven Cooper's reviews were written straight after the broadcast of each episode. I have decided to retain, rather than remove, any speculation on his part as to future events within this series, as I think it's valuable to have a record of what his initial impressions were as each individual episode was broadcast. Indeed, I indulge in quite a lot of speculation myself, because, at the time of writing, the whole story arc has not been completed, as it very much runs into series 6.

For my part, I must say that I have found this to be a very valuable exercise. For instance, on first viewing, there were a few episodes that I didn't really like. However, having watched them again, I began to appreciate them a lot more, especially within the context of the series of the whole. Your perspective of series 5 will change somewhat if you watch all the episodes back to back within a few days, as Steven

Moffat no doubt intended when he crafted such an intricate story line. I must admit that I rather fell out of the habit of repeatedly watching each episode of *Doctor Who* during the series' hiatus, but I'm happy now that Moffat's inspiring work has very much got me back into this habit.

Kevin Mahoney
February 2011

1: The Eleventh Hour

Writer: Steven Moffat
Director: Adam Smith
Originally broadcast: 3 April 2010

Cast

The Doctor: Matt Smith
Amy Pond: Karen Gillan
Rory Williams: Arthur Darvill
Amelia: Caitlin Blackwood
Dr. Ramsden: Nina Wadia
Barney Collins: Marcello Magni
Ice Cream Man: Perry Benson
Mrs. Angelo: Annette Crosbie
Jeff: Tom Hopper
Mr. Henderson: Arthur Cox
Mother: Olivia Colman
Child 1: Eden Monteath
Child 2: Merin Monteath
Atraxi Voice: David de Keyser
Prisoner Zero Voice: William Wilde
Patrick Moore: Himself

Steven's review: This opening episode lives up to its title by being an hour long rather the standard 45 minutes, and introduces our all-new regular cast line-up of Matt Smith as the Eleventh Doctor and Karen Gillan as his new companion Amy Pond.

This is the first episode to be overseen by new showrunner Steven Moffat, taking over from Russell T Davies, the man behind *Doctor Who*'s incredibly successful resurrection over the last five years. Moffat contributed one story to each of the last four seasons, to great acclaim each time. He was the natural and popular choice to take over the top job, and this year he is writing seven episodes (including the Christmas special), overseeing the other seven, and devising the season arc into which they all fit. Naturally, the change of showrunner brings with it one of *Doctor Who*'s periodic shifts in style and emphasis, which is apparent even in this first episode. The Davies era was concerned (particularly at the start) with embedding the essential strangeness of the Doctor within the context of normal urban life that the non-fan audience could relate to - as exemplified by the central character of Rose Tyler. Moffat seems more willing to embrace strangeness for its own sake; his episodes often seemed to stand apart from the overall narrative lines of Davies' seasons (I'm thinking particularly of *The Girl in the Fireplace* and *Blink*). In terms of its basic plot, *The Eleventh Hour* parallels the 2007 season opener *Smith and Jones* - an escaped alien prisoner is hiding on Earth, other aliens pursuing it arrive trying to track it down, and the situation escalates into a threat to the entire planet - but the differences in tone are striking. Instead of taking place in London, the whole story is contained within a quiet English village, with almost no reference to the wider world at all.

We pick up just after *The End of Time* left off, with the wrecked, burning TARDIS tumbling down to Earth. What will be our last sight of the familiar control room has the Doctor dangling from the open doorway and hanging on for dear life, as the console succumbs to gigantic explosions in a "we're never going to be needing this set again" manner. This sequence segues into what turned out to be my least favourite thing in the whole episode - the revamped title sequence. The visuals are mostly fine, with the TARDIS now being tossed around through a much stormier vortex than before, although the big metallic blue font in which our stars' names zap into view (complete with lightning bolts) makes the *Superman*-style zooming in the previous title sequence look like a model of restraint. No, the real problem is the music. I've enjoyed the various orchestral arrangements of the *Doctor Who* theme used over the past five years, but I was hoping for a turn back towards the spooky original Delia Derbyshire version - still the best after nearly fifty years. Instead, Murray Gold has come up with a

Hooked on Classics rendition that buries the actual theme under a pile of extraneous noise. Particularly unwelcome are the brass fanfares blaring over the opening bars, and the drum machine obscuring the melody line. It gets a little better towards the end, with an interesting choral bit, but it's still one of the weakest versions of the theme I've heard. A pity, because I thought Gold's incidental music for this episode was generally excellent.

Of course, the most important facet of this new-look *Doctor Who* is the new Doctor himself. Everyone was waiting to see how relative unknown Matt Smith would cope with the task of taking over the role from the incredibly popular David Tennant. Most of the misgivings were over his age - at 27, he is the most youthful Doctor ever. For all Moffat's statements about how Smith had blown them away in his audition, instantly getting the character of the Doctor, the concerns remained - just how believable could this guy be playing a 900-and-something-year-old alien?

Well, after just this one episode, I'm prepared to deliver a verdict - Moffat and co. have got it *spectacularly* right. Matt Smith has absolutely grabbed the role of the Doctor and made it his own, with an assurance and confidence rivalling that in Tom Baker's arrival 35 years ago. He certainly doesn't play it as young in any way. In fact, he seems to me a quieter, more cerebral Doctor than either Eccleston or Tennant, with his mind constantly whirring away observing and making connections, staying one step ahead of everyone else; I had no trouble believing he could be the smartest guy in any room. Combined with this is an amusing eccentricity in his movements - an "elegant shambles," to use Moffat's own excellent description - that makes him continually watchable. It's a truly impressive performance, and I'm genuinely looking forward now to seeing where he takes the Doctor over the course of this season.

One thing the producers did to help him was to employ the strategy also used back in 1982 when Peter Davison (at that time, the youngest Doctor ever) had the same challenge, following on from the iconic Tom Baker. Davison filmed three later stories, allowing him to fine-tune his characterisation and performance, before going back to tackle his debut adventure. In the same way, episodes 2 through 5 of this season were in the can before *The Eleventh Hour* started filming. It'll be interesting to see over the next few weeks whether there's any sign of tentativeness or indecision in Smith's earlier episodes, because he seemed totally in command of his performance through every moment of this one.

He's also helped by the structure of the script, which gives him the space to show off what he can do by starting with an uninterrupted fifteen-minute section where we see only his Doctor, interacting with one other character. The TARDIS ends up crashed on its side in the garden of a home-alone seven-year-old Scottish girl, Amelia Pond, who has been praying for someone to come and fix an odd crack in her bedroom wall. She's initially wary of the strange man who climbs out of the box demanding apples and falls to the ground ("Who are you?" "I don't know yet. I'm still cooking"), but his manner is so direct and child-like that they immediately connect, and he sets off to investigate the crack - though not before walking straight into a tree. ("Early days... steering's a bit off.")

In the kitchen, the physical comedy continues as the girl tries to keep up with his cravings for various foods - apples, yoghurt, bacon ("You're Scottish, fry something"), baked beans, bread and butter - with him deciding he hates each one and spitting them out or making disgusted faces. My favourite part was the flinging of the plate of bread and butter out into the night ("And *stay* out!") - followed, naturally, by off-screen crash and yowling cat noises. He finally settles on a couple of quintessential childhood foods, fish fingers and custard - together. They sit down companionably to eat at the kitchen table, where we learn that Amelia is an orphan, living with her aunt. So far this scene might seem like a prolonged comic diversion, but now comes a great payoff:

The Doctor: "You're not scared of anything. Box falls out

9

of the sky, man falls out of a box, man eats fish custard...
and look at you. Just sitting there. So you know what I
think?"

Amelia: "What?"

The Doctor: "Must be a hell of a scary crack in your wall."

The last line, suddenly pulling us back to the plot with a
suitably ominous musical cue, is perfectly played by Smith.
It was not long after this point that I realized any worries I'd
had about whether he was up to the role had completely
disappeared.

Steven Moffat is a master of using fears children can relate
to to fuel his stories - in *The Girl in the Fireplace* it was
monsters under the bed; here it's a weird crack in a bedroom
wall through which strange noises can be heard. The Doctor
discovers that it's a "crack in the skin of the universe"
leading to another place entirely, and they hear an alien
voice saying, "Prisoner Zero has escaped." This leads to
another creepy idea, of some presence lurking in your house
unseen, never able to be glimpsed except out of the corner of
your eye.

But before the Doctor can investigate further, the TARDIS
cloister bell sounds, warning that the machine faces
imminent destruction. The Doctor rushes back inside;
Amelia asks to come with him, but he says it's not safe yet,
making a fateful promise to her that he'll be back in five
minutes. The TARDIS vanishes; Amelia rushes to pack a
little suitcase, takes it down to the garden, and sits on it,
waiting for her friend to return...

Doctor Who hasn't always had the best fortune with child
actors, but they really lucked out with Caitlin Blackwood as
young Amelia. She gives a perfect natural, open
performance - especially impressive considering she had no
prior acting experience. (She's also, incidentally, a cousin of
Karen Gillan, and the family resemblance really helps to sell
the idea that they're the same person.) I particularly loved
her deadpan delivery of "What...a real one?" when the
Doctor told her his box was actually a time machine.

The TARDIS returns, belching smoke and needing to shut

down and rebuild itself. The Doctor manages to not notice that it's now daylight outside as he runs into the house yelling for Amelia, having realized that this "Prisoner Zero" must have been hiding in there. Someone knocks him out from behind, and he wakes up to find himself handcuffed to a radiator by an attractive policewoman wearing a very non-regulation short skirt. She is, of course, the now grown-up Amy Pond. Most of the Doctor's female companions tend to get tagged with the description "feisty" (actually, is there any young female lead character who isn't described as "feisty" these days?) but rather than just present that as a given, the story shows us how she got that way. This time, the Doctor has managed to change the course of his companion's life even before she joins him.

She eventually has to abandon the pretence of being a policewoman, crying "I'm a kissogram!" before pulling off her hat and letting loose a mass of ginger hair with a swish worthy of a shampoo advert. Karen Gillan and Matt Smith have a tremendous chemistry together, batting Moffat's comic dialogue back and forth ("Why a policewoman?" "You broke into my house - it was this or a French maid!") while showing how the initial spikiness between them slowly eases as the Doctor wins Amy's trust. This culminates in a hilarious scene where Amy, still not quite believing that this man is her childhood friend come back, traps the Doctor's tie in a car door in order to get him to talk sense. In a typical piece of Moffat cleverness, he wins her over by producing an apple that Amelia gave him earlier. It's a lovely bonding moment between them, which works even in spite of the director resorting to slow motion and lens flares in a misguided attempt to make it "magical".

Apart from the sheer enjoyability of Moffat's dialogue (I've had to severely resist the temptation to quote more of my favourite moments, or this recap would end up twice as long), there are any number of places where lines will link up with or reflect others elsewhere - this script has clearly been polished to within an inch of its life. For example:

The Doctor: "Who's Amy? You were Amelia."

Amy: "Yeah, and now I'm Amy."

The Doctor: "Amelia Pond. That was a great name!"

Amy: "Bit fairytale."

This is an ironic reference back to the kitchen table scene, where the Doctor delightedly told young Amelia Pond her name was "like a name in a fairytale." What an efficient way of showing how the disappointment of the Doctor's failure to return for her would lead Amy to grow up burying her dreams beneath a brittle, somewhat cynical personality. Or there's this, which will come back at the end:

Amy: "You told me you had a time machine."

The Doctor: "And you believed me."

Amy: "Then I grew up."

The Doctor: "Oh, you never want to do that."

Once Amy's trust is regained, we get into the actual plot part of the story - the Doctor tracking down Prisoner Zero before the pursuing aliens, the Atraxi, lose patience and burn the planet. Although the plotting fizzes along with Moffat's usual ingenuity, this stuff can't help but be less interesting, partly because the only real characters in the story are the Doctor, Amy, and Amy's "kind of" boyfriend, Rory. Everyone else is strictly functional, even when they're being played by Annette Crosbie, Nina Wadia, or Olivia Colman - and not forgetting a bonkers cameo from the great Patrick Moore. The Doctor quickly hacks into a worldwide videoconference call to release a computer virus that will reset all clocks and displays to zero in order to get the Atraxi's attention. It's interesting that neither Torchwood nor UNIT, which loomed so large in the previous era, are so much as mentioned - Moffat seems to be recalibrating the world of the show away from the situation that developed over the last five years, where pretty much everyone in the world was aware of both the existence of aliens and the organizations that deal with them.

Prisoner Zero itself makes for a somewhat underwhelming foe - rather like the skeletons in spacesuits in *Silence in the Library*, it tends to not actually *do* anything apart from look menacing. The concept of a shape-changing creature that can look like multiple creatures at once, e.g. a man and a dog, is very good, and it's nicely unsettling when the man and dog keep moving their heads in sync. Later, it takes the form of a mother and her two girls, and it's momentarily chilling when the mother's voice comes out of one of the children's mouths. And I liked the final twist where it takes the form of the Doctor, thanks to its link with Amy, and young Amelia peeks out from behind him (again, cleverly reflecting a shot from earlier). But the creature's natural form is a rather unimpressive CGI snake, and the idea of having the human disguises suddenly open their mouths to reveal the alien's fangs gets way overused. (While I'm on the subject of the CGI, the Atraxi ships themselves are one of the goofiest designs ever seen in *Doctor Who* - basically a giant eyeball inside a spinning snowflake. It almost works in spite of itself out of sheer oddness.)

The intricate plot mechanism finally works itself out as Prisoner Zero, tracked to a hospital where it has been using coma patients as sources for its disguises, is tricked into reverting to its natural form, when it is detected and recaptured by the Atraxi. Before it disappears, however, it provides some mysterious hints of something big to come. "The universe is cracked. The Pandorica will open. Silence will fall." What does that mean? At this stage, I've no idea...

Up until now, the Doctor has been borne along by the plot, but now, with his regeneration almost complete, he finally takes control. First, he orders the Atraxi to come back and face him because of their threat to burn "a fully established Level Five planet". Then he casts off the persona of the "Raggedy Doctor" as he finds some new clothes in the hospital lockers (following a precedent set by the Third and Eighth Doctors). Up on the roof of the hospital, he confronts the Atraxi.

Matt Smith is given an iconic moment, as he tells the Atraxi to check whether the Earth is protected, and they project holograms of the ten previous Doctors. He walks through the image of David Tennant to reveal the Eleventh Doctor, complete at last in his professorial costume with tweed jacket, braces and bow tie, ready to see off these aliens with one simple line:

The Doctor: "Hello. I'm the Doctor. Basically... run."

With the threat over, the Doctor is delighted to discover that the TARDIS has finished repairing itself. Immediately forgetting everything else, he dashes off. Amy runs after him, but to her astonished dismay the box dematerialises in front of her.

In the next scene, Amy is woken in the night by the sound of the TARDIS arriving back in her garden. The Doctor apologizes for rushing off - he was only taking his brand new time machine on a "quick hop" to the moon and back. But - surprise! - erratic navigation has struck again... "That was *two years ago*!" As the saying goes, history repeats itself, first as tragedy, second as farce.

Finally, Amy gets her chance to enter the magic box. But she's no longer sure she really wants to.

The Doctor: "You wanted to come fourteen years ago."

Amy: "I grew up."

The Doctor: "Don't worry. I'll soon fix that."

With a snap of the fingers, the Doctor opens the door (a nice callback to Moffat's *Forest of the Dead*). The new interior is a warmer, more magical space than the single echoing chamber of the previous era. There are now multiple levels, stairways leading off to other areas, and a console full of strange objects - levers, gauges, hot and cold taps, a typewriter, even an old gramophone horn.

These last few scenes are played perfectly by Smith and Gillan. They already seem like a great Doctor/companion team, falling into an easy banter, and yet they are both keeping information from each other. Just as the Doctor is promising he had no ulterior motive for asking Amy along, the TARDIS scanner screen beside him is showing an image of a line in the exact same shape as the crack in the bedroom wall. Cue ominous music...

And Amy asks him to agree to get her back tomorrow morning, but won't say why - "Just...you know, stuff." After the TARDIS has left, we pan across Amy's room to reveal...

a wedding dress hanging in her wardrobe. She has run away on the night before her wedding…why? For one final childhood adventure before she has to finally grow up? Or for some other reason? I can't wait to find out.

Steven's Classic Who DVD Recommendation: *Robot*, starring Tom Baker in his very first story as the Doctor. As I mentioned above, Baker's performance in this story, where he just completely inhabits the role of the Doctor from the off, came strongly to mind when I saw Matt Smith's debut.

Kevin's review: *The Eleventh Hour* is a splendid introduction for Matt Smith's Eleventh Doctor. "Cometh the Hour, Cometh Who da Man!" one might say in the light of Steven Moffat's incredibly witty script. So sublime is the dialogue that it comes as a great surprise to read in *The Brilliant Book of Doctor Who 2011* that Moffat found *The Eleventh Hour* to be the most difficult script to write of Matt Smith's first series, because it had to be written in such a short space of time. However, one suspects that Moffat has had much of this dialogue running around his head for many years, such as when the Doctor exclaims "Who da man!" Hurt by the lack of reaction to this outcry, the Doctor decides that he's never going to say this again.

Which is probably just as well, because on closer inspection, this exclamation only works if one has heard of a certain TV programme called *Doctor Who* (which obviously doesn't exist in the Doctor's universe), since "Doctor Who" is not the Doctor's actual name. Although this didn't stop supercomputer WOTAN calling him "Doctor Who" in the 1966 adventure *The War Machines*, and author Bill Strutton also mistakenly used this appellation throughout his novelisation of another Sixties adventure, *The Web Planet*. So, it's not surprising that there's no reaction from Amy and Rory to the Doctor's outcry, as it makes no sense when one dissects it in detail. However, such is the exuberance of Steven Moffat's dialogue, that we let him get away with it, especially since it very much fits the spirit of the script and the characterisation of the Eleventh Doctor. It goes without saying that Moffat himself, with his great love of *Doctor Who*, would know that having the Doctor say "Who da man!" is technically an error, but it's such a great line full of contemporary verve that it would have been a crime not to use it. I didn't mean to start off this review by examining such a short line in great forensic detail. However, Moffat's very great attention to detail was one of the main reasons why this book was commissioned, as there is a great deal to be discovered and discussed about even the most minor of features in each episode.

The first adventure of any Doctor can be rather a hit and miss affair. There have been some disasters, such as Colin Baker's *The Twin Dilemma* (which suffered from poor production values and script, along with a rather foolhardy decision to deliberately make the new Doctor unlikeable), while both Sylvester McCoy's *Time and the Rani* and Tom Baker's *Robot* were silliness personified. Tom Baker got over the indignity of having to dress up in a poor Viking costume to hold the record of appearing in the most episodes of the show. Colin Baker never really recovered from that bad start, especially since it portrayed him trying to strangle his assistant Peri in a moment of post-regenerative angst. There was also the fact that the production team decided to have his first adventure broadcast immediately after Peter Davison's final one, with the result that viewers ultimately had to wait 9 months for Colin Baker's next adventure to see whether they really liked him or not. Michael Grade, the BBC Controller at the time, didn't like either Colin Baker or the programme, which led him to put the series on hiatus for 18 months, and to slash the number of episodes for future series by half. It was this that ultimately led to the Classic Series' demise. So the first adventure of each Doctor can really be life or death affairs.

I think the best first Doctor adventure is probably the original, *The Power of the Daleks*, in which Patrick Troughton made the role his own, winning over both his suspicious companions and the viewers with his sparklingly impish personality. The device of having the Doctor regenerate was an ingenious one, which, probably more than anything else, enabled the series' longevity. A lot of *Doctor Who* fans rate Patrick Troughton's second Dalek adventure, *The Evil of the Daleks* more highly, but I've always thought that *Power* portrayed the Daleks at probably their most intelligent and menacing, as they pretend to be servants to human colonists while subtly building up their numbers in secret, a tactic that they later re-adopted in this series' *Victory of the Daleks*.

Peter Davison's debut, *Castrovalva*, was a subtle and intelligent piece. Since there'd only been 4 previous Doctors, Davison demonstrated his range by adopting the persona of each forebear in this story, which was especially poignant as the programme neared its 20th anniversary. This is obviously something that Matt Smith couldn't do (although his tone of voice often reminds me of Davison, as well as his youth) as impersonating 10 previous Doctors would have been extremely wearisome, and would have lost the majority of viewers who hadn't watched it throughout its nearly 50 year history. So, having the Atraxi project an image of Matt Smith's predecessors was an excellent workaround, especially since it ended with the Eleventh Doctor truly asserting his new persona for the first time.

The most action-packed debut for a Doctor was Jon Pertwee's *Spearhead from Space* in 1970. In another departure for the series, this was the first adventure broadcast in colour. Thanks to some timely BBC industrial action, this story was shot entirely in film, which gave it even more of a glossier sheen. Robert Holmes, who is widely recognised to be the best writer of the Classic Series, wrote the script. *Spearhead from Space* is a rollicking adventure that is only let down by the appearance of a extremely rubbery monster at the end, and the expression on Pertwee's face is perhaps too comedic as this Nestene tries to strangle the Doctor. It could be however, that the single eye of the Nestene peering from out of its tank is what influenced Moffat's depiction of the Atraxi. Certainly, as

Steven has noted in his review above, the trait of the Doctor stealing clothes in a hospital was first seen in *Spearhead from Space*.

This is something the Eighth Doctor did also, although, like the Third Doctor, this is understandable as both were both were in hospital as a result of their respective regenerations. However, unlike Pertwee, Matt Smith's Doctor appears to be devoid of a cobra tattoo… (Perhaps one day we can have a mash-up with Stieg Larsson's fiction entitled *The Time Lord with a Cobra Tattoo*?) And of course, *Spearhead from Space* was the first adventure to feature the Autons, who would go on to appear in the Ninth Doctor's debut adventure, *Rose* (albeit not a regeneration story), and this series' *The Pandorica Opens*. *Spearhead from Space*, like *Rose*, also heralded an era in which most of the stories were set on Earth. The Third Doctor was assisted by the 'UNIT family', albeit Brigadier Lethbridge-Stewart and Sergeant Benton only really started as foils for the Doctor, rather than fully rounded characters such as Rose, her mother, and Mickey Smith.

One great departure from his predecessor is Moffat's decision to present Amy as an orphan, so while Rory is there as a 'sort-of' boyfriend, Amy doesn't have a mum or dad to fall back on, unlike Rose (who of course, does eventually run into her missing father). In Amelia's case, it's both her parents who are missing (although, in a strange episode that we may return to in the 6th series, Amelia does relate that she remembers her mother giving her apples with strange Halloweenesque faces carved into them).

In the *Doctor Who Confidential* that accompanied the succeeding episode (*The Beast Below*), Moffat revealed that the main reason why he had chosen to introduce the Doctor to Amy first as a little girl, and then as an older woman, was due to the fact that the Eleventh was the first Doctor to regenerate without any companions present. Thus, Amy's reluctance to recognise this man as the "Raggedy Doctor" from her childhood mirrors the viewer's reluctance to let go of their identification of the Doctor with the previous incumbent (David Tennant). So, in *The Eleventh Hour*, Matt Smith endeavours to convince both Amy and us that he is indeed the Doctor. On a pedantic note, it must be pointed out that Patrick Troughton's Doctor regenerated into Jon Pertwee's with no companions present. In this instance, the Time Lords were kind enough to drop him into the lap of casual acquaintance Brigadier Lethbridge-Stewart, who also took some persuading with regards to the Doctor's true identity.

When Steven Moffat was first announced as the new showrunner, I was initially concerned that this would lead to an abundance of children appearing in the series, as many of his stories have featured kids. Who can forget the boy with a gas mask seemingly glued to his face asking, "Are you my mummy?" in Moffat's first episode *The Empty Child*? As its title would suggest, *The Girl in the Fireplace* featured a very young Madame de Pompadour in the beginning, while the scenes with the young girl are the only parts of *Silence in the Library/Forest of the Dead* that don't really work.

Very few children appeared in the Classic Series of *Doctor Who*, despite the fact that the programme's often regarded as being mainly focused at kids. Admittedly, the Doctor's first companion, his granddaughter Susan, was presented as a 15-year-old schoolgirl, but the 23-year-old Carole Ann Ford played her. The character of Adric, played by Matthew Waterhouse from 1980-1982, was a teenage prodigy and a kind of prototype for *Star Trek: the Next Generation*'s Wesley Crusher, who was disliked by some fans for much the same reasons. Although when I was 10, I thought Adric was okay, and even snivelled once or twice following his epic demise in *Earthshock*. However, I really liked the portrayal of Amelia in *The Eleventh Hour*, and as Steven writes, the *Doctor Who* production team were very lucky to discover the best possible actress to play the young Amelia, Karen Gillan's own cousin, Caitlin Blackwood. Although I did struggle to understand everything that Amelia was praying to get from Santa, possibly due to her Scottish brogue.

Unlike many fans, I didn't mind the rearrangement of the *Doctor Who* theme music, as I've heard and seen many bastardisations of the opening titles throughout the years, and this is far from being the worst. The most hideous *Doctor Who* opening titles and music belongs to the Sylvester McCoy years, especially when he breaks the fourth wall and winks at the viewers. Now that all TV programmes are produced in the letterbox widescreen format, one would have thought that the reintroduction of *Doctor Who* would been the ideal time to bring back Tom Baker's title sequence, which many people (like me) consider to be the best. The lightning strikes in the new title sequence are rather silly, but otherwise it's much on a par with that introduced along with the new series in 2005. Having written that, I do think the new "DW" TARDIS logo is a very neat piece of design.

However, there is one design innovation of the fifth series that I very much did not like, and that was the TARDIS' new look. I was appalled in the run-up to the new series when I read that Moffat was a great fan of the way the TARDIS looked in the 1960s Peter Cushing *Doctor Who* movies, because it seemed absurd that anyone would wanted to reproduce that jumbled mess. Then again, the appearance of the TARDIS doors in the console room from 2005 already seem to have been influenced by Peter Cushing's films. In the event, it seems that the Cushing inspiration was restricted to the reappearance of the St. John's ambulance badge on the door.

What I didn't like is the fact that the TARDIS has degenerated even further into a Heath Robinson contraption that looks fit to be only flown by a mad Victorian scientist. Admittedly, the Doctor does often appear to be such a mad Victorian scientist, but when the show first began, the TARDIS was an alien, futuristic machine. Now its controls have been replaced by antique typewriters and phones, and by a pinball machine! All of which are very human, rather than alien inventions. Yes, we all know that the Doctor is very preoccupied by us humans, but this is taking things too far.

Indeed, the only futuristic device on the console later turns out to be the new green-tipped sonic screwdriver, which the TARDIS can now apparently regenerate at will. Gone are the days, it seems, when the Doctor is left traumatised by the destruction of his sonic screwdriver, as the Fifth Doctor was in the 1982 adventure *The Visitation*. The production team of the day decided on this brutal act, as they thought the sonic device made it too easy for the Doctor to get out of tight situations - no such problem for the Doctor now, as he has an everlasting supply of sonic screwdrivers. Perhaps he should have asked the genie for an everlasting pint of Guinness too?

In the accompanying *Doctor Who Confidential*, Moffat was very excited about the fact that the TARDIS is now far vaster. And yet, to my eyes, it doesn't look any bigger than the 2005 design, and it's a bit odd that the area directly beneath the console floor is so small in height that Matt Smith has to crouch down while moving around there. I think in the case of the TARDIS, that less is more. We could believe it was vast before because we were told that it was so.

The production crew in the early 80's did an impressive job of embellishing this to the extent that they revealed the bedrooms that the companions inhabited. While you don't want every episode to be dominated by the companions wandering around TARDIS corridors, it would be nice for us to finally see a convincing TARDIS swimming pool (unlike the one that featured in 1978's *The Invasion of Time*, which was obviously a public facility). On this point, it's interesting to note that Michael Moorcock recently stated that the production team wouldn't allow him to include a scene in Amy's TARDIS bedroom in his *Doctor Who* novel *The Coming of the Terraphiles*. Could Moffat be saving the appearance of this room for a future adventure? Or does he want it to be left to the viewer's imagination? Obviously there is also the issue that Rory might share this room with her... The current TARDIS set looks really unhomely though - you couldn't imagine someone living there, as

21

comfort seems to have been left behind in the bid for wackiness.

In Steven Moffat's defence though, you could argue that this is the only TARDIS set that's been created to reflect the very character of the Doctor. Indeed, it was the Doctor's regeneration that literally sparked this rehash, although we've never seen his regenerative energy wreak such havoc with the TARDIS before. Of course, this is merely a device that Moffat has employed to justify the redesign. However, with the budget cut for this season, one would have thought that there were higher priorities for the cash than this ugly mess. In addition to this, Moffat has paved the way for future production teams to chip away at the TARDIS' foundations in the same way.

You could accuse me of being a reactionary conservative who wouldn't like any change, but I would argue that an attempt at continuity has always been part of *Doctor Who*'s success. Change has also always been vital, as previously discussed in terms of the Doctor's regenerations, but one is still entitled to judge whether any particular development is successful. Of course, the current wackiness of the TARDIS console can be traced back to the 1996 Paul McGann *Doctor Who* TV movie. While this story was criticised by many fans at the time, it did play an important role in breaking certain taboos, and created several precedents that the series has relied on since its revival in 2005. But more of this later...

One very important change that Steven Moffat has established here is that his Doctor is up and about and walking immediately after regenerating, rather than going for a prolonged kip as previous Doctors did (with the unsuccessful exception of Colin Baker). Admittedly, this is partly due to previous showrunner Russell T Davies' preference to convey that Time Lords now regenerate standing up, rather than lying on the floor as they did previously. The main reason for this device is that it enables the new Doctor to show off a bit of his character immediately in the final minute or so of the series finale, since we won't see him again until some months later.

I thought both such scenes featuring David Tennant and Matt Smith to be quite unsuccessful, as to display such a lot of character within the space of a couple of minutes has tended to result in a rather hyperactive and manic display that has little bearing on the Doctor's eventual character. Indeed, I wasn't won over by either actor when watching just these first scenes. Matt Smith's involved such verbal dexterity that it produced an unsightly amount of spittle, and some oversensitive members of the audience found themselves offended by the Doctor's declaration that he was disappointed to discover that he was still not ginger.

Of course, perhaps one of the major controversies of this series has centred on the shortness (or not) of Amy's skirts. In this light, it's amusing to see Amy endeavouring to perform a kind of Picard manoeuvre on the bridge in Leadworth to make her WPC's skirt longer, with the inherent message being that Amy is definitely not interested in any kind of physical relationship with the Doctor in the early stages of this story. In a similar light, it's interesting to see that the Doctor's manhood is nearly removed by a spike at the top of St. Stephen's Tower when the TARDIS skirts over the Houses of Parliament at the beginning of the episode. No doubt kids would find this amusing also, but this threat to the new Doctor's potency is also something that adults in the audience would no doubt pick up on.

There are also more subtle messages here that some viewers may miss on their first viewing of this episode. For instance, in the accompanying edition of *Doctor Who Confidential*, Steven Moffat explained that Rory has been trying to live up to Amy's dream of the "Raggedy Doctor", but could only make the grade as a nurse, rather than a doctor proper (Rory's ambition is articulated further later on in the series during his dream in *Amy's Choice*).

Just as the TARDIS scanner has an image of the crack in the universe indicates that the Doctor has some hidden motivation for inviting Amy into the TARDIS, so the weird image of the sun caused by the Atraxi forcefield could well be intended as a foreshadowing of the TARDIS' fate at the end of this series... Another unexplained anomaly is this: why do the coma patients cry out for the Doctor? Are they somehow aware of his presence, or are they vocalizing some anxiety about our favourite Time Lord from Prisoner Zero?

One great indication of how big *Doctor Who* is now is that the splendid Nina Wadia only has a minor bit role as Dr. Ramsden. Admittedly, she was probably limited timewise due to her commitments on *EastEnders*, and her appearance smacks of a desire to please one of her kids by appearing in their favourite TV programme - she wouldn't have been the first famous name to appear in *Doctor Who* for this purpose! The great Olivia Colman, of *Peep Show* fame, also makes a too brief appearance as Prisoner Zero, who Steven Cooper rightly describes as "underwhelming". However, at least Prisoner Zero's role as oracle did mean that Olivia Colman's lines regarding the Silence would achieve much more resonance later on in the series.

The fact that the Doctor has all his wits around him makes all the difference in *The Eleventh Hour* (even if he hasn't got his steering quite right yet). The main reason the Atraxi aren't really all that much of a menace, and why Prisoner Zero isn't all that threatening, is due to the fact that *The Eleventh Hour* is mainly a character piece rather than a rollicking adventure. Indeed, Moffat has done a fantastic job of introducing the new Doctor with his fabulously witty script. This episode also sets in play the main narrative that will run throughout this series - and the next!

Steven Moffat is obviously a man who likes to think big, and we must applaud him for that. Moffat must also be commended on his energy, for he has evidently put a great deal of effort into creating this season long narrative, easily overshadowing Russell T Davies' rather lame attempt to do the same in his first season with regards to the "Bad Wolf" motif. And it's also great to see that Moffat has the clout to persuade the powers-that-be to give a little extra running time for his baby, if that's what's required for the story, as *The Eleventh Hour* goes on for an unusual 65 minutes. And, as Steven has noted, Moffat and his fellow producers have made an outstanding choice of actor for the Eleventh Doctor in Matt Smith.

Did You Know? The Eleventh Hour was the most watched programme on the BBC's iPlayer in 2010, with 2.2 million viewings (that's 600,000 more viewings than the next most popular programme!) Matt Smith's debut was also broke the record for the most viewed programme on BBC America with 1.2 million viewers.

2: The Beast Below

Writer: Steven Moffat
Director: Andrew Gunn
Originally broadcast: 10 April 2010

Cast

The Doctor: Matt Smith
Amy Pond: Karen Gillan
Liz 10: Sophie Okonedo
Hawthorne: Terrence Hardiman
Mandy: Hannah Sharp
Timmy: Alfie Field
Morgan: Christopher Good
Peter: David Ajala
Poem Girl: Catrin Richards
Winder: Jonathan Battersby
Voice of Smilers/Winder: Chris Porter
Churchill: Ian McNeice

Steven's review: *The Beast Below* is an episode that surprised me. It starts out as a futuristic "romp" that seems to have no particular deeper purpose, but at the climax suddenly turns its focus onto the relationship between Amy Pond and the Doctor, and how she proves herself to be a worthy companion. Not as polished and coherent as *The Eleventh Hour*, with some unusually exposed plot holes by Steven Moffat's standards, I nevertheless found it to be quite moving by the end.

Doctor Who episodes are nominally forty-five minutes or so long, but given 2009's series of specials, this is actually the first standard-length instalment since *The Stolen Earth* nearly two years ago. With it following on closely from the previous episode, and the next one gatecrashing the ending as well, the actual story is told in not much more than half an hour. It feels not so much like a story in its own right as a brief interlude in a continuing journey.

The setting is impressively strange right from the opening shot, which shows what looks like a huge collection of tower blocks on a piece of "land" floating through space. This is the *Starship UK*, 1300 years in the future, created as a space-going refuge for the people of Britain when the Earth became uninhabitable due to solar flares in the 29th century. However, anyone expecting a nuts and bolts, science-fictional depiction of a future society would be disappointed. There are two main reasons for this: the first is that the budget limitations of *Doctor Who* simply don't allow for the sort of CGI integration and panoramic shots that would convince the viewer that this ship is a real place with miles of corridors and thousands of inhabitants. In that respect, this story is no more successful at establishing a credible vision of the future than *The Long Game* from Christopher Eccleston's season in 2005, which took a similar approach to realizing its setting with a CGI exterior and a few interior sets redressed multiple times.

But the second reason is that writer Steven Moffat is trying for a different effect, which simply doesn't require such a realistic environment. He and his fellow executive producers, Piers Wenger and Beth Willis, have said in interviews that one of their key touchstones for the feel of this season is "dark fairytale," and this episode certainly establishes an exaggerated, Roald Dahl-style environment, with the nominal setting of a far-future Britain serving in fact to contain a microcosm of current Britain, with the accent on familiar iconography - flags everywhere, red post boxes, London Underground signage, etc. The off-kilter element is introduced with the sinister Smilers that watch over everyone and everything - mannequins with heads that spin around to change their expression from smiling to frowning whenever someone does something wrong.

In some ways it's a pity that the Smilers were emphasized so much in all the pre-publicity for the season and for this episode, making it seem like they were a major new foe for the Doctor. In fact, they're more like the Nodes in *Silence in the Library* - a subsidiary element of the story that is there mainly for macabre effect. They're still successfully creepy, though, particularly when you consider the fact, which the story never makes a point of emphasizing, that they have two faces, but three expressions: smiling, frowning, and demonic. So they can't just be inanimate dummies - something's happening out of sight when those heads spin around…

Another way in which the story maintains a fairytale atmosphere is by foregrounding children. The pre-credits sequence shows a boy falling foul of the Smilers by scoring zero on a test, and being punished by having to walk home. When he disobeys and takes the elevator instead, the nearest Smiler turns demonic and the floor underneath him opens, sending him "below," as described in a strange poem chanted by a girl who appears on the elevator's screen:

"A horse and a man, above, below,

One has a plan but two must go.

Mile after mile, above, beneath,

One has a smile, one has teeth.

Though the man above might say hello,

Expect no love from the beast below."

Unfortunately, although last week the show found an extremely good child actor to play a crucial role, this episode does not fare so well. The child with the main role, Mandy (Hannah Sharp), is good, but the other children are not. In particular, the girl who reads the poem quoted above is dreadful - almost unintelligible, in fact.

Into this weird setting arrive the Doctor and Amy, and the fairytale aspect of Amy's adventure is emphasized with the striking opening shots of her floating in space outside the TARDIS, as she discovers that the Doctor's police box really is a spaceship. She is also still in her nightie from last week, and in fact keeps wearing it all through this episode - an explicit callback, as Moffat himself has said, to Wendy from *Peter Pan*, having left home the night before her wedding to go adventuring with the friend from her childhood.

It's another strong performance from Matt Smith as the Doctor. In the early scenes, as he and Amy investigate, he shows the Doctor's mind working at top speed, instantly deducing the police-state nature of the environment and the role of the Smilers. There's a lovely moment of eccentricity as he suddenly grabs a glass of water from a table and puts it down on the floor, observing it closely. He disarms the protests of the patrons at the table with "Sorry, checking all the water in this area. There's an escaped fish." When Amy asks why he just did that, he just says, "Dunno. I think a lot, it's hard to keep track."

The interaction between the Doctor and Amy continues to be very good. At the start, in the TARDIS, he spins her a line about observing but never interfering in the places he visits, which he of course immediately contradicts by rushing over to comfort the crying Mandy.

Amy: "So is this how it works, Doctor? You never interfere in the affairs of other peoples or planets... unless there's children crying."

Of course, to a near-immortal Time Lord, practically everyone else in the universe counts as children... And this line will turn out to inform the conclusion of the story in a typically clever Moffat way. Amy is sent off by the Doctor to follow Mandy, and they find a locked-off passage, which Amy wants to see inside ("I never could resist a KEEP OUT sign"). She picks the lock and looks inside, to see a strange root-like tentacle thrashing around. She is captured and knocked out.

In a lower area of the ship, the Doctor finds something mysterious - this is a starship with no engine. His experiment with the glass of water earlier showed that there was no engine vibration to be detected, and now he discovers that power cables that should be linked are disconnected, and the space where the engine should be is hollow. He also draws the attention of a mysterious masked woman who calls herself Liz 10 and seems to be familiar with him.

Amy wakes to find herself in a voting booth, faced with a bank of monitors and three buttons - PROTEST, RECORD, and FORGET. She is amused when the computer looks her up and gives her age as 1306, and intrigued when her marital status is given as... "information unavailable." The question being put to the voters is a simple one - whether they approve or disapprove of what has been done to save the people on this ship. If just one percent of the voters protest, the voyage will end. She is given the necessary information in the form of a video of the history of *Starship UK*, but we don't get to see it; we only see her choosing vehemently to hit the FORGET button. Then a recording appears of herself - upset, urging her to find the Doctor and leave this place immediately. The direction is rather unnecessarily confused here - it took me a while to realize that she must have used the RECORD button to create the message for herself, and then pressed FORGET. Whatever she saw in that video, it clearly distressed her.

There's a partial similarity in this strand of the episode to a famous 1973 short story by Ursula K. Le Guin, *The Ones Who Walk Away From Omelas*, where the citizens of a utopian city are required to come to terms with the dark secret at its heart. In this case, however, people are given the opportunity to forget, which allows Moffat to indulge in some political satire via the Doctor on the eve of a general election in Britain (just as happened with *Aliens of London* back in 2005): "And once every five years, everyone chooses to forget what they've learned. Democracy in action."

Also in this scene, Amy discovers more of the Doctor's background - stuff which we already know, but which every companion must sooner or later find out. When the subject of the Time War comes up, Matt Smith does a fine job of showing that the Doctor now seems to have moved on from the survivor's guilt of Eccleston and the angst of Tennant. The fact that the one thing the Doctor never does is forget "bad stuff" will, in Moffat fashion, come back strongly at the end. For the moment, he simply says, "Hold tight. We're bringing down the government." He hits PROTEST, and the floor opens.

They find themselves unceremoniously dumped into a dark, cavernous space filled with revolting sludge and scraps of rotting food. "It's a rubbish dump - and it's *minging*!" cries Amy, bringing a fine old Scottish term of disgust to a wider audience. The Doctor realizes they are in an enormous mouth, belonging to a creature being fed by implanted tubes like the one through which they have just fallen. What with the earlier remark to the Doctor from Liz 10, "Help us, Doctor - you're our only hope," it's easy to keep up a running commentary of *Star Wars* lines through this section - "What an incredible *smell* you've discovered!" "This is no cave..." And, of course, "I have a bad feeling about this..." (Also, at the end of the story, there's another obvious homage with an ostentatious cinematic wipe-style scene transition.) The Doctor manages to get them vomited from the mouth back up through an "overspill pipe." I loved the way he nervously adjusts his bow tie as he says, "Right, then. This isn't going to be big on dignity..."

The area where they end up is guarded by a couple of Smilers, but they are rescued by Liz 10, who reveals that she knows of the Doctor having heard stories of him from her family growing up. "Vicky was a bit on the fence about you, weren't she...knighted and exiled you on the same day. And so much for the Virgin Queen, you bad, bad, boy." It seems like the Doctor was telling the truth in *The End of Time* about his casual dalliance with the flower of Tudor royalty... Elizabeth the Tenth guns down another couple of pursuing Smilers before posing for her signature line, which will have you either laughing or groaning: "I'm the bloody queen, mate. Basically, I rule."

The idea of the British monarch being this Cockney-accented, masked, caped, gun-toting undercover vigilante is hilarious in itself, but Oscar-nominated Sophie Okonedo (*Hotel Rwanda*) really makes the most of it, bringing a wonderfully funny, cheeky quality to Liz 10. Unfortunately the episode's other major guest star, Terrence Hardiman, well known to children of the 1990s as *The Demon Headmaster*, is stuck in the thankless role of the chief of her functionaries, the Winders, and has very little to work with.

Liz 10 explains that she is certain her government has been

keeping things from her, and she is proved right when the Winders revolt against her, taking her and the others to the Tower of London - the lowest level of *Starship UK*. To her confusion, the Winders tell her they are acting on "the highest authority." The secret at the heart of the ship is revealed - the giant creature's brain is being repeatedly shocked to force it to fly the ship. The Doctor discovers that Liz 10 has been on the throne for a lot longer than the ten years she thinks - she's almost 300 years old, and she has repeatedly been led here over the decades, to a choice like that of her subjects, between FORGET and ABDICATE. A video message from her original self (which, in a nice touch, has a much more refined speaking voice than her current accent) lays out her dilemma. The giant beast is actually a completely benign space-faring creature called a "Star Whale," which arrived "like a miracle" in the time of the solar flares when Britain's people were dying; they trapped it and built their ship around it.

Liz 10: "If you wish our voyage to continue, then you must press the FORGET button - be again the heart of this nation, untainted. If not, press the other button. Your reign will end, the Star Whale will be released, and our ship will disintegrate."

The ethical dilemma itself is well presented, but the set-up unfortunately really strains the willing suspension of disbelief. You find yourself asking questions like, why couldn't Britain build a ship with a functioning engine when every other nation apparently could? The script doesn't do enough to answer (or encourage the audience to not ask) such questions, which is an unusual misstep for Moffat, whose stories are usually much more tightly constructed.

Fortunately, this is the point where the episode takes a more interesting and original turn. So far, it's followed the predictable structure where the Doctor and companion arrive in a strange place, investigate, penetrate to the heart of the situation, and identify an injustice to be corrected. Now is the point where the Doctor should come up with the solution. But this time, he has no easy answer. Either he leaves things unchanged, with the innocent Star Whale being tortured, or he releases it, which will doom all the humans on the ship. He eventually decides on the least bad option, which is to pass a massive electrical charge through the Star Whale's higher brain centres, rendering it still able to fly the ship, but no longer knowing anything about it.

Matt Smith and Karen Gillan are excellent in these scenes. The Doctor/Amy relationship, which was threatening to become quite cosy, is suddenly full of conflict. Amy realizes that this knowledge is what she voted to forget, so that the Doctor would not be faced with an impossible choice. The Doctor, in turn, is disappointed - and angry.

The Doctor: "When I'm done here you're going home."

Amy: "Why? Because I made a mistake? One mistake, I don't even remember doing it. Doctor!"

The Doctor: "Yeah, I know. You're only human."

Smith, who has been great with the Doctor's humorous and eccentric sides, now shows that he is also up to handling the anger and authority of the character. When Liz 10 presses him that there must be another way, he suddenly yells, "Nobody talk to me. Nobody *human* has anything to say to me today!" with an intimidating rage worthy of Tom Baker's Doctor. Gillan shows Amy crushed at the thought that she has destroyed her voyage of discovery before it's barely begun.

But then, Amy gets her chance to retrieve the situation. There are children down here performing various menial tasks, including the boy who was sent below in the opening sequence - apparently, the beast refuses to eat children. She sees some of them touching and playing with one of the creature's tentacles, and suddenly puts the pieces together. She grabs Liz 10's hand and presses the ABDICATE button. The ship is rocked as the Star Whale is released... but nothing further happens. The Star Whale chooses to stay with the ship, as it had originally chosen to come to Earth and offer itself to the people there to save them - their trapping and torturing of it was, tragically, not just wrong but needless.

I liked the cleverness of this script in coming up with a plausible way for the Doctor to be beaten to the solution by Amy. The Doctor is of course a genius, but he can't see himself from outside. Amy, with the advantage of having spent fourteen years obsessing about him, can spot the similarity between the lone Time Lord and the lone Star Whale. "What if you were really old, and really kind, and alone. Your whole race dead, no future. What couldn't you do then? If you were that old, and that kind, and the very last of your kind, you couldn't just stand there and watch children cry." It's true that the script loses all subtlety here, hammering the point home no less than three times in succession, but I think it's sufficiently important and significant that Amy proves herself worthy of being a companion, not just tagging along but providing a viewpoint for the Doctor that he can't provide for himself.

The Doctor: "But you couldn't have known how it would react."

Amy: "You couldn't. But I've seen it before. Very old and very kind, and the very very last. Sound a bit familiar?"

And now it's back to the TARDIS, and a bit of humour as we come back to that wedding that Amy's running away from. Matt Smith plays the Doctor's bantering here quite ambiguously, as he watches her stumbling through nearly telling him about it. Bearing in mind the strange image of the crack on the TARDIS scanner at the end of the last episode, it's possible he already knows more about Amy than he's letting on.

In any event, she is interrupted when the TARDIS phone rings. It's Winston Churchill, calling from next week's episode, and summoning the Doctor back in time as the shadow of a Dalek appears on the wall beside him. Apparently it's not only former companions who have the Doctor's phone number... The TARDIS fades away, to a poetic voiceover from Amy:

"In bed above we're deep asleep,

While greater love lies further deep.

This dream must end, this world must know,

We all depend on the beast below."

We have one final view of *Starship UK*, which shows - surprise! - a crack appearing in its hull the exact same shape as the one from last week. There's no doubt now that some silent menace is following the Doctor and Amy around... but just what is going on?

Steven's Classic Who DVD Recommendation: To see what happened to another group of humans affected by the solar flares referred to in *The Beast Below*, check out *The Ark in Space*, starring Tom Baker, with Elisabeth Sladen and Ian Marter.

Kevin's review: Steven Moffat's preceding *Doctor Who* scripts have been of such high standard that there's hardly a bum note in any of them, which is why he was the favourite to take over from Russell T Davies as the showrunner. However, having been previously limited to sculpting one or two excellent scripts a year, this series saw Moffat writing many more episodes while also operating as one of the show's executive producers and endeavouring to construct a very intricate and complex story arc. No one can be uniformly excellent all the time, so it's hardly surprising that Moffat has something of a blip with regards to his script for *The Beast Below*.

It all starts promisingly enough, with those fantastic shots of Amy floating outside the TARDIS, with her long red hair waving this way and that due to the lack of gravity. Moffat does very well at conveying Amy's awe at her discovery that the TARDIS is also a spaceship as well as a time machine. Amy does indeed blink in astonishment when she steps out of the TARDIS for the first time in a new location. I think these scenes are much better at catching the wonder of the TARDIS than the actual redesign, as discussed in my review of the previous episode. However, you can only really do such scenes once a season, otherwise they would get tiresome for veteran viewers. Rory's reading up on time travel and relative dimensions certainly saves the story some time in *The Vampires of Venice*, even if his casual reaction to the TARDIS somewhat disappoints the Doctor. And it's just as well that the TARDIS only flies over the top of *Starship UK* (and that the Doctor doesn't do a thorough scan of this curiously shaped ship), otherwise there would have been no central mystery for this story.

I like Moffat's concept of *Doctor Who* as being a form of "dark fairytale"; however, there are some aspects of its execution that I'm not too partial to. For instance, I really disliked the fact that the make-up of the *Starship UK* was conveyed as being much the same as late Twentieth Century Britain. It gave the impression - probably intended - that this society had not made any great progress since then (although this is quite hard to believe in a story set a thousand years after our time).

In Moffat's defence, he's probably drawing on the tradition of representing a 'blue collar future' in science fiction films such as James Cameron's *Aliens*, whose futuristic marines are very similar in dress, weaponry, and motivation to their modern day counterparts. Indeed, Moffat very successfully utilises this very motif in *The Time of Angels/Flesh and Stone*, albeit with British rather than American soldiers. The main motivation behind this device is to ensure that the viewers aren't alienated from the protagonists on screen due to the fact that they are wearing some peculiar futuristic fashion. Conveying soldiers and workers of the future in their uniforms and overalls works because this is gritty, while displaying a girl in a bright red pristine school uniform, as we have here, is just bourgeois and therefore ultimately boring.

So my main bone of contention with Steven Moffat here is that *Doctor Who* isn't, in essence, a "dark fairytale" but "pure escapism", for which there is no more perfect a vehicle than the TARDIS, which can go anywhere in time and space. We don't want to go to the 'Other' only to discover that it's full of red metallic benches that wouldn't look out of place at a Network Rail station in the UK, or that it features a kid watching TV just like us (as in Moffat's 2008 script *Silence in the Library*). The big dark wood is an alien, forbidding place for a child, yet still they feel a sense of thrill that compels them to explore it... Instead of this sensation in *The Beast Below*, all we get is a lazy tyke who decides to get the lift home, rather than walk home as he's been told to by the one of the Smilers (whose profile, when first seen sitting down, curiously looks like of Davros, the creator of the Daleks).

It's likely that the main reason why all this Twentieth Century paraphernalia was thrown into *The Beast Below* was because the Smilers themselves might have jarred otherwise. They very much resemble the dummies of a laughing policeman that used to feature in British fairgrounds, and they are another instance of Steven Moffat taking an image from everyday life and drawing on its more sinister aspects, such as the Weeping Angels. I think it's fair to say that these monsters would have been distinctive enough on their own. Indeed, they would have been even more imposing had they not been surrounded by the modern everyday tat. I mean, there's a great deal that's not explained with regards to the Smilers: such as their origins, and why at least one of the Winders appears to be half human/half Smiler in the single decent use of CGI in this episode.

Indeed, *The Beast Below* does appear quite impoverished when compared to some of the more lavish episodes in the series, and could have done with some more cash splashed at it. Take, for instance, the CGI model of the *Starship UK*, which is very poor and hideous. No doubt it's supposed to look impoverished and rundown, but there's no disguising the fact that it's actually a very shoddy model that's been weakly executed. To some extent, Moffat also appears to be following Russell T Davies' lead too well, as a similar vessel to the *Starship UK* formed the basis for Rose's first trip in the TARDIS in 2005's *The End of the World*; however, the staging of the latter is positively opulent in stark contrast to *The Beast Below*'s poverty. Having written that, the staging of the scene where the Doctor and Amy first explore the *Starship UK* must have been hideously expensive, although it doesn't really stand out as being so, as the props are too all familiar to us, as previously discussed. There are also possibly more references to *Star Wars* in this episode alone than in a whole series of *Lost*.

Another *Doctor Who* story that appears to have influenced Moffat's writing of *The Beast Below* was Tom Baker's second adventure, *The Ark in Space*. This 1975 story also had budgetary constraints, which meant that it had to share the set of space station Nerva with another story from the same year (*Revenge of the Cybermen*). The low budget meant that the special effects team had to be very creative, which often led to them employing new innovative materials. In the days before video recorders, this didn't really matter, but the illusion of a man turning into an alien here is somewhat spoiled when you realise that the green stuff on his arm is that now relatively common office staple: bubble wrap. The exterior model shots of the Nerva Beacon are also quite shoddy and wobbly, and were suitably replaced by CGI in its original DVD release.

However, despite the lack of money, the 1975 production team arguably provided a more convincing image of the future in *The Ark in Space* than the current one (dodgy 1970s coiffures aside). Indeed, although the station and the people within it date from exactly the same time as those on *Starship UK* (since they too were escaping from the solar flares), their culture is very much different from that depicted in *The Beast Below*. For instance, this is a far more organised society, which managed to preserve its people in cryogenic pods. Admittedly, the people who were saved were selected, but it appears that they were chosen according to their skills rather than say, class. And the voice of the female High Minster makes it clear that their acquiescence with this process was regarded as a sacrifice for them (for each one would never see their friends and family again) rather than an unseemly, desperate bid for survival. When they emerge from their pods, these people also appear to be consummate professionals, logical and unemotional - until an infestation by the insect-like Wirrn threatens their fragile existence (the similarly insect-like antennae that break through the *Starship UK*'s hull are indeed mistaken by Liz 10 to be evidence of an alien invasion). The scale of these humans' achievements takes the Fourth Doctor aback; so much so, that he famously exclaims:

Homo sapiens, what an inventive, invincible species. It's only a few million years since they crawled up out of the mud and learned to walk. Puny, defenceless bipeds! They've survived flood, famine and plague. They've survived cosmic wars and holocausts. Now here they are out among the stars waiting to begin a new life, ready to outsit eternity. They're indomitable, indomitable.

When the Eleventh Doctor discovers just what's been powering the *Starship UK*, he understandably has a somewhat dimmer view of humanity, to the point that he self-righteously exclaims "Nobody *human* has anything to say to me today!" In this instance, Steven Moffat shares the same pessimistic view of humanity's future that I depicted in the *Doctor Who* scripts I submitted to the production team in the late 80's (which were, sadly for me if no one else, never commissioned). Admittedly, the Doctor was also upset due to the fact that Amy had taken it upon herself to decide that this was one dilemma that the Doctor could not resolve. It is indeed startling to see the Doctor address one of his companions in this way, with real, justifiable anger, as he threatens to take her right back to Leadworth.

Although, in essence, Amy's right, as the Doctor busies himself with bringing about the Star Whale's brain death. So this denouement reveals precisely what this episode was really about: more character development. This time, it's Amy who first disappoints, and then wonderfully surprises the Doctor to win the day. Although, as Steven points out, this point is rather hammered home by Moffat. However, the fact that Amy has been programmed to forget her agonising vote, would appear to be the first sign that memory and remembrance are going to play an important part in this series.

The idea that the Doctor only ever gets involved when he hears children crying is the kind of sentimental hogwash that I'd hoped had ended with Russell T Davies' era. Then again, it was in the Russell T Davies scripted *Torchwood: Children of Earth* miniseries that Gwen Cooper speculated that the Doctor didn't intervene in that episode as he was no doubt disgusted with humanity's use of its own children as bargaining chips. There was no hint of him making an appearance to prevent Captain Jack's grandson from being sacrificed in this unusually dark and cynical Russell T Davies story. Obviously, trying to make the Doctor's actions appear consistent is impossible over a fifty-year period, and Steven Moffat's focus on children (as discussed in the previous review) is essentially a device to make the show even more family friendly.

In this episode, Moffat seems to be mainly addressing a neglected part of the *Doctor Who* audience: parents (which is fair enough). However, as my fellow reviewer Steven has noted, the child actors in this episode aren't as good as Caitlin Blackwood. In one especially jarring scene at the end, Mandy asks Timmy how he is, to which she receives no reply. So the actor playing Timmy (Alfie Field) just stands there awkwardly. Admittedly, this could be down to poor direction on Andrew Gunn's part (since the main focus of this scene is on the fact that the Star Whale pets rather than assaults them), or it could be read that the Winders have somehow turned these otherwise rebellious children into mute drones. Having written that, Mandy does stand around like a spare part for ages preceding this, as her role in Steven Moffat's script is somewhat limited.

His creation of Liz 10 is rather more wonderful, brilliantly brought to life by the sublime Sophie Okonedo. It's a real coup to have such Oscar nominated actors as her on the show. Glammed up here, she practically steals every scene that she appears in, especially when she rescues the Doctor and Amy from the Smilers. However, it's a shame she feels compelled to hide her voice as well as her face when out and about in public, so the scenes where she really "rules" are few and far between. She's also more muted as the Doctor and Amy bustle around saving the day at the end, yet she's still a real highlight in an otherwise dull episode.

Just like Robert Holmes with regards to the message from the High Minister in *The Ark in Space*, Steven Moffat gets the tone of voice for the recorded bureaucrat in the voting booth just right, as well as the more refined language that Liz 10 employed in her earlier days of office. The idea of "forgetting everything you've learnt" in the previous five years when voting is rather cynical on the eve of a British election (but is all the more splendid for that).

I was somewhat appalled to discover in this episode that there would still be a Northern Ireland in a thousand years' time, but this may be Moffat's point, as it's exactly this kind of ugly compromise - that was only supposed to be temporary - which forms the crux of this episode. It's also amusing to see the Union Flag so prominently displayed around the *Starship UK*, despite the fact that Scotland decided to go its own way. No doubt they were right to do so, as the *Starship UK* seems to have been cobbled together in very much of a hurry! The dilapidated ship is certainly shown to have an all-too familiar crack in its hull... Interestingly enough, *The Brilliant Book of Doctor Who 2011* describes this crack as a "crooked smile" in its entry on *The Beast Below*, and Karen Gillan uses this same term to describe the cracks in her interview in the book.

Did You Know? The exterior of the Queen Vic pub from the BBC soap *EastEnders* is just one of the many features on the *Starship UK*'s promenade!

3: Victory of the Daleks

Writer: Mark Gatiss
Director: Andrew Gunn
Originally broadcast: 17 April 2010

Cast

The Doctor: Matt Smith
Amy Pond: Karen Gillan
Churchill: Ian McNeice
Bracewell: Bill Paterson
Blanche: Nina de Cosimo
Childers: Tim Wallers
Dalek 1: Nicholas Pegg
Dalek 2: Barnaby Edwards
Dalek voice: Nicholas Briggs
Lilian: Susannah Fielding
Todd: James Albrecht
Air Raid Warden: Colin Prockter

Steven's review: Every Doctor sooner or later has to face the Daleks. The great space dustbins are so fundamental a part of *Doctor Who* that they have appeared every year since the series was revived in 2005. The notion introduced by Russell T Davies that the Daleks were the opponents of the Time Lords in the great Time War which destroyed both species cemented their status as the Doctor's greatest enemies, but also meant that the writers had to keep finding new ways of bringing them back from total extinction, only to be defeated again by the Doctor. This story finally breaks out of that cycle of the Daleks repeatedly being completely-but-not-really destroyed by giving them, as the title suggests, an actual, unambiguous victory. Unfortunately, although *Victory of the Daleks* successfully accomplishes this main purpose, it has so many flaws elsewhere that it's clearly the weakest episode of the season so far.

The episode is bizarrely structured, falling into three quite separate pieces that hit completely different levels with regard to tone, atmosphere, and effectiveness. The first third is by far the best part, taut and gripping as the Doctor and the Daleks manoeuvre around each other - the Doctor *knows* the Daleks are up to something, but can't figure out what, or convince anyone of the danger. The middle stretch is when the Daleks' plans reach fruition and the Doctor leads the fight against them in a silly but fun action sequence. But then everything goes pear-shaped, and the climax of the episode is a terrible, mawkish miscalculation, probably the worst misstep since the ending of *Fear Her* four years ago.

By coincidence, the structure of the first part of this season corresponds closely with that of the Christopher Eccleston season back in 2005, with the showrunner writing the season opener to introduce the new Doctor and companion, then following that up with a weird far-future adventure, and then an excursion into history written by Mark Gatiss (and, to complete the analogy, Steven Moffat is back next week writing the first two-parter of the season). Back then, *The Unquiet Dead* gave us Charles Dickens fighting ghosts in Cardiff; here, it's Winston Churchill leading Britain through the dark days of World War Two. As usual, the BBC design, costume, and make-up departments have done an excellent job of recreating the period setting. Much of the episode takes place in the Cabinet War Rooms underneath central London, and the narrow, drab corridors, the cramped rooms packed full of people and smoke, the dust drifting down as German bombs impact overhead, are all perfectly depicted.

Ian McNeice presents a Churchill who is very much the legendary icon - all cigar-chomping, bulldog determination, in bowler hat and bow tie - rather than a realistic portrait of the complex, contradictory man he actually was. I suspect this is partly because the story makes the interesting choice of having the Doctor already well-known to Churchill; in fact, they're almost old cronies, with Churchill totally unfazed by his changing appearance or his TARDIS - as we saw last week, he was even able to phone the Doctor far in the future and call him back to Earth. They wrangle, but not in an unfriendly manner, over the Doctor's refusal to put the TARDIS at Churchill's disposal for the war effort. It's all very cosy.

The Doctor is taken outside the Cabinet bunker to witness an incoming squadron of German bombers being wiped out by Britain's new secret weapon - a very familiar-looking death ray. One of the "secret weapons" trundles into view - a Dalek, looking surprisingly fitting in this environment in khaki colours with a Union Jack painted underneath its eyestalk; I particularly loved the little blackout covers placed over its head lights. Horrified, the Doctor demands to know what the Daleks are doing here, but it shows no sign of recognizing him, simply repeating, "I-AM-YOUR-SOLDIER."

The scientist who apparently developed these weapons, Professor Edwin Bracewell, explains how his "Ironsides" will win the war. The Doctor immediately declares to Churchill that the Daleks are aliens and Bracewell must be some kind of dupe, but the PM replies with the story of how Bracewell approached the government some months ago with the plans and blueprints for the machines. As they argue, the Daleks in the background are keeping a careful watch on the Doctor.

This first section is very reminiscent of *The Power of the Daleks*, a classic story from the 1960s, which introduced Patrick Troughton as the Doctor and showed the Daleks at their scheming best. The basic ideas of Daleks pretending to be subservient to humans for their own purposes (the repeated "I-AM-YOUR-SOLDIER" here corresponds to a similar refrain of "I-AM-YOUR-SERVANT" in the older story), and the Doctor's warnings of danger going unheeded, are reused, and are just as effective. In *Power*, they played on human greed in order to buy time to make themselves stronger; here, they are relying on Churchill's desperate need to seize any advantage he can find to defend against the Nazis. When pressed by the Doctor, he makes this explicit (neatly making use of a famous quote from the real-life Churchill, about allying with Stalin):

The Doctor: "The Daleks have no conscience, no mercy, no pity. They are my oldest and deadliest enemy. You cannot trust them."

Churchill: "If Hitler invaded Hell, I would give a favourable reference to the Devil. These machines are our salvation."

The Doctor can do nothing but watch as the Daleks glide around with impunity, carrying out their menial tasks (and hearing a Dalek voice asking "WOULD-YOU-CARE-FOR-SOME-TEA?" is actually quite unsettling). He also discovers something even more disturbing, when he tries to get Amy to warn Churchill about the Daleks.

The Doctor: "Amy. Tell me you remember the Daleks."

Amy: "Nope... Sorry."

The Doctor: "That's not possible..."

Clearly something has happened to the timeline that has meant that, for Amy (and perhaps for her entire world), the events of *The Stolen Earth* didn't happen. No doubt this is related to the "cracks in the universe," which have appeared in both the last two episodes, and will be further developed over the rest of the season...

Eventually the Doctor's frustration at not being able to convince anyone of the danger boils over. He grabs a huge wrench and attacks one of the Daleks ("YOU-DO-NOT-REQUIRE-TEA?"), taunting the creature and demanding that it acknowledge him. Matt Smith is good throughout the episode, but is particularly excellent here, managing to conjure up the same combination of frenzied fear and loathing as Christopher Eccleston showed when his Doctor met a Dalek for the first time in 2005. You really get a sense that the Daleks unleash something frighteningly primal in the Doctor.

The Doctor: "You! Are! My! Enemy! And I am yours! You are everything I despise. The worst thing in all creation. I've defeated you time and time again... I sent you back into the Void. I saved the whole of reality from you. I am the Doctor, and *you* are the Daleks!"

And now the Daleks make their move. The one he attacked

simply replies, "CORRECT." They transmit the Doctor's "testimony" about their identity to their waiting ship, hiding behind the moon, and teleport away after revealing to the shocked Bracewell that, far from being the Daleks' creator, he is in fact an android created by them and programmed with human-seeming memories.

The Doctor quickly uses the TARDIS to travel to the Dalek ship, where he holds off the Daleks by pretending that a jammie dodger (a jam-filled biscuit) is a TARDIS self-destruct switch. I really liked this bit of whimsy - recalling a time when Tom Baker's Doctor once held a group of savage warriors at bay with "a deadly jelly baby" - and especially the punchline when his bluff is eventually called, taking a bite from it and saying, "All right, it's a jammie dodger. But I was promised tea!"

While they are engaged in this standoff, the Daleks reveal what they are up to. They are the only survivors from their last encounter with the Doctor (*Journey's End*), trying as usual to rebuild their race. But this time they have found a Progenitor device, an ancient Dalek gene bank (presumably dating from the Time War) that can be used as the source for a whole new army of Daleks. There's only one problem - the Progenitor doesn't recognize them, since they are not pure Dalek (the ones we saw in *Journey's End* were created by Davros using his own cells), and will not function for them. Hence the whole elaborate scheme to lure the Doctor to them and obtain the "testimony" of the Daleks' great enemy that will confirm to the Progenitor their identity. I thought this was a very clever idea, and certainly the craftiest the Daleks have been for years.

The Doctor can only look on as the Progenitor gets to work, and eventually out from the machine emerges "a new Dalek paradigm." Deciding to launch a redesigned version of the Daleks was a risk for the show to take - not only has the original been a design icon for decades, but it had been reintroduced to a whole new generation of viewers with massive success - and it has to be said that the new Daleks have received a more negative reaction than just about anything else in the new series so far. They're significantly larger than the old ones, which can make them look nicely imposing, particularly when they're shot from a low angle, but also gives them an unwanted ponderous, lumbering quality. The idea of having them in different colours to differentiate them into functional categories (scientist, drone, soldier etc.) harks back to the earliest Dalek stories - and in particular, to the two cinema films, *Doctor Who and the Daleks* and *Daleks: Invasion Earth 2150 AD*, starring Peter Cushing and made in the mid-'60s at the height of the Daleks' initial popularity. However, the bright primary colours chosen make them look rather plastic and lightweight next to the metallic bronze Daleks we've gotten used to, not to mention raising the suspicion that merchandising considerations may have played a part ("Hey kids, collect the whole set!"). My least favourite change, though, is the alteration to the proportions of the creatures. From the front they're fine, but in profile they now present a rather hulking, even humpbacked appearance, thanks to the increased size of the back section. Maybe it's just the unfamiliarity, and I'll get used to them over time (I initially complained about the new theme tune, but I have to report that it's now beginning to grow on me), but I really don't see them as an advance on the originals. It is a nice touch, though, that their first action is to exterminate the previous versions for being "impure," and that the old Daleks immediately accept their fate with no argument.

Meanwhile, back on Earth, Amy and Churchill talk the shattered Bracewell out of killing himself by telling him they need his advanced technical knowledge to find a way of attacking the Dalek ship. Earlier he had talked of possibilities for hypersonic flight and "gravity bubbles" enabling flight into space, and what do you know, that's exactly what's needed to soup up a squadron of Spitfires so that they can take on a Dalek spaceship. It's best not to dwell on the question of how this advanced tech progressed from a theoretical possibility to being deployed in actual airplanes over the course of a couple of scenes - we've crossed over fully into pulp adventure serial mode now. Murray Gold provides a fine *Dam Busters*-style score as the Spitfires strafe the Dalek ship with cries of "Tally ho" and "Let's go, chaps" - and there's a lovely *Where Eagles Dare* reference ("Broadsword calling Danny Boy") stuck in as well. With the Doctor helping by deactivating its shields, the planes eventually threaten to destroy the Dalek ship.

And now the story takes a *really* crazy turn, as the Daleks buy time to escape the Spitfire attack by suddenly revealing that the Bracewell android is powered by something called an "oblivion continuum" which they threaten to detonate - effectively making him a massive bomb that can destroy the entire planet. This is supposed to set up the critical dilemma for the Doctor - let the new Daleks escape, to rebuild their forces anew, or destroy them forever (again) but allow the Earth to be shattered. Unfortunately, despite Matt Smith's best efforts at showing the Doctor's anguish, the scene falls flat, because (a) we've seen the same situation at the climax of *The Parting of the Ways*, where it was much more personal and emotional for the Doctor; (b) the ridiculous technobabble ("oblivion continuum" - really?) makes it impossible to take seriously; and (c) the whole situation is thrown in with absolutely no foreshadowing, as if the writer had suddenly discovered that the script was running short.

Anyway, the Doctor calls off the attack, returns to Earth, and with one punch knocks down Bracewell and starts trying to defuse him, since the Daleks have naturally triggered the countdown to detonation. This turns out to involve getting him to talk about his human memories and feelings, since somehow if he becomes more "human" then the Daleks won't be able to remotely explode him. The idea of talking a bomb out of exploding is frankly impossible to take seriously, especially for anyone who's seen John Carpenter's *Dark Star*, which did the same thing as a comedy. The only reason the whole scene doesn't fail completely is Bill Paterson's performance - he manages to make Bracewell's bewildered desperation compelling despite the preposterous situation.

After the Doctor fails to stop the countdown with appeals to Bracewell's humanity and pushing him to recall memories of his early life, his parents' deaths, and so on, Amy asks him, "Ever fancied someone you know you shouldn't?" with a glance at the Doctor. This prompts Bracewell to reminisce about an old flame named Dorabella, which somehow proves to be enough to abort the countdown. (As I mentioned at the top of this review, this resolution brought back unwanted memories of the sickly sentimental "power of love" ending to *Fear Her.*) With their bomb having failed, the new Daleks head off into the universe to rebuild their forces, no doubt in preparation for a resumption of hostilities further down the line this season or the next.

As with last week's episode, Amy ends up providing the solution by contributing a viewpoint that the Doctor lacks. She's turning out to be surprisingly competent at this adventuring business, but I only hope her look toward the Doctor here doesn't indicate that there's another Doctor/companion romance on the cards. We've had quite enough of that for the time being. Karen Gillan is once again excellent, although it's pushing the bounds of belief that her miniskirt barely attracts a second glance from anyone in 1940. Perhaps it has its own inbuilt perception filter.

There's a drawn-out ending, or rather a string of endings - first some business with Churchill once again trying to get the TARDIS key before going back to his war, then some rather laboured comedy with the Doctor, having removed all the advanced Dalek tech Bracewell created, deciding not to dismantle the android and letting him go instead. Finally, back at the TARDIS, the Doctor returns to a matter that's been nagging him:

Amy: "You're worried about the Daleks?"

The Doctor: "You didn't know them, Amy. You'd never seen them before. And you should have done. You should."

And so the episode finishes on an unresolved note, as the TARDIS vanishes, leaving another crack in the universe behind - unfinished business. The Daleks have their victory. But it must be said, it's a rather hollow one.

Steven's Classic Who DVD Recommendation: I'd love to be able to recommend *The Power of the Daleks*, but unfortunately it no longer exists in the BBC archives. For those who'd like to check out the soundtrack (recorded off-air at the time of transmission, and carefully cleaned up for commercial release), it is available on audio CD, and the story is actually strong enough to stand up even without its visuals. But, sticking with DVDs, to see how the Classic Series visited World War Two, try *The Curse of Fenric*, starring Sylvester McCoy and Sophie Aldred.

Kevin's review: *Victory of the Daleks* is a rather strange affair that appears to have both too much and too little going on in it at times. As the accompanying *Doctor Who Confidential* makes clear, this episode is very much a joint creation by both Mark Gatiss and Steven Moffat, with the former appearing to have some initial reservations about the premise. Moffat and Gatiss also work closely together on the new highly praised BBC series *Sherlock*.

Unlike most viewers, I had several reservations about this reinvention of Sherlock Holmes, as at times it appeared quite shambolic and incoherent, especially Mark Gatiss' dire last episode, *The Great Game*. The first episode, written by Steven Moffat, was okay, but I thought the best of the run was *The Blind Banker*, by Steve Thompson (which is just as well, as he's written an episode for *Doctor Who*'s sixth season). While the casting of Benedict Cumberbatch is very good, I think that Martin Freeman makes a poor Watson, and that his portrayal of an Afghanistan veteran was simply unbelievable (Matt Smith, who also was in the running to play Watson, would have been far more convincing from this point of view). However, my main objection to *Sherlock* is that it's an unnecessary distraction for Moffat that will only detract from his work on *Doctor Who*. It's a great shame that the BBC seems to have adopted the US trait of getting your very successful showrunner, such as Joss Whedon, to create a new show, while simultaneously still playing a hands-on role on the original show. The end result is usually that the maestro's attention is necessarily diluted, and that both shows suffer as a result.

Admittedly, US serials tend to have twice as many episodes as their UK counterparts. However, it must be said that the very energetic Russell T Davies' efforts did very much seem to diminish when he also became involved in running *Torchwood* and the *Sarah Jane Adventures*, as well as *Doctor Who*. Steven Moffat famously gave up his role of writing the remaining two Spielberg *Tintin* films to work on *Doctor Who*, in recognition that he could not possibly do both. My impression is that Moffat's focus is so intense (particularly with regards to creating such a complex storyline for this series of *Doctor Who*) that it literally wears him out at times. I suspect that the splitting of the sixth series of *Doctor Who* into two parts is as much to do with giving Moffat a break, as well as moving the show from an unsuitable early summer slot. However, Steven Moffat has gone on the record to state that this is not so, as the BBC has given him exactly the same amount of work in 2011 as they did in 2010.

Back to the episode itself, *Victory of the Daleks* starts well enough. As Steven Cooper has written, the Daleks do very much fit into the Second World War setting, almost as if they were an artefact of this conflict, as they appear to be miniature tanks. This isn't a particularly original insight on behalf of the current production team, as the legendary 1975 adventure *Genesis of the Daleks* explicitly conveyed the fact that the Daleks were created by a fascist culture that appeared and behaved almost exactly like the Nazis, especially with regards to their uniforms, to the extent that one of them even wore a German Iron Cross. This story was also mainly set in an underground bunker. So, the idea of the Daleks being related to Second World War Nazis was one that was set in stone by the scriptwriter that originally created them, Terry Nation. However, the appealing twist here is that the Daleks seem bent on serving the Allied cause, rather than the Nazis, their more natural allies.

Indeed, the presentation of the Daleks here as being subservient to the extent of serving tea, is brilliantly executed here, and (as Steven notes) is a splendid reflection of a tactic that the weakened Daleks first adopted in the sublime *Power of the Daleks* (written by David Whitaker, who'd been *Doctor Who*'s first script editor). By behaving this way, the Daleks appear more scary and cunning than ever, because you've no idea what they're planning... This tactic also gives an all too rare insight into the Daleks' intelligence, and provides a reminder that they can also be subtle as well as bombastic.

The Doctor's comment that Bracewell has a positronic brain is another nod back to *The Power of the Daleks*, in which David Whitaker borrowed the concept of the positronic brain developed by Isaac Asimov in his *Robot* stories. I also very much liked another scene where a Dalek trundles down a corridor in the bunker holding a box file, which seems to be a flashback to the dexterity they first demonstrated in their original adventure, *The Daleks*, from 1963. Such attention to detail is quite exquisite, and is also displayed by the rather splendid and authentic "To Victory!" poster featuring a Dalek that Churchill shows off to the Doctor.

However, Ian McNeice's performance as Churchill is not the most convincing that I've seen, especially as he only seems to hit the right tone in fits and starts. One thing that really jarred with me was Churchill's employment of the rather bizarre motto "KBO" ("Keep Buggering On"). At first sight, this appears to be a quite inappropriate saying that Mark Gatiss had included in the script, possibly for his own amusement. However, as shown in *Doctor Who Confidential*, Mark Gatiss did do a great deal of research for this story, and Google confirms that "KBO" (and its attendant meaning) was indeed an acronym that the real Churchill was inordinately fond of, to the extent of using it to end most phone calls! So, this is perhaps an early example of how this series has returned to *Doctor Who*'s roots by becoming educational once more. Maybe it's just me, but

Matt Smith's performance of the Doctor seemed quite flat in this episode. Also jarring was Colin Prockter's portrayal of the Air Raid Warden, which did not hit quite the required tone. And, despite the fact that the Daleks created Bracewell, he manages to mispronounce their name throughout the episode.

Obviously, the Spitfire attack on the Dalek saucer defies all logic, science and belief. However, this bit of CGI is excellently executed, and you can see why the production team could not resist creating this sequence. In contrast to the poor budget of the Classic Series, *Doctor Who* can now afford to be a spectacle, and to show off as such every now and then. One suspects that the production team of the early 70's would have been ecstatic had they been afforded a similar opportunity to mount such a battle. And the assault of Danny Boy et al is indeed spiffing good fun. However, maybe it's just me, but I thought the phone that the Doctor uses to communicate with Danny Boy is different from the one that Amy picked up when Churchill called at the end of the previous episode?

Of course, the biggest departure in this adventure is the design of the new Daleks, which I still hate. As previously discussed, Edward Thomas' 2005 redesign of the "old Daleks" still looks splendid, and indeed, they were particularly formidable in the early part of this episode. Admittedly, they were rather on the short side (*with Doctor Who Confidential* revealing that they were originally designed so that their eye stalk would be level with Billie Piper's eyes), but then the Daleks have always been vertically challenged. It seems rather bizarre that one of the main reasons for a redesign is to enable the Daleks to look the Doctor (or one of his companions) directly in the eye, as Doctors and companions can obviously increase and decrease in stature!

Steven Moffat has stated that he wanted to return the Daleks to return to the way they looked in the two Sixties movies starring Peter Cushing. This, in itself, would have been fine, as they looked pretty imposing in these two features, aside from their "fire extinguisher" guns. However, I think the real problem with these new Daleks is that they look too plasticky, and thus weaker than their previous metallic image, as it seems like a blast from a flamethrower would be all that's needed to melt them away. Obviously, one could argue that the Autons, masters of the plastic form, are menacing enough in this medium, but this is usually because they bear haunting and uncanny facial features. And the Daleks are the one monster this series that you can't make more scary by adding fangs to them. Having written that, several World War II warplanes had shark fangs painted on them to make them look scarier, so perhaps the Daleks could adopt this tactic?

As many others have previously observed, these new Daleks have evidently been produced to appeal to the toy market. Indeed, their main design fault (that strange out-of-proportion back panel) looks as though it's an ideal fit for the bit that would break off from a plastic mould, so maybe toy manufacturers were too involved in the production of these new models?

According to the *Brilliant Book of Doctor Who 2011*, this aperture is supposed to conceal a whole variety of new weapons. In *Doctor Who Confidential*, Steven Moffat revealed that these new Daleks were supposed to have fleshy eyeballs. These would indeed have made the new Daleks scarier, but you can't see them in this episode, as the *Brilliant Book* reveals that this design aspect was removed because the production team felt that it would have been too scary for children. Indeed, also in the *Brilliant Book*, Moffat referred to the new look Dalek as just being a "prop". Well, I can refute this with a well-known Sarah Jane Smith quote from *Genesis of the Daleks* - "We're talking about the Daleks. The most evil creatures ever invented!" - so it does very much matter what they look like.

Admittedly, I've always initially disliked the portrayals of Davros after Michael Wisher's original masterclass performance in *Genesis of the Daleks*, but got used to them in the end (after the initial shock). However, I don't think the same epiphany will occur for me with regards to the new look Daleks. Steven Moffat has since stated that the old Daleks will return, and it's telling that that when the new Daleks did reappear in *The Pandorica Opens*, they looked far more threatening when covered in crud... Andrew Gunn was very gushing in *Doctor Who Confidential* when he made evident his pride of being the *Doctor Who* director who managed to get eight Daleks on screen at one time (although I don't think he actually managed to get them all in one shot). However, as with the TARDIS redesign, the show's limited new budget could have papered up a few other cracks here and there with the money they spent on these new Daleks. They're also rubbish shots, seemingly unable to hit a moving target like the Doctor. (Perhaps they haven't got the steering quite right yet?) In addition to this, the Doctor addresses the Dalek Supreme even more disrespectfully than usual: "Don't mess with me, Sweetheart!" This sounds almost like something that a certain River Song would say...

Victory of the Daleks ends with the kind of sentimental maudlin moment that marred many an episode of *Star Trek: the Next Generation* (specifically the recurring desire of many of the aliens or androids within it to become more "human"). To be fair to Mark Gatiss, he did signal earlier on that this might happen when he got Churchill to challenge Bracewell with the question of whether or not he was "a man" (i.e. strong and brave).

There was also a similar mawkish moment at the end of the 2005 episode *Dalek* (which saw the first appearance of Edward Thomas' brilliant redesign of the Daleks), where the last Dalek in the universe did a lot of unusual soul searching. The scene where Bracewell is about to explode is given its own *Doctor Who* twist also, since the alien Doctor unwittingly appeals to the Dalek (rather than the human) inside Bracewell, by reminding him of how angry the death of his parents and the massacres in the First World War made him. So, it's down to Amy to save the day again, by getting Bracewell to recount some experiences and emotions that Daleks have never felt, such as unrequited love. (In *ST:TNG*, Bracewell may well have asked that cliché, "What is this thing you call *love*?") It's somewhat ironic that, just an episode after berating humanity, the Doctor is now hoping that it's Bracewell's latent humanity that will save the day.

The Doctor's casual threat to blow up the TARDIS on the Dalek ship could well serve as a foreshadowing of this actual event at the end of this series... Which is a shame, as when the Doctor and Amy lean up against his time machine at the end of this episode, we can see that the regenerated TARDIS has now got an unusually rich lacquer. The TARDIS then dematerialises to reveal this series' ubiquitous crack in the universe appearing on the wall behind it...

Did You Know? Bill Paterson (Bracewell in *Victory of the Daleks*) starred opposite Michael Gambon (of *A Christmas Carol* fame) in *The Singing Detective*, playing Philip Marlow's psychiatrist.

4: The Time of Angels

Writer: Steven Moffat
Director: Adam Smith
Originally broadcast: 24 April 2010

Cast

The Doctor: Matt Smith
Amy Pond: Karen Gillan
River Song: Alex Kingston
Alistair: Simon Dutton
Security Guard: Mike Skinner
Octavian: Iain Glen
Christian: Mark Springer
Angelo: Troy Glasgow
Bob: David Atkins
Marco: Darren Morfitt

Steven's review: Now that's more like it. After a couple of lesser episodes over the last two weeks that failed to match the level reached by *The Eleventh Hour*, showrunner Steven Moffat returns with the kind of story he used to provide once a year for the Russell T Davies era - virtuoso plotting, brilliant dialogue, and an emphasis on scares and surprises. Indeed, this one builds directly on two of those previous high points: 2007's *Blink* and 2008's two-parter consisting of *Silence in the Library* and *Forest of the Dead*. With a top-quality script from Moffat, combined with excellent production values, *The Time of Angels* is the highlight of the season so far.

The marvellous pre-titles sequence is a classic five minutes of *Doctor Who*. It shows Moffat's plotting at its most exuberant; right from the get-go he's tossing out one plot element after another at high speed, keeping the audience off-balance and challenging us to keep up. It opens with a deliberately baffling shot of a dazed security guard (an improbable cameo from British rapper Mike Skinner) staggering around in an open field, approached by a tuxedo-wearing man named Alistair. The *James Bond* feel of this opening is only enhanced by the fact that the suave Alistair is played by Simon Dutton, alias TV's *The Saint*. In reality, they are not in a field but in the metal corridors of a spaceship; the guard has been affected by "hallucinogenic lipstick... She's here." Cut to a woman striding along in an evening gown and a pair of killer stiletto heels. She comes to a locked door, takes out a futuristic pistol, and shoots it open. Inside is a box-like piece of equipment; her pistol converts into a cutting torch, and she begins carving strange letters into it.

Then suddenly, a caption pops up which could surely only appear in *Doctor Who*: "12,000 years later." As he did in *The Girl in the Fireplace* and *Silence in the Library*, Moffat is using temporal trickery at the beginning of an episode to draw the audience in. The Doctor, accompanied by a bored Amy Pond, is looking through a museum when he discovers the box - now ancient and decayed, but with the letters still visible - and tells her it's a flight recorder from "one of the old starliners."

Amy: "So?"

The Doctor: "The writing. The graffiti. Old High Gallifreyan! The lost language of the Time Lords. There were days... these words could burn stars, and raise up empires, and topple gods."

Amy: "What does this say?"

The Doctor: "...'Hello, Sweetie.'"

Those of us who remember *Silence in the Library* will immediately know what those last words portend - and why the Doctor says them with such hilarious resignation in his voice. The woman is River Song, using the flight recorder to send a message to the Doctor across time. Back in the TARDIS, they replay the recorder's security footage, showing Alistair and his guards confronting River at an airlock door. She tells him she wanted to see what was in the ship's vault, and warns, "This ship won't reach its destination." Then she simply says, "As I said on the dance floor… you might want to find something to hang on to," blows the airlock open, and is launched into space. Naturally the TARDIS is there to catch her, and she lands in the Doctor's arms, jumping up with a cry of "Follow that ship!" And so the adventure begins…

It's a perfect teaser, somehow seeming like quintessential *Doctor Who* while at the same time having a style and pace that are quite new, and more akin to some of Moffat's sitcom work. I'm thinking especially of *Coupling*, where he would often play with techniques like out-of-sequence storytelling, or multiple viewpoints, or in one case even have a whole episode in split-screen. The sitcom style continues into the first part of the episode, which is dominated by the comic sparring between the Doctor and River Song. When we met her previously in the Library story, it was obvious that she had had a long and intimate relationship with the Doctor, even though for him, it was his first meeting with her. As he says here, "Time travel - we keep meeting in the wrong order." In that story she mentioned "the crash of the *Byzantium*" as something in her past, and now we get to see it.

So this is a younger, more playful version of River, who delights in constantly scoring points off the Doctor. Smith and Kingston seem to fall with great ease into a very funny "bickering married couple" dynamic, despite their twenty-year age difference. The Doctor is most annoyed when it turns out she can fly the TARDIS better than him. When she parks it with great precision next to the wreck of the *Byzantium*, he is hilariously discomfited:

The Doctor: "But… it didn't make the noise."

River: "What noise?"

The Doctor: "You know. The…" *(makes wheezing, groaning sound)*

River: "It's not supposed to make that noise. *You* leave the brakes on."

The Doctor's habit of calling Amy by her surname ("Come along, Pond!") was apparently something Matt Smith came up with in rehearsals, and it fits his "mad professor" persona very well. By this stage, it's almost alarming how quickly I've come to accept Smith as the Doctor - there's hardly been a single moment in all the episodes so far where he struck a false note.

This two-parter was actually the first story filmed for the season, but you'd never know it from the assurance of the performances, and the direction. The production team took the risk of going with an entirely new team of directors for this season, and Adam Smith (who also directed *The Eleventh Hour*) is a real find for the show. The whole story is filled with memorable, beautiful images; in particular, the stupendous effects shot of the enormous crashed ship, sticking up vertically out of an ancient temple set into a cliff face. I gather that, due to the current recession, the budget for *Doctor Who* has been trimmed somewhat compared with previous years, and it's true that in the first three episodes of this season, some economizing seems to have been made - for instance, compare the bare, empty set for the Dalek ship in last week's episode with similar sets in *The Parting of the Ways* or *Journey's End*. This story, though, looks as though it's had a decent amount of money spent on it - and it certainly deserved it.

It turns out that River is here to meet up with a team of soldier-clerics, led by Father Octavian. The idea of religious fighters of course resonates with medieval orders such as the Knights Templar, but I suspect Moffat simply wanted the amusing incongruity of a "bishop second class" in modern-day camouflage gear barking orders like, "Verger, how're we doing with those explosives?" Octavian and his men are here on a mission to neutralize the dangerous creature in the vault of the *Byzantium* - a Weeping Angel.

In 2007, Moffat scored a huge success with *Blink*, creating an episode which appears on many people's Top Ten lists, and also won him a third consecutive Hugo award. A large part of its success was due to the stunningly original Weeping Angels. A creature which can only move when you're not looking at it, otherwise it's frozen into stone - a wonderful concept, executed brilliantly in the form of beautiful statues which can turn, literally in the blink of an eye, into hideous fanged monsters. However, when the news came that the Angels would be returning in this new story, there was some concern that Moffat might simply be repeating himself, attempting to take advantage of a previous success by churning out a lesser sequel. He avoids that danger, though, by putting the Angels in a completely different setting and introducing several new abilities for them, providing just as many scares - but in new ways - as their previous episode.

In particular, the very image of an Angel now becomes dangerous. River provides a four-second loop of security camera footage of the Angel in the ship's vault, and Amy discovers that, impossibly, the recorded image keeps changing. According to a book about the Angels discovered by River, "That which holds the image of an Angel becomes itself an Angel" - and Amy, trapped in a locked shuttle pod with the recording, finds herself unable to escape as the Angel starts to actually come out of the screen, as in the climax of the horror movie *The Ring*. Then the creepiness gets amped up even further. Whereas in *Blink* if you made sure to keep staring at an Angel it was harmless, now if you stare at an Angel's eyes for too long you can become "infected" - as the Doctor reads, "The eyes are not the windows of the soul, they are the doors. Beware what may enter there." Amy manages to deactivate the recording of the Angel, but she starts to experience hallucinations such as a stream of stone dust falling from her eye (an excellently done effect) and her hand turning to stone.

Karen Gillan, like Matt Smith, gives an excellent performance in her first-filmed episode. She is greatly intrigued by River and quickly bonds with her, and enjoys teasing the Doctor over his attitude towards her. When River asks the Doctor to "sonic her" to boost her communicator's homing signal for the clerics and he grumpily complies, her delivery of "Oooh Doctor, you *sonicked* her" is a delight. Amy is so direct and child-like (as if part of her is still very much the seven-year-old girl she was when she first met the

Doctor) as she asks the questions we all want answered, in one of my favourite sequences of the whole episode:

Amy: "Is River Song your wife?"

The Doctor: *(sigh)*

Amy: "'Cause she's someone from your future. And the way she talks to you, I've never seen anyone do that. ... She's Mrs Doctor from the future, isn't she? Is she gonna be your wife one day?"

The Doctor: "Yes... you're right. I am definitely Mister Grumpyface today."

Matt Smith perfectly times the last line there, leaving a long enough pause after "Yes" for Amy (and the audience) to think for a moment that he might actually be answering her question about River Song. In fact, rather than answering questions, the episode introduces still more mysteries about River; when Amy directly challenges her about being the Doctor's future wife, she replies, "This is the Doctor we're talking about - do you really think it could be anything that simple?" She certainly has one particular secret she's keeping from the Doctor, as a conversation between her and Father Octavian reveals:

Octavian: "He doesn't know yet, does he? Who and what you are."

River Song: "It's too early in his time stream."

Octavian: "Well, make sure he doesn't work it out, or he's not going to help us."

The party find their way into a labyrinth of passages leading up from the base of the cliff to the crashed ship, and begin to make their way through the maze. It's a "mortarium" created by the Aplans, the dead-and-gone native species of this planet, and is filled with decayed statues - an ideal hiding place for a stone Angel. As with the earlier exterior matte shot of the crashed ship, the wide shots of the labyrinth interior, illuminated by a floating "gravity globe" (a nice bit of future-tech continuity with Season Two's *The Impossible Planet*) are eerily beautiful.

We have the familiar, but always effective scenario of a small group trapped in hostile territory, being picked off one by one. Several of the cleric cannon-fodder succumb to the hidden Angel as the tension increases. And unlike the ones in *Blink*, which didn't kill people but just banished them backwards in time, this Angel definitely kills its victims, nastily. Amazingly enough, Moffat managed to write eight episodes before this one without a single character being killed on screen - most unusual for *Doctor Who* which, even though it's often thought of as a kids' show, generally has at least one character meeting a horrible fate each episode.

And he's still expertly controlling the mix of light-hearted adventure and sudden shocks. The Doctor is busy cheerfully burbling on about how he once had dinner with the chief architect of the Aplans, and how the Aplans all had two heads. Then, suddenly, he and River simultaneously come to the realization that all the statues they've seen only have one head... One quick experiment with momentarily switching their torches off, and the truth is revealed - all the statues are Weeping Angels. Their decayed state means that they can only move slowly - in a neat continuation of the "image" theme, the fact that they've lost their image means they have also lost most of their power. At least, for the moment - it becomes clear that the Angel in the *Byzantium* deliberately caused the crash of the ship into the temple so that these Angels could drain the ship's power and recover their own.

One of the clerics left behind to guard the entrance, Bob, is used by the Angel to communicate with the Doctor and Octavian. This could be considered another case of Moffat recycling a previous idea - the data ghosts from the Library story, which also provided a means for characters to speak from beyond death. But it's not quite the same, and in any case it's a supremely creepy moment as his calm voice emerges from the communicator.

The party finally reach the top of the maze, but the base of the crashed ship is thirty feet above them, out of reach. With no way out, the Angels surrounding them and their torches and gravity globe being drained, it's up to the Doctor to find a way out. "Angel Bob" continues taunting him over the communicator, telling him how Bob died in fear and pain,

63

and how the rest of them will suffer the same fate now that they are trapped. In response, the Doctor borrows Octavian's gun and delivers a rousing, *Bad Wolf*-style speech to lead up to the cliffhanger. It's an effective enough ending, but its impact is somewhat reduced for anyone who has seen it constantly in trailers for the past month or so:

The Doctor: "Didn't anyone ever tell you? There's one thing you never put in a trap, if you're smart... If you have any plans about seeing tomorrow, there's one thing you never ever put in a trap."

Bob: "And what would that be, sir?"

The Doctor: "Me."

He fires at the gravity globe, which explodes. What happens next? Tune in next week to find out...

Steven's Classic Who DVD Recommendation: *The Key to Time* boxset, consisting of six stories making up *Doctor Who*'s sixteenth season. Principally because of the relationship between the Doctor and his assistant, Romana, which is very reminiscent of his sparring here with River Song.

Kevin's review: That's more like it! *The Time of Angels* is a splendid return to form for Steven Moffat's *Doctor Who*. From the off, we're reintroduced to the splendid River Song, who's found an ingenious way to send an SOS to the Doctor, albeit one that is highly redolent of her very individual voice: "Hello Sweetie". Thus we learn that River has knowledge of the Doctor's tongue, Old High Gallifreyan, which looks to have more characters than our alphabet. As an aside, it's interesting to note that the TARDIS doesn't translate this message into English for Amy - perhaps it keeps some things for the Doctor's eyes only?

For the first time this season, the TARDIS materialises at exactly the time that the Doctor had intended it to (although there is a significant delay between the airlock blowing and the TARDIS' appearance, so River didn't get much use of the air corridor that she'd asked the Doctor to provide). It's very amusing that River is able to pilot the TARDIS far better than the Doctor has ever done. River says that she was taught by an expert, and jokes that the Doctor was busy that day. So, sometime in the future, the Doctor does finally gain mastery of the TARDIS, to the extent probably, of not leaving the brakes on and thus making that wheezing groaning sound. This makes a great deal of sense, as TARDISes were originally supposed to blend into the background when landing on alien planets, so a very noisy, trumpety arrival would have been unwarranted.

Having written that, most other Time Lords that the Doctor has encountered evidently also liked leaving the brakes on - perhaps as a form of 'macho' engine revving? Although, like the Doctor, most of these were renegade Time Lords who probably hadn't been properly instructed on how to fly a TARDIS. River isn't fazed by the fact that this current TARDIS console seems to have been greatly rejigged to suit the character of the latest Doctor, so it may be that the console doesn't change so much by the time 'her' later Doctor comes around, or that she's just very adaptable.

Looking at the Doctor's face, River comments that this meeting is still early on for him. As this is only the second time that we have encountered River, this must mean that this is indeed one of the Doctor's first meetings with her, although it could also be read as stating that the Doctor has many more regenerations after this. So, the idea that the Doctor has only 13 regenerations may well have been shelved as far back as the Doctor's first encounter with River in 2008's *Silence in the Library*.

River is again working with a team of people, although this time it's a squad of military clerics. When Father Octavian greets River, he complains that she had promised him an army. Obviously, his anxiety is probably related to the threat at hand, namely the Weeping Angel, or it could refer to a bigger crisis. In addition to the inspiration of the Japanese horror film *The Ring*, there's also a definite nod to James Cameron's *Aliens* in this episode, as Father Octavian and his troops are the rather British equivalent of the more American marines in that movie. Steven Moffat's depiction of a 'blue collar future' is far more bourgeois than that of James Cameron; Octavian has quite a patrician bearing, although his squaddies are still working class. One of the subplots in *Aliens* involved a clash between the grunts and their high born, but incompetent, commander. However there's no time in *The Time of Angels/Flesh and Stone* for a similar class war. Like *Aliens*, the planet on which the Angel has crashed the *Byzantium* has recently been terraformed. However, the Doctor et al have arrived before the Weeping Angel has any opportunity of suborning the local population. In a nice contrast to *Aliens*, the soldiers here are terrorised by Angels, rather than demonic aliens (although some of the decaying Angels do look quite decadent and nasty).

It's not made clear which church Father Octavian and his clerics are members of. The *TARDIS Index File* wiki suggests that 'Sacred Bob' may be a reference to the supposed founder of the faux church of the SubGenius (1). However, there are several St. Roberts in the Catholic Church, with the most notable being Robert Bellarmine, who was the first to ask Galileo to recant his views on heliocentrism, upon the instructions of the Pope. Christian and Angelo are obviously names related to Christianity, although the naming of the latter is more than a tad ironic on Moffat's part.

'Octavian' is a troublesome name from a Christian point of view, especially as it was the original name of the antipope Victor IV. However, the most famous Octavian was the great nephew of Julius Caesar, who would later become the first Roman emperor under his adopted name of Augustus. The Romans granted Augustus godhood upon his death. So, it may be that these militant clerics are not Christian, if they regard the pagan Octavian as being sacred. There could be a class distinction here, as Octavian's troops have modern Italian names, while his is rather more ancient. The naming of the starliner as 'Byzantium' continues the Roman theme, as this was the name of the city that became the capital of the long lasting Eastern Roman Empire. It's also great to see such a brilliant actor as Iain Glen providing some excellent gravitas for the role of Father Octavian. He does very much remind me of Bernard Horsfall, who played several prominent roles in the Classic Series.

The naming of the Aplan catacombs as the 'maze of the dead' could be a reference to the similarly entitled 1970 Philip K. Dick novel *A Maze of Death*, although, beyond the obvious science fiction theme, there's not much similarity in plot. Admittedly, it does involve a small group of people who are picked off one by one by mysterious assailants, but the murderers turn out to be some of the remaining members of the group. However, it turns out that these events only happened in a virtual reality dream world created by their spaceship's computer to help the crew pass the time while the ship is effectively crippled, unable to return them home with no hope of rescue. Yet the twist is that one of the godlike beings from the simulation turns out to be real... The Doctor mentions that he had dinner with the Aplans' Chief Architect, which appears to be a reference to Steven Moffat's first *Doctor Who* script, a spoof adventure called *The Curse of Fatal Death* from 1999, which was broadcast during a *Comic Relief* telethon.

Moffat repeats the device of having a disembodied dead voice over a radio creeping everyone out, which as Steven Cooper has pointed out, was already employed in *Silence in the Library/Forest of the Dead* (which is also an advance from the similar tactic of his utilising a haunting kid's voice distorted by a gas mask in Moffat's 2005 script *The Empty Child*). It's still very effective here, mainly down to some excellent voice acting by David Atkins. Steven Moffat seems to instinctively know what will scare people, beyond the obvious employment of sudden loud noises and gore. Obviously, it's not a device that you can use too often, as regular viewers of the show would no doubt get fed up with it, but it's still very powerful here.

Matt Smith gets to show off his footballing prowess by giving the gravity globe a good kick. In addition to this, he claims to have been on Virginia Woolf's bowling team. And despite the greater competence that River shows in flying the TARDIS, and the mystery that surrounds who she really is, the Doctor still has the capacity to surprise her. This is first shown when the Doctor demonstrates that he knows exactly what the conditions are like on Alfava Metraxis just by sticking his head out of the TARDIS door for a moment, without having to rely on the TARDIS' analysis. River also tells Octavian that the Doctor is the equivalent of an army. So even the very resourceful River has no option but to look askance at the Doctor in the light of their seemingly helpless plight at the end of this episode...

Did You Know? The climax of this episode was spoiled for many viewers in the UK by the appearance of an animated trailer on screen for the Graham Norton hosted show *Over the Rainbow* (which sought to find an unknown actor to play Dorothy in a new stage production of *The Wizard of Oz*). A Graham Norton voiceover also interrupted the first episode of the *Doctor Who* revival in 2005!

(1).http://tardis.wikia.com/wiki/Bob_(The_Time_of_Angels)

5: Flesh and Stone

Writer: Steven Moffat
Director: Adam Smith
Originally broadcast: 1 May 2010

Cast

The Doctor: Matt Smith
Amy Pond: Karen Gillan
River Song: Alex Kingston
Octavian: Iain Glen
Bob: David Atkins
Marco: Darren Morfitt
Pedro: Mark Monero
Phillip: George Russo

Steven's review: *Flesh and Stone* maintains the high quality displayed by the first half of this two-parter, *The Time of Angels*. To start with, it's a straightforward, satisfying continuation and conclusion, as the story of the Doctor and Amy, with River Song and her party of solder-clerics, being pursued by Weeping Angels through the crashed spaceship *Byzantium* makes for an exciting, action-packed roller coaster. But as the episode progresses, more and more elements of what is obviously a much larger, season-spanning arc come to the fore, and although the story ends with the immediate threat defeated, many questions remain unanswered.

The first part of the episode is all action. Last week's cliffhanger is quickly resolved, as the Doctor's shooting out of a "gravity globe" provides the party with the impetus needed to reach the base of the ship, thirty feet above them. As with *The Time of Angels*, director Adam Smith provides top-notch visuals throughout. In a lovely effects shot, the picture rotates to show them standing upside-down on the hull of the ship, held there by its artificial gravity. They have escaped the Angels for the moment, but the respite is only temporary - the Angels are still absorbing power from the ship to restore themselves, and before long they are right behind the party as the Doctor struggles to open the internal doors of the ship.

They make it through to the secondary flight deck, where the Doctor settles into an amusingly *Star Trek*-like command chair to have a chat with 'Angel Bob' - the soldier whom the Angels killed last episode and reanimated to use as a mouthpiece. The idea of giving the Angels a voice was a risk on the part of writer Steven Moffat; their silent, inscrutable nature was a major part of their success in their first appearance (2007's *Blink*), and by allowing them to communicate with the Doctor, their menace could well have been diminished. I think it works, though, because of Bob's calm, almost apologetic demeanour. The Doctor has some fun mocking the Angel's seriousness, but you never get the sense that he's not worried about the situation.

Then things take a sinister turn as the Doctor realizes that during the last few minutes Amy has been injecting numbers randomly into her dialogue, counting down from ten without realizing it. Bob admits that the Angels are behind it - Amy's experience in the last episode of looking into the eyes of an Angel has affected her, and the Angels are in her mind.

Bob tells the Doctor that the Angels are laughing at him for not realizing what's going on - notably, using almost the same phrasing ("The Doctor in the TARDIS hasn't noticed") as Prisoner Zero did in similar circumstances in *The Eleventh Hour*. Suddenly, the overarching season plot moves into the foreground as a crack in the universe like the ones we've seen in previous episodes opens up in the wall, with bright light spilling through it.

The four previous seasons of *Doctor Who* under Russell T Davies also had season-long arcs, but always very loose ones which didn't really have much impact on the individual stories - mostly just a quick mention of something (like "Bad Wolf" in Season 1) which would be tossed into each story but not paid off until the season finale. The most substantial of these arcs was probably the Saxon thread in Season 3, but even there it tended to hover around the edges of the stories, touching minor characters but going unnoticed by the Doctor and companion. Here, Moffat is deliberately calling attention to the ongoing plot and placing it front and centre - in fact, the crack ends up being crucial to the resolution of this episode's threat. It could be said that this is a long-overdue innovation for *Doctor Who* - for well over a decade now it's been standard practice in sci-fi series to have long-running arcs threaded through a season's worth (or more) of episodes. It will be interesting to see whether this more complicated season structure results in any reduction of the casual, non-genre audience - which is very much in the majority, in the UK at least.

The Doctor stays to examine the crack, while he sends the others to find a way through the ship's oxygen factory to its primary flight deck. This provides another lovely visual, as a wall slides up to reveal a huge forest that occupies the heart of the vessel. The concept of "treeborgs" - trees with technology embedded, sucking in starlight for power and giving out oxygen, is brilliant. Fundamentally this story is mainly a simple chase, with the Angels in pursuit of our heroes, but the variation in setting - from caves, to corridors, and now to this dense forest - stops it from becoming monotonous.

The Doctor discovers that the crack is releasing pure time energy into the universe, which can erase the existence of anyone it touches ("Oh, that's bad. That's extremely very not good"). Then he looks up to discover he is surrounded by Angels; in the course of carefully making his way out from among them, one of them grabs him. Up until now we have never seen an Angel move on screen, so it's a nearly subliminal moment of shock - it happens so quickly you almost doubt your own eyes - when we see the hand of one of them suddenly close on his collar. But the Doctor manages to escape into the forest after the others, and the Angel is left holding just his jacket.

In the forest, Amy collapses, with the image of an Angel now visible in her eye. The praise I gave last week for Matt

Smith, Karen Gillan and Alex Kingston's performances applies equally to this episode. Smith is again excellent at showing the Doctor's mind working at top speed, and he's not afraid to have the Doctor be abrupt and shouty with Amy - knowing she has only seconds left, he simply tells her to shut up while he's thinking. He realises that Amy must now keep her eyes closed in order not to succumb to the Angel within her, so the Doctor has to leave her in the forest while he and River go ahead to the primary flight deck. Father Octavian insists on accompanying River, and - much to her horror - tells the Doctor her secret:

Octavian: "Doctor Song is in my personal custody. I released her from the Stormcage containment facility four days ago, and I am legally responsible for her until she's accomplished her mission, and earned her pardon."

Later on, Octavian will warn the Doctor not to trust River Song, revealing that she was in prison because she killed a man - "a good man, a hero to many." It's beginning to look less and less likely that the relationship between the Doctor and River will turn out to be a simple case of time-crossed lovers, as most people assumed before this story.

With a brusque "Later," the Doctor heads off after the others, leaving Amy sitting alone, eyes closed. And then, strangely, he's right back there again, holding Amy's hands and telling her she needs to start trusting him. The first time I watched the episode, this sequence seemed a bit odd and out of place, but I thought nothing more of it. It was only after subsequent viewings that I grasped what Steven Moffat is up to here. This *isn't the same Doctor* as the one who just left; it's all shot in extreme close-up, to disguise the fact, but if you look carefully you'll see that he's wearing a different watch, and a jacket (and not the same one that got taken by the Angels, either). He's quite different in manner, too, almost desperately tender as he tells Amy it's vital that she remembers what he told her when she was seven. Clearly this is a later Doctor who has crossed back into his own timeline here, for some dire reason to do with Amy's memories, which will be revealed at the appropriate time (probably in the season finale). I suspect that once the whole season is over, all sorts of earlier events that might have seemed weird at the time will take on new meanings. For instance, remember last week's joke scene about the TARDIS making its characteristic noise because the Doctor leaves the brakes on? What if it wasn't there just for the joke, but as a way to give the Doctor a way to arrive silently if he needed to? Moffat even goes so far as to make the Doctor muse about an event from back in the 2008 Christmas special (*The Next Doctor*):

The Doctor: "It's been happening all around me and I haven't even noticed. … The CyberKing - a giant Cyberman walks over all of Victorian London and no one even remembers!"

Is Moffat cleaning up something that I remember many people complained about at the time as needing just too much suspension of disbelief? Or did he get together with Russell T Davies and plant some seeds for this season two years ago? Or is he just having a laugh? I guess we'll find out in a few weeks' time…

In the forest, the Angels are closing in on Amy and the clerics - they are attacking the treeborgs in order to destroy their light, leading to the wonderfully surreal line, "The trees are going out!" - when another crack appears. The Angels disappear, apparently scared of the uncontrolled time energy the thing pours out, and the clerics are mysteriously drawn, one by one, to investigate the crack. As they get close, they vanish, erased from time, and their remaining comrades cannot even remember them. I found the creepiness of this sequence very well done, and reminiscent of one of my favourite episodes of the original *Twilight Zone*, *And When the Sky Was Opened*, where a group of three pioneering astronauts likewise disappear one by one, yanked out of existence. At last, Amy is left alone.

As Father Octavian, Iain Glen has been very good throughout this story, making the most of a part that doesn't actually have all that much for him to do. He's mostly just a smoothly competent military leader, albeit with the interesting wrinkle that he's a leader of clerics - and it's refreshing to have a character whose religion is portrayed positively, yet not overemphasized. In his final scene, he is at last given some material to work with. The Doctor has used River's computer to pinpoint the moment of the cataclysmic explosion which caused these cracks all through time; he tells Octavian, "Never mind the Angels, there's worse here than Angels." The lights go out momentarily, and when they come back up Octavian replies, "I beg to differ, sir," as an Angel has its arm in a stranglehold around his neck. It's a moment of brilliantly combined laughter and shock. The Doctor realizes there's no way out - while the Angel is frozen, Octavian is trapped, but the moment he looks away it will be free to kill him. He sombrely obeys the cleric's command to leave him.

The Doctor: "I wish I'd known you better."

Octavian: "I think, sir, you know me at my best."

The cast of characters has now been whittled down to just the Doctor and River in the primary flight deck of the *Byzantium*, and Amy alone in the forest, surrounded by Angels. She still can't open her eyes, so she has to use her communicator as a proximity detector as she attempts to join the others. This section was the weakest part of the whole story for me, for a couple of reasons. Firstly, Moffat is rather gratuitously changing the rules as we understood them from *Blink*. In that episode, the Angels' freezing into stone when they were observed was an unalterable, involuntary aspect of their nature. But now, it seems to be something they can control - which immediately makes them much less original and interesting. Also, one of the cleverest ideas in *Blink* was that the Angels didn't move while we the audience could see them, even if none of the characters in the story were observing them. That idea is also discarded here, as Amy stumbles and falls to the ground, and several Angels slowly turn their heads to look at her. The movement is creepy and well done, with nice grinding-stone sound effects, but again it's an original idea being thrown away in favour of something more commonplace.

Secondly, in order to explain why the Angels don't simply attack Amy, there's a speech from the Doctor about how they are more interested in running from the crack than they are in her, and that if she simply walks as though she can see then the Angels will believe her and "their instincts will kick in." It's an uncharacteristically weak justification by Moffat's standards, made more annoying by the fact that the whole sequence turns out to have no significance at all - it's just a bit of time-filling jeopardy for Amy, until River eventually manages to teleport her to the flight deck in the nick of time. At least the scene does end with a nice exchange between the Doctor and River: "River Song, I could bloody kiss you." "Maybe when you're older."

The final defeat of the Angels, though, is a very nice piece of plotting by Moffat, making use of the fact that the viewer has probably forgotten (I certainly did) that they've actually been moving up through a vertical ship all this time. Indeed, near the beginning of the episode he puts the solution right out there in plain sight, disguised with humour:

Amy: "What if the gravity fails?"

The Doctor: "...we'll all plunge to our deaths. See, I've thought about it."

As the Angels drain away the last of the ship's power, the artificial gravity disappears and they fall back into the advancing crack. River gets another opportunity to display her cleverness and quickness of understanding - all that's needed is for the Doctor to tell her to "Get a grip," and she instantly gets what's about to happen. She, Amy, and the Doctor hold onto the flight deck consoles for dear life as the Angels tumble away from them through the suddenly side-on forest (another wonderfully memorable visual) into the crack, which closes.

In the mop-up, there's a farewell - or rather, an *au revoir* - to River on the beach, as the Doctor confronts her with what he learned from Octavian. She admits that she was in prison for killing "the best man I've ever known." From her reluctance to give any further details, the implication is clear that she means the Doctor, but I'm quite sure there are many more twists in this tale to come. You get the sense that these two have come to enjoy sparring with each other. She tells the Doctor that they'll meet again soon, "when the Pandorica opens" - a name that was previously mentioned by Prisoner Zero in *The Eleventh Hour*. The Doctor dismisses the Pandorica as a fairy tale, to which River teasingly replies, "Aren't we all?"

And so they part, with River's future leading to an ending we already know, while the Doctor is heading into the unknown toward their next meeting ("I look forward to it." "I remember it well.") The Doctor, left brooding on the beach after her departure, seems to cheer up at the thought that "time can be rewritten." Is he thinking about River's fate?

The final scene closes the first part of the season's story as the Doctor and Amy return to Amy's bedroom five minutes after she left at the end of the first episode, and she shows him the wedding dress hanging in her wardrobe. She confesses she's getting married to Rory in the morning, and shows the Doctor her engagement ring. And then she moves into territory not previously entered by any of the Doctor's companions, in displaying an obvious sexual interest in him - which he hilariously fails to pick up on until she actually goes to kiss him.

The Doctor: "Amy, listen to me, I am 907 years old. Do you understand what that means?"

Amy: "It's been a while?"

As a long-time *Doctor Who* fan I should probably have been having palpitations at this point, but I'm afraid I was too busy laughing. Anyone familiar with Moffat's comedy work will recognize this sort of scene, and Smith and Gillan, with their brilliant chemistry together, play it perfectly. But it's not just thrown in as a joke out of nowhere - Amy's direct, uninhibited character was established back in the first episode as she watched approvingly while the Doctor was changing clothes, and her near-death experiences on the *Byzantium* have only sharpened her desire to seize the moment.

No doubt to his vast relief, the Doctor is able to divert Amy's attack when he suddenly realizes that the day of her wedding is the day of the explosion which created the cracks in time. The last shot is a flashback to River Song's computer screen, showing the critical date, 26-06-2010 - the date on which the finale of this season is scheduled to be broadcast in the UK, and no doubt the date on which Moffat's grand design will be revealed.

The Doctor: "Mad, impossible Amy Pond! I don't know why... but quite possibly the single most important thing in the history of the universe is that I get you sorted out right now..."

Steven's Classic Who DVD Recommendation: As for the previous review, the six-story Key to Time boxset makes a good companion to this two-parter. Not only does the Doctor have a rather River Song-like assistant in Romana, but the third story, *The Stones of Blood*, even has monsters of living stone.

Kevin's review: *Flesh and Stone* is another brilliant episode by Steven Moffat. Having written that, the beginning is a bit odd - why would a spaceship need gravity on its hull? I guess it would help in the servicing and maintenance of the hull, but one wouldn't have thought that this feature would need to be switched on all the time.

Having the clerics fire at the Angels in the airlock created a suitably scary moment, as this showed us the Angels creeping up on our heroes, staccato fashion. Octavian blames River for the loss of his men, and threatens to tell the Doctor who River really is if he loses any more. Amy's countdown is scripted perfectly by Moffat, especially her frustration when she keeps saying "five" instead of "fine". The limited budget for this season isn't in evidence here, as the forest on the starliner is brilliantly realised - such a *mise-en-scène* is redolent of a Hollywood production.

Having sent the others ahead, the Doctor is caught by the Angels. However, they seem mesmerised by the crack on the wall, allowing the Doctor to escape while making a comment about how it's never a good idea to let him talk. Yet all the Doctor's enemies do tend to want to have a good chinwag with him, with the Angels especially having gone to extremes to allow this to happen. Obviously, their main purpose is to taunt their victims, to convey their power by verbally abusing them, and yet they do also find the Doctor engaging. Then again, having previously expressed regret for Bob's loss of life, the Doctor now seems to relish taunting this fact in return; although, obviously, he's talking to the Angels, rather than Bob. The reappearance of the crack in Amy's bedroom wall is disturbing enough for both her and the Doctor, yet it's made even more so by the fact that this "crooked smile" seems to grimace (like a mouth) in anticipation of the Doctor's noticing of it.

The Doctor's party attempt to escape from the Angels by heading in the forest. Unlike the metaphorical *Forest of the Dead* that followed the Doctor's first encounter with River in *Silence in the Library*, this is a real Forest of the Dead, in which deadly Angels stalk them. This is also the most literal representation of the "dark fairytale" theme in the series. Having written that, this forest is well lit by the treeborgs; that is, until the Angels start ripping the lights out. These are almost Biblical scenes, since they feature angels in a paradisiacal forest.

Amy's predicament is very ably presented, and the idea that there's an Angel ready to climb out of her (and therefore kill her in the process) is well executed. Viewers of a particularly sensitive disposition may well have nightmares of Angels doing the same to them, especially as they can't help but look into the Angels' eyes when they are advancing on screen. There is also the mantra that whatever contains the image of an Angel is an Angel itself... I've heard that a viewer of the Japanese horror film *The Ring*, which plays with a similar concept, put a blanket over his TV in order to prevent any ghostly girls from crawling out of the screen to get him, so it would be amusing if any viewers of the previous episode, *The Time of Angels*, have the same reaction.

Although the resolution of *Blink* suggested that the Angels could take the form of any statue, all the ones we see on screen here are Angels. What isn't explained is why the Angels took this form in the first place. Of course, Angels are common to Judaism, Christianity, and Islam, so these figures are recognisable to the majority of humanity. Indeed, angels are regarded as being messengers from God, and thus would be seen as beneficent by most people, so it could be that this is something that the Angels utilise to fool their prey. And yet, taking the form of stone angels makes them redolent of Death, as such statues are most commonly found in Victorian gothic graveyards…

The solution to Amy's deadly dilemma is simple and elegant enough. However, the Doctor then abandons Amy to head for the secondary flight deck, on the belief that she would slow the whole party done, despite Amy pointing out, reasonably enough, that there are enough people there to help speed her up. So, the main function of this is to allow the Doctor to have some more jawjaw with River and Octavian. And to enable the staging of the very strange scene when the Doctor apparently returns and asks Amy to remember what he told her when she was 7. Which left dedicated viewers scratching their heads wondering what he meant. Of course, as my fellow reviewer Steven correctly predicted, this scene has everything to do with the series finale.

Octavian refuses to let River out of his sight, which leads the Doctor to ask if they're engaged. Octavian, keeping his pact with River, suggests that he and River are indeed engaged. Which may have been intended by Moffat to inject some sexual tension into the proceedings, although the viewers already know that this isn't true, and that Octavian is effectively River's gaoler. And it isn't long before Octavian reveals their true relationship, and the fact that River is in his custody. Soon after, there is Octavian's very dignified death scene, in which he warns the Doctor not to trust River, as he doesn't know who or what she is, and that she was being held in the Stormcage for killing a man, "a hero to many". I agree with my fellow reviewer, Steven Cooper, that this probably means that River will someday kill the Doctor... And yet, would she really be let out of gaol to immediately meet up with a man she's just killed? Octavian, as late as the airlock scene at the beginning of this episode, evidently didn't trust the Doctor, and stated that only River could "control" him. So, if the "good man" is indeed the Doctor, then this is a realisation that Octavian has only gradually come to over the course of this episode.

So, the mystery as to who River is deepens. The puzzle concerning her true identity is reminiscent of that from the early days of the programme, which is still reflected in the title: *Doctor Who*. Over the past 50 years, we've learnt a great deal about the Doctor, and although it seems that we won't ever truly know who he is, a lot of the mystery surrounding his origins has evaporated. There are still some known unknowns, such as the Doctor's real name (which apparently, River knows if no one else does). Thus it's great to see this element of mystery returning to the programme. In my idle moments, I've speculated who River could be.

Maybe she's the Doctor's mother rather than his lover? Then again, the strange woman played by Claire Bloom in *The End of Time* was supposedly the Doctor's mother, and besides, the Doctor would instinctively recognise that he'd met a fellow Time Lord. Perhaps River Song is a future incarnation of the Doctor, and having her appear in the show early on is a clever way of Steven Moffat to get the audience accustomed to a female Doctor? However, the Doctor always appears to recognise versions of himself, and River died without regenerating at the end of *Forest of the Dead*. Then again, this could be explained away by her being the Doctor's final incarnation... She does keep saying that the current Doctor is early on in his timestream, and has also stated that "her Doctor" is a truly formidable opponent, and the very mention of her name had the Dalek in the series finale begging for mercy...

Admittedly, she did stand around looking clueless at the

Doctor at the end of *The Time of Angels*, but then again, Octavian later implied that she was manipulating the Doctor is some way. She also manages to fix the teleport on the flight deck, despite the fact that the Doctor had declared this to be impossible. This is the second occasion that we've seen her willing to offer up her life for the benefit of others, and out-Doctors the Doctor in this respect, as he's none too keen at giving himself up to the "crooked smile". And River seems to care about Amy as much as the Doctor does... No doubt I'm wrong, but such wild speculation is part of the fun, and proof that Steven Moffat has really captured our imaginations with the creation of River Song.

The Doctor's analysis of the crack in the universe reveals that the explosion that caused it is due to occur on the 26th of June 2010, which many an alert viewer would have surmised to be the airdate of the season finale... This was very brave of Steven Moffat, as airdates and schedules are subject to change at very short notice nowadays, especially due to early summer sporting events. So, the fact that Moffat was able to pick an airdate for the series finale shows what clout he has. However, it's rather a shame that he can't control the weather, as *The Big Bang* coincided with the only nice bit of the British summer, which reduced the viewing figures for the actual broadcast of the finale.

Just prior to Octavian's death, the Doctor gets a bit too excited about the fact that there weren't any ducks in the Leadworth duck pond during *The Eleventh Hour*, but you never know, this might have some significance during series 6... The Doctor comes to the realisation that Time can be "unwritten", not just "rewritten" - and there's a strange sound effect as he waves his finger in the air clockwise and anti-clockwise, and indeed, this realisation will play a vital role in *The Big Bang*. Amy has independent verification of what the Doctor's saying due to the fact that the various clerics seem to be actually forgotten by their squad leader, Marco, when they investigate the strange light that has so frightened the Angels. It appears as if the clerics concerned have never been born, something that will resonate with

Amy even more at the end of the later episode *Cold Blood*...

Once Amy is finally on her own, stumbling through the forest to get to the flight deck with her eyes closed, we get to see the Angels move in real time. I know that my fellow reviewer Steven feels that some of the Angels' logic was twisted to realise this scene, but I thought it made sense in the spirit of the moment. Like many predators, it seems that the Angels react to what their prey are doing. So, acting as though you can see is a tactic that could work, especially while the Angels are distracted by the crack in the universe.

Doctor Who Confidential revealed that most of the Angels seen on screen are actually actresses, rather than real statues. I guess if any of these actresses were 'resting' after finishing work on *Flesh and Stone*, then they could always have borrowed the costumes and make-up to do some street performances! This scene is the epitome of the "dark fairytale", and it can't be a coincidence that Amy is wearing a red hood throughout these episodes (although there's no sign of a Big Bad Wolf).

Matt Smith gets to display some real anger as he anxiously waits for Amy to stumble through the forest, most of which is aimed at River, simply because she is present with him on the flight deck. This is also because he knows that only a complex space/time event, such as himself, will be enough to close this particular "crooked smile". In many ways, this is reminiscent of the Doctor's behaviour during his Fifth incarnation. He and the Eleventh Doctor could get away with such outbursts of anger because they are otherwise quite charming and approachable, whereas similar scripts didn't work for the Sixth Doctor, as he was rather less endearing all round.

Much like Amy's closing of her eyes, the resolution of this episode hangs on a rather simple twist. The Angels, having drained practically all the power from the *Byzantium*, fall to their 'deaths' when the ship's artificial gravity fails. They literally become Falling Angels as they are unwittingly dispatched from Paradise... We don't get to see the Doctor, Amy, and River leaving the *Byzantium*, so I rather imagined that the gravity came back on after the Angels had been wiped from history. However, the Doctor states that they did have to climb out of the wreck.

River tells the Doctor that she's already lived through the events occasioned by the opening of the Pandorica, thus revealing that they have met out of sequence once more. Amy asks the Doctor why she can remember the clerics that fell victim to the crack in space and time, and the Doctor speculates that this is probably due to the fact that she now has a different perspective on things than others due to her being a time traveller. Certainly, River's chances of a pardon are slim if all the Angels have been wiped out from space and time, so her only hope would appear to be that there are more Angels lurking out there, somewhere…

The shackled River jokes with the Doctor that their encounters always end with one of them in handcuffs. And the Doctor was indeed bound by handcuffs when River 'died' in *Forest of the Dead*, so does this mean that she is as much aware of her own future as the Doctor's? Then again, she didn't know that she would become a professor when the Doctor blurted this out in *The Time of Angels*. Of course, most casual viewers would have taken nothing more from River's remark than sexual innuendo… Then again, *The Brilliant Book of Doctor Who 2011* explicitly states that River's comment doesn't mean that she has foreknowledge of the circumstances surrounding her death.

Which brings us to the controversial conclusion of this episode, where Amy attempts to seduce the Doctor into having a one-night stand. This is the inevitable conclusion to Grace's kissing of the Eighth Doctor in the 1996 TV movie, which itself was controversial at the time. However, time cannot be unwritten in this instance, and the barrier that prevented intimacy between the Doctor and his companion has well and truly been burnt, especially since it allowed Russell T Davies dramatic licence to explore this area further. Thus we had the Doctor and Rose's love story, followed by Martha's unrequited love for the Doctor.

However, Steven Moffat plays things a rather different

way, as his Doctor is more befuddled by Amy's approach than anything else - he truly doesn't understand what Amy's getting at, despite the fact that she references his unofficial title of "Who" more than once. We have seen this Doctor engaging in some sexual innuendo with River, but never with Amy, so it appears that this Doctor is not completely asexual, but yet his alien emotions are still a barrier to his understanding what is happening in this scene.

It's good that Moffat resists the temptation of getting the Doctor involved in another romantic relationship with one of his regular companions though, as such repetition would have been tiresome. It seems that some viewers may have been fearful that Steven Moffat was approaching the same level of explicitness as *Coupling*, his adult comedy, in this scene. Certainly, Russell T Davies' hard-hitting dramas have tended to be far more sexually explicit than Moffat's comedies. And although Amy's approach is pretty full on, I think that there were much more explicit sexual innuendo throughout Russell T Davies' years, but none of these occasioned the same level of complaints in the British press as this incident did; maybe such critics didn't want to appear to be homophobic by criticising such scenes during Russell T Davies' time?

Whatever the reasons for the complaints, they soon degraded into a rather silly argument in the media as to whether Amy's clothing was too sexually suggestive in the series. Having watched *Doctor Who* for well over 30 years, I know that what Amy wears is far less revealing than Leela's skins in the 70's, and the bikini that Peri got to wear in her debut story. In fact, if anything, Amy's costumes have been rather less revealing than many of the Doctor's female companions, and that's including her policewoman kissogram costume!

Noticing the date on Amy's clock has changed to the 26th of June 2010, the same date that the explosion that supposedly caused the crack in space and time (and which the Doctor has pointedly held back from Amy), the Doctor bundles her back into the TARDIS to "sort her out". It seems that the Doctor is not quite ready to face these events quite yet... Then again, given that the Doctor's next act is to pick up Rory, the fiancé that she plans to marry on this auspicious date, it seems that the Doctor isn't concerned with rewriting or unwriting any such event; instead he seems to be precipitating it...

Did You Know? One of the original episode titles devised for 2008's *Forest of the Dead* (in which River dies) was *River's Run*, which (to me) suggests a missing final word of *Dry*. Certainly, this gives an indication that River's name is metaphorical in part, and it sounds quite Bluesy to me.

6: The Vampires of Venice

Writer: Toby Whithouse
Director: Jonny Campbell
Originally broadcast: 8 May 2010

Cast

The Doctor: Matt Smith
Amy Pond: Karen Gillan
Rory Williams: Arthur Darvill
Rosanna: Helen McCrory
Guido: Lucian Msamati
Isabella: Alisha Bailey
Francesco: Alex Price
Vampire Girls: Gabriella Wilde, Hannah Steele, Elizabeth
Croft, Sonila Vieshta, Gabriella Montaraz
Inspector: Michael Percival
Steward: Simon Gregor

Steven's review: *The Vampires of Venice* is a distinct step
down for the season after the triumph of the Weeping Angels
two-parter. It has some good elements in it, particularly
when it concentrates on the central relationships between the
Doctor and his two companions, Amy Pond and her fiancé
Rory. It's not so good, though, when it comes to providing a
strong and interesting adventure in its own right. Writer
Toby Whithouse previously provided the highly acclaimed
episode *School Reunion* for the 2006 season of *Doctor Who*;
he's also the creator of the supernatural drama series *Being
Human*, so he should know a thing or two about writing for
vampires. Unfortunately this episode works as a good-
looking "romp," but nothing deeper, with its tone veering
uncertainly between sci-fi, horror, and comedy.

After the final scene of last week's episode, when Amy
launched herself at the Doctor, totally ignoring the fact that
she was getting married the next morning, the Doctor
evidently decides that Amy and Rory's relationship needs

working on as a matter of urgency. This strand of the story opens with a bit of pure slapstick, as Rory is talking (or rather yelling) to Amy's answerphone over the noise of his bachelor party while a large cake is being wheeled in. He and his cheering friends are suddenly silenced as out of it emerges, not a bikini-clad girl, but a bowtie-sporting Time Lord, leading to a hilariously awkward monologue. The way the scene just hangs there, letting the embarrassment pile up until the opening titles mercifully cut in, is laugh-out-loud funny. Basically, Toby Whithouse is, as with *School Reunion*, making central to his story an examination of the Doctor/companion relationship, and in particular its effect on the companion once they leave the Doctor and attempt to return to a normal life. Once again, the thesis is that being a companion is such an overwhelming experience that it makes having normal relationships afterwards virtually impossible. In the earlier story, we saw this demonstrated explicitly with Sarah Jane Smith, former companion from the 1970's. Here, the Doctor is trying to prevent that outcome - observing the Amy/Rory relationship already becoming attenuated over just a few episodes, he's decided that they need to be forced back together.

The Doctor decides they need to go somewhere romantic, and so they land in Venice in 1580. The environment is very well realized by rookie director Jonny Campbell, helped greatly by the location filming - not in Venice itself, but in the Croatian town of Trogir, which provided an abundance of authentic buildings and squares to recreate the period setting. As always when the *Doctor Who* team do a story set in Earth's past, the BBC design and costume departments do an excellent job. I think it's one of the most impressive-looking episodes the series has done.

Unfortunately, the story being told in this impressive setting has its problems. Sometimes, the self-contained 45-minute format in which the majority of *Doctor Who* stories are now told works well - and other times, as here, it really works against the story. At the opening of the show, we saw the aristocratic Rosanna Calvierri, who runs an exclusive school for girls, accept the appeal from a lower-class boatbuilder, Guido (another case of an excellent actor, Lucian Msamati, making the most of a rather minor part) for his daughter Isabella to be accepted into the school. As soon as Guido leaves, Rosanna's son Francesco bares his teeth, revealing enormous fangs, and attacks Isabella. Now if the story had two episodes to play with, the intersection of this plot with the Doctor and his companions could have been played out much more naturally, slowly building up the horror atmosphere that all the nicely creepy vampire imagery deserved. Instead, the Doctor stumbles onto the plot almost immediately; as they are wandering through the streets they see Guido accosting the Calvierri girls, who are out promenading with veils covering their faces. He finds Isabella, but she doesn't recognize him, and another of the girls menaces him with fangs like Francesco's.

The Doctor has no difficult in befriending Guido, who immediately tells him his whole story. This leads to him paying a quick visit to the Calvierri mansion, where he encounters a group of the fanged girls. This scene is one of the few times in the whole season so far where I felt Matt Smith was trying too hard to play up the eccentricities of the Doctor; in particular, the bit where he says "Tell me the whole plan!" and follows up with an aside to the camera ("One day that'll work") was just too jarring, really pulling the viewer out of the story. Meanwhile, Amy and Rory just happen to witness Francesco attacking a nameless flower-seller; they rush back to the Doctor with the news of vampires, which he of course already knows. They go and have another chat with Guido, who just happens to have a map and knowledge of a tunnel leading under the Calvierri mansion. The tunnel ends in a sealed trapdoor, so Amy will have to infiltrate the school and open it for them. The story is advancing in an entirely predictable and formulaic way.

Again, this is similar to *School Reunion*, where some fantastic Doctor/companion material was set against a rather simplistic B-story of alien activity in a school setting. It's interesting to compare the similarities between the Doctor's treatment of Rose and Mickey there, and Amy and Rory in this episode. Just as with "Mickey the Idiot," the Doctor tends to be rather unfairly dismissive of Rory, even when he demonstrates some intelligence. In the opening TARDIS scene, Rory immediately accepts the TARDIS interior as a different dimension because after his last encounter with the Doctor he's been doing some reading of the latest scientific theories - and the Doctor is almost angry when he says, "I like the bit when someone says it's bigger on the inside. I always look forward to that." There's less pathos than in *School Reunion*, though, since unlike with Mickey and Rose, the Doctor is definitely not interested in winning Amy's love, and wants to push Amy towards Rory. Hence the relationships can be exploited for comedy.

Arthur Darvill does well at portraying Rory's rather hapless love for Amy and the way it leads him to follow her into danger as she is taken into the school, which requires Rory to bluff Rosanna - or so he thinks - using the Doctor's psychic paper. Later, he will have a "swordfight" with Francesco that, even though it's played for comedy with Rory wielding a broom instead of a sword, still demonstrates the character's bravery. Indeed, he gets to demonstrate a perception that elevates him above the level of comic relief when, upset over Amy's danger, he berates the Doctor: "You know what's dangerous about you? It's not that you make people take risks, it's that you make them want to impress you. You make it so they don't want to let you down. You have no idea how dangerous you make people to themselves when you're around." Of course, he is falling victim to this himself as he follows the Doctor into the school, armed only with a tiny flashlight - which the Doctor immediately trumps by producing a comically huge lightsabre-like device from his pocket. ("Yours is bigger than mine." "Let's not go there.")

Once Amy is inside the school, the story is full of images taken straight from the Hammer gothic vampire movies like *The Brides of Dracula*, with the vampire girls surrounding and menacing her. There's the classic horror movie image of

Amy in a nightdress, carrying a lantern through the darkened corridors of the building as she goes to open the trapdoor for the others - leading to a nice 'jump' moment when Rosanna's steward suddenly appears next to her. She is seized and taken into a sinister "processing chamber" where the only genuinely horrific sequence of the story takes place. Rosanna reveals that she saw through Rory's bluff with the psychic paper immediately, and wants to know what Amy is doing in this "world of savages." Amy is tied down as Rosanna bares her fangs and lunges at her.

She is rescued by the Doctor and Rory, and it's at this point that the story suddenly changes direction, as it turns out that the vampires aren't actually vampires at all. Amy kicks at Rosanna and accidentally hits a device she's wearing - a perception filter - which reveals her true form, an upright lobster-like alien with spindly black limbs and claws. I thought these aliens were a very good piece of CGI design, particularly the match between the alien form and the human disguise - for example, the way the spines around the alien's neck morphed into features of the ornate collar of her dress.

Helen McCrory gives an excellent performance as Rosanna. Her best scene is another one that parallels a moment in *School Reunion* - a face-to-face confrontation between the Doctor and the villain, who offers the Doctor an alliance. In that episode, David Tennant and Anthony Head created some terrific tension as they strove to outwit each other, and here McCrory and Matt Smith do just as well. It also serves to tie this story into the ongoing season arc, as Rosanna tells how they came here: "We ran from the Silence. ... There were cracks. Some were tiny, some were as big as the sky. Through some we saw worlds and people, and through others we saw silence...and the end of all things. We fled to an ocean like ours, and the crack snapped shut behind us." They have made a new home for themselves in the waters of Venice, and are converting the girls in the school into members of their own race in order to provide breeding stock to rebuild their population.

The episode provides sci-fi explanations for the convenient

coincidence that the aliens have the same attributes as traditional vampires - like invisibility in mirrors - with varying degrees of success. It's a cute idea that the perception filter doesn't work in a reflection, and that the brain can't deal with the aliens' true appearance and so leaves the reflection blank. However, while I could believe that humans would be fooled like that, I just couldn't buy the proposition that the Doctor would have that problem - this is a guy with the wisdom of the universe, who's familiar with innumerable alien races; there's probably no one less likely to be fazed by a creature's strange appearance.

Now things have to start moving *really* fast, in order to wrap the plot up within the episode's running time. Rosanna sends the vampire girls to attack the Doctor and co., but they are all conveniently wiped out by the store of gunpowder that Guido just happens to have stashed in his room. Then Rosanna activates some weather-control device that will apparently cause Venice to sink due to earthquakes or tidal waves or something; which leads to an ending with the Doctor having to climb up the side of a high tower to destroy the generator. This brought back memories of *The Idiot's Lantern* and *Evolution of the Daleks* - neither of which are particularly good episodes to be reminded of. In the end, he manages to overcome the aliens' plan literally by simply flicking a switch. In *School Reunion* (again!) this same situation was treated as a joke - but here we're expected to take it seriously.

There are lots of untidy loose ends in the plot. Who is Rosanna's human steward, Carlo, and why is he serving her without any comments about the weird goings-on within the school? How come only male aliens (apart from their leader) survived the passage to Earth, thereby requiring them to start preying on human girls? Most irritating is the way the aliens' vulnerability to sunlight changes from moment to moment to suit the requirements of the story. The sunlight burns Isabella during the escape attempt so badly that she can't bear it and is pulled back inside, but in the very next scene she is standing in full daylight before being pushed into the water to be devoured by the lurking aliens. During Rory's fight with Francesco, Amy somehow causes the alien to explode simply with a reflection from a hand mirror! After the failure of her plans, Rosanna despairs and commits suicide by diving into the water in her human form. Somehow she is able to shed her outer clothes even though they don't really exist - they're a creation of her perception filter. (Of course, the real reason is probably that the production team couldn't afford to damage that very expensive-looking dress.)

So it's probably best to ignore all the stuff about the vampiric alien lobsters, and just concentrate on the interaction between the Doctor, Amy and Rory. In the end, the adventure does seem to have resulted in a change in their relationships. Amy invites Rory to stay with her and the Doctor in the TARDIS, and he's happy to accept. She's happy too, since it means she doesn't have to choose between them - at least, not yet.

Then, as they enter the TARDIS, the sounds of the marketplace around them suddenly vanish - Silence falls. The direction here is a little too arty for its own good, not making it clear whether all the people who were there just a moment ago have simply vanished, or whether they are still there but have somehow been silenced. And in either case, why does the Doctor head into the TARDIS, rather than stay and investigate? The final shot, a zoom into the TARDIS keyhole, may or may not be important - I've seen some comments saying that the shape of the keyhole is similar to the crack in the universe that's been a feature of this season, but I don't see it myself. An appropriately confusing end for an episode that unfortunately never quite lived up to its potential.

Steven's Classic Who DVD Recommendation: For an example of how the Classic Series dealt with gothic horror themes, check out *The Brain of Morbius*, starring Tom Baker and Elisabeth Sladen.

Kevin's review: At first, like Steven, I wasn't a great fan of *The Vampires of Venice*, since I thought that Toby Whithouse, the creator and lead writer of *Being Human*, hadn't strayed far enough from his comfort zone by producing yet another fiction that plays with the concept of vampires that so dominate his most famous work.

My initial perception of his writing was that he's excellent at creating wordy dramatic set pieces; but that the plotting that leads up to such scenes can be quite woolly and flawed. For instance, in the second season of *Being Human*, George is caught out by the clocks being moved back due to the end of British Summer Time, and begins his transformation into a werewolf during a school parents' evening - yet, as everyone knows, you only put the clocks back on during the early hours of a Sunday morning, not on a weekday, as Toby Whithouse's drama dictated in this instance.

While it may seem churlish to criticise something as being unrealistic in a gothic drama, such things do have a tendency to undermine such stories and diminish faith in the storyteller. I was also less than impressed by Whithouse's previous *Doctor Who* script, *School Reunion*, and this was despite the return of Sarah Jane Smith and K9.

In addition to this, I really dislike the tendency of writers to always associate Venice with Death, since this aspect of the city has literally been done to death, what with Thomas Mann's *Death in Venice*, Salley Vickers' *Miss Garnet's Angel*, a multitude of crime novels, and Nicholas Roeg's sublime *Don't Look Now*. Even the accompanying episode of *Doctor Who Confidential* was rather unimaginatively called *Death in Venice*. Although, to be fair to the Doctor, his intention in travelling to Venice was due to one of its other associations, as a splendid location for a romantic break: it's hardly his fault that those cracks in the universe that are following Amy around have led the Saturnynes to Venice. Presumably the aliens are given this name derived from a planet in order to enhance their otherworldly nature, and because they're moody and sullen (i.e. Saturnine - well, Francesco is - he could be the Emo of Venice!).

I was also irritated because, in the accompanying episode of *Doctor Who Confidential*, Toby Whithouse wrecked an idea that I had for an historical episode set in Italy, featuring the Plague Doctors; these mysterious figures, with their long beaky noses, have always looked like aliens to me, and if so utilised, could have represented something far more threatening than just another revivification of the vampire myth. Admittedly, I would also have wanted to include Casanova and Galileo in this episode, despite the fact that they were not contemporaries - but hey, such things can be overcome with the help of a certain guy with a time machine!

Of course, Casanova did get a jocular name check in this episode, as the Doctor mentioned that it was a good job that they wouldn't run into him, as he owed the lothario a couple of chickens (the in-joke being that Matt Smith really wouldn't want to run into a character so predominantly associated with his predecessor, David Tennant). Another possible reference to Casanova is the casting of the sublime Helen McCrory, who played the philanderer's mother in the Heath Ledger film of 2005.

Several weeks after its first broadcast, when my family wanted to watch an old episode of *Doctor Who*, they chose *The Vampires of Venice*, despite my protestations. And you can see why they chose it, as from the outside, it's very rich and lavish, with sumptuous costumes along with a beautiful location. (Never mind Venice, I'm sure many *Doctor Who* fans will be wanting to holiday in Trogir following this episode!) The budget cuts applied to this series of *Doctor Who* are not in evidence here, apart perhaps for the one CGI image of the Vampire Girls' true Saturnyne features while trying to break into Guido's house.

Indeed, the accompanying episode of *Doctor Who Confidential* was criticised in some quarters for being far too lavish, since it was actually filmed in Venice and featured the very distinguished Venetian Francesco da Mosto, along with a special appearance by Matt Smith. In the BBC's defence though, the visual effects crew had to visit Venice anyway, and this programme very much harked back to *Doctor Who*'s original requirement to be educational, since it could easily have been an episode from da Mosto's own TV series, *Francesco's Venice*.

On a separate note, *Doctor Who Confidential* revealed that Executive Producer Beth Willis likes to lead by example, as she leapt into the chilly water prior to the staging of Isabella and Signora Calvierri's death scenes to see if it would be warm and safe enough for the actors to proceed. I very much like a leader whose attitude is that they would not ask anyone to do anything that they would not do themselves.

The Vampires of Venice is very funny, especially with regards to the Doctor's first appearance, bursting through the cake meant for Rory's stripper. In this light, I particularly appreciated Rory's reaction when he reads that he's been put down as Amy's eunuch on the Doctor's psychic paper, since this says a great deal about how he is perceived by the Doctor, Amy, and just about everyone else at this moment! An example of how Rory regards his own potency is revealed by the fact that his stag party shirt is revealed to bear the number 9 in this episode, as, of course, the number 9 shirt in a British football team is usually reserved for that most alpha male of players: the striker. While not wanting to contradict Steven's very valid initial impressions, the truth is, the more you watch it, the more compelling *The Vampires of Venice* becomes.

For instance, there is the Saturnynes' aversion to light, which does seem to be inconsistent in this episode. However, this aversion to light is explained by Amy as a result of them being fish rather than vampires. Yet, to refine it further, one could argue that the Saturnynes are discomfited by strong, hot sunlight rather than just light per se. This could explain why Isabella is able to stand outside during her death scene, as the sky has clouded over from her earlier attempt to escape from Signora Calvierri's school (although the Signora herself has the partial protection of a parasol while Isabella walks the plank). Francesco and his mother do seem to have greater tolerance for light than the more recently converted

Vampire Girls, although Francesco usually does not go out without a heavy cape and a large hat. Of course, Francesco dispenses with these articles of clothing at the end, as he leaps into the canal in his pursuit of Rory and Amy. It may be the fact that he's wet that prevents his discomfort in the daylight here, or that the sky is shown to very cloudy at this moment, even before Signora Calvierri switches on the storm machine. Maybe his perception filter also provides him with some protection? If so, then it's a great mistake when he switches it off.

Thus it is indeed quite lame, as Steven has already recounted, that Francesco is dispatched with just a bright ray of light reflected by Amy's compact mirror, especially given the fact that Amy has somehow discovered the one ray of light in an otherwise cloudy sky! As I wrote earlier, Toby Whithouse's scripts do sometimes contain such glaring errors, usually employed to justify a big set-piece scene. Here, it justifies the explosion of an alien who's served his purpose with an appropriate amount of gunk, which then leads to Amy vigorously kissing Rory, despite (but probably because of) the fact that his attempt to protect her was so inept.

It's also dramatically satisfying to have a good explosion every now and then, as long as it's not too often (you could have timed your watch by the inevitable explosion in the Sylvester McCoy era of *Doctor Who*, while the latest series of *Spooks* was strangely bereft of explosions good enough to get in the title sequence). As a worker at the famous Venetian arsenale, it is probable that Guido would have got his hands on some gunpowder, especially during a time when the city is isolated by plague and the arsenale is presumably not that busy. As Guido states, he originally purloined the gunpowder as part of his plan to break into the school.

The fact that the Saturnynes' true teeth are displayed despite their perception filters is explained away as being due to the primal fear of their victims, which leads them to construct an image that they can understand. It could also be that such monsters have the ability to bypass their perception filters and to display their teeth to terrify others, as Prisoner Zero also seemed to do in *The Eleventh Hour*. At the end of the day, the display of such sharp teeth is a staple ingredient of many dark fantasies, so you can't really blame the show's production crew for defying logic in their bid to be entertaining. For instance, being chased down a corridor by a mum and her two daughters wouldn't have been frightening at all during *The Eleventh Hour*, if it were not for the display of their bright, spiky teeth…

Unlike Steven, I thought the explanation as to why the Doctor couldn't see the Vampire Girls' reflection was reasonable enough. However, it is quite improbable that Venetians, famed for their seafaring at this time, would have taken Signora Calvierri's word for it that all other cities nearby had the streets piled high with corpses due to the plague, despite their understandable fear of disease.

It also is more than a tad strange that the Saturnynes are so intent on flooding Venice - I mean, it's well known that this is something that the Venetians have always feared - but what on Earth would the Saturnynes do with the flooded city? Live in it? Surely the water would ruin all the lavish tapestries and paintings? Like many a Venetian, I suspect that Venice-under-Water would be far less appealing than the modern day city. And since when has the sonic screwdriver had the ability to heal flesh wounds? The way our favourite Time Lord deals with the fang marks on Amy's neck is more suggestive of 'Bones' McCoy from *Star Trek* rather than *Doctor Who*.

I think the focus on the TARDIS keyhole at the end is meant as a metaphor of the crack in the universe, rather than that the cracks themselves emanated from this possible weak point of the TARDIS as the result of its explosion at the end of the series (*The Brilliant Book of Doctor Who 2011* also suggests that the gap in the clouds that heralds the end of the storm metaphorically resembles one of the cracks in the universe). So much happens in *The Vampires of Venice*, that Steven missed the reason why Lady Rosanna's human steward, Carlo, hung around, despite the shenanigans in the school and his seeing her without her perception filter, as someone (presumably Carlo) is seen exiting the school rapidly at the end with a bundle of pilfered loot... Although Guido and Isabella are proud Venetians, the city's power hunger in its early days led to the sacking of Constantinople and the plundering of its art, a less noble tradition that the steward continues here.

As in the case of Rory's number 9 shirt, *The Vampires of Venice* does display an intricate attention to detail (both visual and literal) that no doubt emanates from Steven Moffat's overall story arch. I, for one, was so totally fixated on the concept of the cracks in the universe, that I didn't really pay any attention to the Silence, despite Signora Calvierri's fear of it, and the fact that it now (in hindsight) features so prominently at the end of this episode. So, it could be that *The Vampires of Venice* will very much turn out to be very much an integral part of the overall story arc, which justifies the money lavished on it (which is also signalled by the fact that at 50 minutes, it's very much longer than the average episode). For instance, Rory's anger at the fact that people put themselves at risk on the Doctor's behalf, while directed at Amy's desire to put herself into danger in this episode, could very much also be a hint to Rory's own eventual demise... And in the final episode of this series, *The Big Bang*, it was revealed that the threat of the Silence has not gone away with the cracks in the universe...

Did You Know? Johnny Campbell, who helmed this episode, also directed the 2006 Ant and Dec vehicle *Alien Autopsy*.

7: Amy's Choice

Writer: Simon Nye
Director: Catherine Morshead
Originally broadcast: 15 May 2010

Cast

The Doctor: Matt Smith
Amy Pond: Karen Gillan
Rory Williams: Arthur Darvill
Dream Lord: Toby Jones
Mr Nainby: Nick Hobbs
Mrs Hamill: Joan Linder
Mrs Poggit: Audrey Ardington

Steven's review: "Hold on tight. This is going to be a tricky one." With those words, the delightfully twisty *Amy's Choice* kicks off a high-concept mindbender of an episode that also provides a crucial turning point in the journey our three regular characters - the Doctor, Amy, and Rory - are taking over the course of this season. After the problems some earlier stories (e.g. *Victory of the Daleks* and *The Vampires of Venice*) have had with fitting into the 45-minute running time of a single episode, *Amy's Choice* is an object lesson in how to get it right. Like a well-crafted prose short story, it sets up a self-contained situation for our heroes, follows the logic of that situation through to its end, and leaves the characters definitely changed from where they were at the start.

One of the major threads running through this season has been Amy's relationships with the Doctor and her fiancé Rory. Given that she spent most of her life fixated on her memory of meeting the Doctor when she was seven, and that when he finally turned up again she happily went away adventuring with him on the night before her wedding, Rory could be forgiven for wondering about just how deep her commitment to him is. In the last episode, they did seem to come together again when the Doctor took them to sixteenth-century Venice, and Rory had the opportunity to share in the weirdness of her life with the Doctor. But that only postponed, rather than resolved, the issue of Amy having to decide whether or not she is fully committed to a life together with Rory. As the episode title suggests, the emotional heart of *Amy's Choice* is the final working out of that issue.

At the start, though, it seems that the matter has already been fully settled. We open with a pastoral shot of a country cottage, inside which a heavily pregnant Amy is happily at work making cupcakes. Rory, her husband of five years - and sporting a hideously tragic ponytail - arrives just in time to see the TARDIS materialize in their garden. The Doctor has dropped in for a visit to his old friends' quiet existence in the village of Upper Leadworth. It's all very relaxed and peaceful - but then loud, insistent birdsong is heard, as the three of them simultaneously drop off to sleep...

...and wake up inside the TARDIS, realizing that they have all just had the same experience. The Doctor dismisses it as some sort of freak "psychic episode," but then the same birdsong is heard in the TARDIS control room, as the three of them simultaneously drop off to sleep...

...and wake up back in the village. Both worlds, the village and the TARDIS, feel absolutely real, but that's clearly impossible. As the Doctor says, "Listen to me - trust nothing. From now on, trust nothing you see, hear or feel. ... Are we flashing forwards, or backwards?" Which world is real?

This episode is one of only two this season to be the work of a writer new to the series. In this case, Simon Nye (best known as the creator of 90's sitcom *Men Behaving Badly*) has come up with an excellent script whose working out bears comparison with showrunner Steven Moffat's time-twisting plotting, while at the same time having quite a different feel to it. Rather than playing tricks with time, we are rapidly hopping from one setting to another as the Doctor is increasingly desperate to work out exactly what's going on, and it becomes imperative to make a choice as to which world to accept as real. And as with some of Moffat's best episodes, the ending sheds a whole new light on what has gone before, showing that what was *actually* happening was quite different to what initially appeared to be the case.

Nye fills every scene with characterizing humorous detail for the regulars. A favourite of mine is the first TARDIS scene, where the Doctor and Amy both surreptitiously check the back of Rory's head for a ponytail, while Amy is less than pleased that the "nightmare" the Doctor speaks of having turns out to be the tranquil scene they've all just shared. The Doctor is not at his best in a quiet English village with nothing to do - later, he yells that he can't get his brain working to solve the problem because "this village is just SO DULL! I'm slowing down, just like you two…" Amy immediately trumps him by pretending to go into labour, leading to the hilarious sight of the Doctor with a look of clueless terror on his face, hands poised beneath her to catch a baby emerging at speed. When Amy reveals it was a hoax and snaps, "This is my life now, and it just turned you white as a sheet. So don't you call it dull again, ever," she has definitely scored a point over the Time Lord. Amy's pregnant state is the source of quite a few nice gags ("Now we all know there's an elephant in the room…" "I *have* to be this size, I'm having a *baby*!"), including her inability to keep up as the Doctor goes rushing around investigating ("Ohhh…can we *not* do the running thing?").

But there's a lot more going on than just some clever comedy. After a couple more switches between realities, they find themselves in a dead TARDIS, growing ever colder, unable to even find out what's outside. Suddenly a man appears in the control room - a short guy wearing an outfit very much like the Doctor's. He calls himself the Dream Lord, and tells them he is setting them a test. "So here's your challenge. Two worlds - here, in the time machine, and there, in the village that time forgot. One is real, the other's fake." What's more, in each world they will face a deadly threat. In the village, the population of the old peoples' rest home turn out to be infected with alien

101

parasites, while in the TARDIS, the ever-increasing cold is caused by an impending impact with a "cold star". Both threats - an army of zombie pensioners, and a star radiating cold - are *outré* enough that they could be dismissed as the stuff of dreams (or nightmares). But as the Doctor says, it's a big universe, and he doesn't know everything, so the mere presence of something as ridiculous as a bunch of old people with green eyestalks in their mouths, or a star "burning cold" doesn't automatically indicate unreality. A more subtle approach is required.

Dream Lord: "If you die in the dream, you wake up in reality. Healthy recovery in next to no time. Ask me what happens if you die in reality."

Rory: "What happens?"

Dream Lord: "You die, stupid. That's why it's called reality."

The Dream Lord is played by Hollywood star Toby Jones (among many other credits, he provided the voice of Dobby in the *Harry Potter* films, and is in the forthcoming *Tintin* movie written by Steven Moffat and directed by Steven Spielberg). He puts in a mesmerizing performance, having been given by far the best guest part so far this season. There's never any doubt that he's in control of the situation, and has the measure of the Doctor and his companions. Initially content to simply throw snarky quips, he becomes steadily more menacing throughout the episode, particularly after he separates Amy from the others. He takes a delight in prodding her about her conflicted feelings towards Rory and the Doctor.

As Rory perceptively pointed out earlier, the two worlds are effectively set up to highlight possible futures for Amy with either Rory or the Doctor. Rory's world encompasses a quiet existence in a peaceful little village, with him having passed his exams and become a doctor, married his childhood sweetheart and started a family. The Doctor's, by contrast, is a world of adventure and weird encounters out there in a huge universe of wonders. But as it turns out, neither Amy nor the others have to make a choice between the worlds at all - because *neither* world is real.

The Doctor: "The Dream Lord has no power over the real world. He was offering us a choice between two dreams."

Amy: "How do you know that?"

The Doctor: "Because I know who he is."

After it's all over, the Doctor reveals some specks of "psychic pollen" which apparently caused all the trouble by falling into the time rotor. As an explanation, it ranks alongside the ending of the very early first Doctor story *The Edge of Destruction*, where the TARDIS crew are put through a similar hallucinatory experience as the result of a spring on the console getting stuck (yes, really). Fortunately, what would otherwise be a cheap "it was all just a dream" ending is just a stepping-stone to the real revelation - that the Dream Lord was a manifestation of the Doctor himself.

The Doctor: "Psychic pollen, it's a mind parasite. Feeds on everything dark in you, gives it a voice, turns it against you. I'm 907; it had a lot to go on."

It's well worth watching the episode again once you know the Dream Lord's true nature. His taunts to all three of the characters take on a whole new meaning. In particular, of course, his sparring with his other self reveals a self-loathing that the Doctor usually keeps well hidden.

A character piece like this, without any big effects or action set pieces, stands or falls on the performances of the cast, and they are on top form here. I've already heaped praise on Matt Smith throughout this season, but here he was even better than in previous episodes; perfectly in control of his performance at every moment. His ability to play against his youth and embody the age and wisdom of the Doctor is continually amazing. It's worth noting that this episode was almost at the end of the production schedule - the second-last filmed for the season. If the maturity and confidence of Smith's performance here is any indication, *Doctor Who*'s future is looking extremely good.

Karen Gillan is naturally the focus of the episode, and she gives a superb performance. Apart from handling the comedy expertly, in the second half she is given a whole range of emotional material to work with. She portrays very well the making of Amy's real choice in this episode - the choice between the Doctor and Rory. At the start, in the face of the Dream Lord's taunts, Amy breezily reassures Rory that she has chosen him, but she doesn't yet believe that Rory is her soul mate (note the clever way the direction at that moment has her positioned closer to the Doctor than to Rory). But in the village, Rory is shockingly, suddenly killed by one of the zombies, and Amy is brought to the stricken realization of how much she really loved him. Gillan is brilliant as she bitterly says, "Then what is the *point* of you?" when the Doctor tells Amy he can't bring Rory back. From that moment she drives the action - literally in fact, as the Doctor steps back to allow her to end the dream by deliberately crashing a van into a wall. When she later confesses to Rory that she didn't know whether it was a dream - and didn't care - her obvious sincerity finally cements the two of them together as a couple.

The direction from newcomer Catherine Morshead is mostly straightforward - the nature of the episode doesn't really allow for directorial showing off, although the scenes in the darkened, icy TARDIS were suitably atmospheric, and there's a notable shot at the end of the teaser with the camera circling several times around the characters as the Doctor realizes the situation. The main thing I noticed about the production is that they must have had lots of trouble with terrible weather on location. Normally rain is hard to see on film or video, but there were several scenes here where the cast had to pretend that they weren't standing outside in a downpour - in particular, the scene of the Doctor, Amy and Rory watching the children playing looked completely ridiculous.

As we head into the home stretch of the season, I suspect it will become increasingly difficult to discuss the episodes as entities in themselves, without referring to the overarching plot elements of the season. There was no appearance of the "crack in the universe" this episode, but since everything up until the last scene was not real, that's not surprising.

However, the final shots provide a twist of their own, as the Doctor momentarily sees the Dream Lord's reflection instead of his own in the console. Is this just a directorial flourish, or a hint that the Dream Lord may play a further role in later episodes?

Looking back, it's curious how many times dreams have been referenced this season. In *The Eleventh Hour*, Prisoner Zero refers to "poor Amy Pond, still such a child inside - dreaming of the magic Doctor she knows will return to save her." In *The Beast Below*, Amy's final voiceover (and just what *was* that beginning and ending narration about, anyway?) contained the phrase, "This dream must end, this world must know..." Then in *The Time of Angels*, River Song reads from a book about the Weeping Angels: "What if we had ideas that could think for themselves? What if one day our dreams no longer needed us?" Finally, and perhaps most pertinently, Rosanna in *The Vampires of Venice* tells the Doctor to "remember us. Dream of us," to keep the memory of her race alive. Knowing how much Steven Moffat enjoys building up intricate plot structures that suddenly take on whole new meanings once some crucial fact is revealed, I'm wondering whether *Amy's Choice* will in the end turn out to be even more central to the whole season than it currently appears.

Hold on tight. This is going to be a tricky one.

Steven's Classic Who DVD Recommendation: There were a couple of occasions when the Classic Series had stories that employed dreamscape or otherwise surreal elements, and probably the best of them is *The Mind Robber,* starring Patrick Troughton, Frazer Hines and Wendy Padbury.

Kevin's review: At first viewing, I didn't like *Amy's Choice* much. Perhaps initially because I was expecting that a collaboration between Simon Nye and Steven Moffat, both noted comedy authors, would be full of belly laughs rather than pregnant pauses and bellies. I also wasn't a great fan of the intrusive birdsong, which I found irritating. However, this was no doubt intentional, and having the birdsong signal when the TARDIS crew were dreaming was a good piece of defamiliarisation, as this sound is usually associated with waking up, rather than falling asleep. Yet, on my second viewing of this episode, I (unlike the Doctor and his companions) warmed to the dark humour, and did indeed laugh out loud at the image of one of the pensioners holding a whirring, upside down lawn mower like a chainsaw in the assault on Amy's cottage.

I thought the Eknodine were laughable at first, and couldn't take them seriously. Which indeed, was no doubt Simon Nye's intention with regards to these zombie wannabes. Their choice of weaponry is fascinating from a Cultural Studies point of view, as it's very phallic, to the extent that it seems to be the complete opposite of the dentata imagery that's so popular in horror films, i.e. any shot of a fanged mouth that evidently wishes to consume the hero or heroine. Interestingly enough, quite a lot of these feature in this series of *Doctor Who*, namely with regards to Prisoner Zero, the Vampire Girls, the Weeping Angels, and the "crooked smile" itself, since the jagged edges of the crack are made to look like teeth in *Flesh and Stone*. This may or may not be an intentional theme in Steven Moffat's conception of the "dark fairytale". However, the dentata myth does derive from folklore, in myths that usually warn young men not to sleep with strange women that they don't know. The dentata imagery is defamiliarised here due to such a phallic object protruding from toothed (probably dentured) mouths, so it could be an expression of the dangers of extreme potency here. So phallic are these Eknodine probes that Rory wonders aloud whether they have any more of them sticking out from other parts of these bodies, presumably referring to their nether regions. Since these green protuberances look like eyes on stalks, it's a bit strange that the new Daleks' eyes, which sounded quite similar in design, weren't realised because the production team thought that they would be too scary.

The depressed weather conditions on location were

106

obviously a hindrance to the filming of this episode. Indeed, such is the large presence of snow and sleet in each dream world, that *Amy's Choice* could have made a splendid (if rather dark) Christmas episode (since the TARDIS team were evidently freezing in both worlds). Obviously, the sleet in Upper Leadworth wasn't planned for, but I think it added to the bleak atmosphere of the episode, and helped make the village even duller visually.

My initial impression was that Simon Nye wasn't all that familiar with *Doctor Who*, and that's why he wrote an episode that departed from the norm. Indeed, as my fellow reviewer Steven has noted, the plot bore more than a passing resemblance to one of the earliest adventures of *Doctor Who*: *The Edge of Destruction*, made when the original production team was still exploring what the show was all about. To save on costs, this 1964 psychodrama was set entirely in the TARDIS, and possibly the same reasoning applied here, due to this season's limited budget. *Amy's Choice* is the one episode in this run that really utilises the new TARDIS set. Having seen more of it, I must confess that I still haven't warmed to it (indeed, it looked much better as a frozen icebox). All those strange juxtaposed platforms and pointless cubbyholes and spaces really don't fire the imagination for me, for the set looks as though it's only been half built, and it really lacks atmosphere. Perhaps the design team could have constructed something more like M. C. Escher's never-ending staircase for the interior? Realising this optical illusion would have been tough, but it was done quite successfully in the 1982 adventure *Castrovalva*. Although this episode very much features dreaming, there's again no sign of Amy's bedroom here, or any space on the TARDIS that could be described as "domestic".

I was quite disappointed to see that even a temporary generator utilised by Rory in this episode looked like a bathroom appliance. I guess one way you could justify the appearance of all these human household items in the TARDIS could be a result of the chameleon circuit going even more haywire, to the extent that it has affected the interior of the TARDIS as well as its exterior. This may be because the exterior doors are now very visible from the inside. If the TARDIS chameleon circuit were ever to work again, it would involve having to reconfigure the whole exit from the TARDIS console room so that it no longer resembles the interior doors of a police box...

As to why the TARDIS became stuck as a police box in the first place? Well, my musing is that this was a direct consequence of the Doctor's kidnapping of schoolteachers Barbara and Ian back in 1963. Due to the unprecedented presence of these aliens, the TARDIS decided to stick to the image that was already familiar to Barbara and Ian, rather than transform to anything more suited to its new Neolithic surroundings, thus creating a dilemma that neither the Doctor nor the TARDIS has ever resolved.

Another of my gripes is my concern that the interior of the TARDIS has been infantilised. Which, from the production team's point of view, is fair enough, as Steven Moffat et al evidently made a decision to aim the series more at children this year (while still very much appealing to adults). A possible explanation for the new console is that the TARDIS was influenced by the fact that the 7-year-old Amelia Pond was the first alien to encounter it while it was still "cooking", and thus created an eccentric interior that would very much lived up to her image of the "raggedy Doctor". Having written that, the new TARDIS console is not a huge departure from the one that graced the series' revival in 2005.

At first glance, this episode also hasn't much to do with the overall story arc of the crack in space and time. Having written that, the Dream Lord taunts Amy by saying that the Doctor hasn't really let her close to him at all, and hasn't even told her his name... Yet, there is one woman who does know the Doctor's name, and who is quite intimate with him: River Song. Obviously, only dedicated viewers will recall this fact (unknown to Amy) from *Silence in the Library/Forest of the Dead*. Before I watched this episode again more closely, and read my colleague Steven's review of this episode for a second time, I had been gradually coming to the same conclusion as he: that dreams could play a vital role in this current story arc (in which I also include series 6).

As mentioned in my review of *The Time of Angels*, there's a Philip K. Dick novel called *A Maze of Death*, which is a very similar name to that that the Aplans gave their catacombs: the Maze of the Dead. Again, in Dick's novel, the crew of the spaceship are stuck in a never-ending virtual reality dream world as the ship's computer seeks to amuse them while they are adrift with no hope of rescue. And who is the one character in *Doctor Who* that we know whose spirit and consciousness is stuck in such a virtual reality dream world? It's River Song. Note also that the episode that introduced her was called *Silence in the Library*, and it's apparently the Silence that is the main threat in series 6... Oh, and added to this is the dreamlike way in which the Doctor is returned to us at the end of *The Big Bang*, an episode in which River Song is the only character that has evidently not forgotten the Doctor...

Also, there's also the fact that the Doctor "explodes" the TARDIS at the end of this episode, just as he threatened to do so during *Victory of the Daleks*. This is obviously quite an important motif, which is employed to highlight the explosion that will eventually cause the crack in the universe in *The Big Bang*. The explosion of the TARDIS in this episode isn't that traumatic, because it's not the real thing. In this light, the Doctor's revelation that he is the Dream Lord is even more interesting.

I postulated in my review of *Flesh and Stone* that the Doctor's motive for collecting Rory at the beginning of *The Vampires of Venice* is that he very much wants to bring about his union with Amy on the 26th of June 2010. Not particularly because he wants them to be happy, but that he wants to put all the pieces in place for the event that precipitates the explosion that creates the crack in the universe. The most likely explanation for this being that he wants to control this event as much as he can, rather than actually being the agent behind it himself. Amy and Rory's rapprochement in *The Vampires of Venice* wasn't convincing enough, so maybe the Doctor placed that psychic pollen in the time rotor himself, to unleash his unscrupulous dark side, the Dream Lord, who would finally force Amy to uncover her real feelings for Rory? And thus bring into fruition the wedding and explosion date?

It's neat that the Dream Lord taunts Amy here that the Doctor always leaves her alone in the dark, since this appears to be a direct reference to *Flesh and Stone*, where the Doctor (bizarrely) did exactly that. One of the key themes of this episode is the Doctor's tendency to abandon his companions once he has finished with them (with the exception of Sarah Jane Smith, and the Tenth Doctor's companions). The beginning of this episode greatly emphasised the Doctor's boredom and itchy feet when he accidentally arrived back in Amy and Rory's lives, to find them living the stereotypical rural idyll where nothing ever happens. The Dream Lord's suggestion that "Anything could happen" when he's left alone with Amy is made all the more arch and funny by the fact that he's ironically dressed as a gigolo at this point.

When I first watched this episode, I initially thought that the Dream Lord could be the Master of the Land of Fiction, last seen on screen in the 1968 adventure *The Mind Robber*, the first episode of which ended with the TARDIS exploding in a very surreal way... (We only get a disappointing white flash on screen to signal the TARDIS' destruction in this episode.) There has also been some fan speculation that the Dream Lord could be an early manifestation of the Valeyard, the dark side of the Doctor from between his Twelfth and "final" incarnation, who appeared in *Doctor Who*'s longest serial, 1986's *The Trial of a Time Lord*. Much of this adventure was revealed to have taken place within the Matrix Data Bank: the repository of all Time Lord souls, so whether the Valeyard actually existed in "reality" is debateable. The Matrix Data Bank is also the epitome of the virtual reality environment now inhabited by River Song...

Maybe the Matrix survived the Time War? Yet again, this is all speculation on my part, but I do very much agree with my fellow reviewer Steven that *Amy's Choice* could very well be a more important part of Steven Moffat's overall story arc.

Did You Know? Toby Jones, the actor who plays the Dream Lord, is the son of Freddie Jones, an actor well known to genre fans from his appearances in David Lynch's *Dune* and *The Elephant Man*.

8: The Hungry Earth

Writer: Chris Chibnall
Director: Ashley Way
Originally broadcast: 22 May 2010

Cast

The Doctor: Matt Smith
Amy Pond: Karen Gillan
Rory Williams: Arthur Darvill
Alaya: Neve McIntosh
Nasreen Chaudhry: Meera Syal
Tony Mack: Robert Pugh
Ambrose: Nia Roberts
Mo: Alun Raglan
Elliot: Samuel Davies

Steven's review: In all four previous seasons of the revived *Doctor Who*, the second two-parter of the year turned out to be one of the highlights of the season - see, for example, Steven Moffat's *The Empty Child* in 2005, or Paul Cornell's *Human Nature* in 2007. Unfortunately, this year that run of success is broken. Appropriately for an episode that centres around an underground drilling operation, *The Hungry Earth* is a slow-moving bore. While not actively dreadful, it functions mostly as a prologue for next week's conclusion, and struggles to fill its running time with meaningful plot and incident. Most of the good bits are repeats of moments and concepts that have been seen before in *Doctor Who* - some from decades ago.

In 1970, *Doctor Who* was undergoing one of its periodic upheavals that shook up the series and sent it down an entirely different path. Not only was Jon Pertwee taking over the role of the Doctor from Patrick Troughton, as the show transitioned from black-and-white into colour, but the whole setting and rationale for the Doctor's adventures was being radically changed. At the end of the previous season, the

Doctor had been captured by the Time Lords and exiled to present-day Earth with his TARDIS rendered non-functional; for the forseeable future, out would go the freewheeling adventures in time and space, and instead the Doctor would be working with the UNIT military organization in a series of contemporary thriller stories. Writer Malcolm Hulke, on being briefed by script editor Terrance Dicks about the new set-up, was aghast that the production team had deliberately given up the ability to go anywhere in the universe, and restricted themselves to, as he put it, precisely two stories - "alien invasion" and "mad scientist." Dicks immediately challenged him to devise a way around that restriction, and the two of them came up with an ingenious idea - an "alien invasion" story where *we* are the invaders, because the "aliens" are a reptilian species which once dominated the Earth, but went into hibernation millions of years ago, after which human civilization developed and took over the planet. Now these reptiles, known as Silurians, are waking up, and they want their world back. The stage is set for a struggle between two irreconcilable factions, each with a valid claim to the Earth, with the Doctor in the middle trying to broker a solution that both sides can live with.

Despite being destroyed at the end of *Doctor Who and the Silurians*, the reptiles, or rather an aquatic variant of them, returned two years later in *The Sea Devils*, and then rather less successfully a decade after that, in *Warriors of the Deep*, with Peter Davison as the Doctor. In each case, the Doctor found his efforts at making peace between humans and reptiles going for naught. Now, forty years after the original story, writer Chris Chibnall presents another iteration of the same basic concept.

Many of the elements of this story have their roots in the Pertwee era. The setting, a scientific drilling project in the near future (2020), immediately recalls the story *Inferno* - except that where that story was set in a believably huge industrial installation with dozens of characters and extras, *The Hungry Earth* slims down its cast to a mere handful. We do see some extra technicians milling around in the teaser, but soon they're all sent home for the weekend, leaving the project in the hands of its chief scientist, Nasreen Chaudhry, her assistant Tony Mack, and Tony's family - his daughter Ambrose, her husband Mo, and their little son Elliot - who are conveniently the only local inhabitants of the area. Indeed the night shift, incredibly, consists of just Mo, and the story proper starts when the drilling control room is suddenly shaken and a mysterious hole appears in the concrete floor. Mo investigates the hole and, to the surprise of absolutely no one, gets pulled by some strange force into the earth.

The TARDIS arrives, with the Doctor apparently having promised Amy and Rory a trip to Rio. He immediately senses something strange about the ground, but they are distracted by two figures on a distant hillside waving to them. The Doctor peers through binoculars at them, and announces that it's Amy and Rory's future selves. The way this crossing of their own timeline is presented so casually feels very odd, particularly since nothing further comes of it this episode. I understand *The Hungry Earth* seriously overran its allotted running time and had to be quite severely edited down; there was some additional material with the Doctor and Amy discussing the appearance of her future self and her relationship with Rory, and it does feel that something's been lost here. Obviously, the fact that the scene was left in is a blatant clue about events next week, but I'll leave off discussion of that for now.

After the events of *Amy's Choice*, Rory and Amy are clearly a couple now, and they have a nice bantering relationship during the early scenes. The plot contrives to separate them by having Rory suddenly become concerned that she might accidentally lose her engagement ring and decide to take it back to the TARDIS; however, this does have the good effect of giving Rory some screen time to himself. When leaving the TARDIS again, he encounters Ambrose and Elliot, who take him to be a plain-clothes police officer. Ambrose wants him to investigate a grave whose body was discovered to have somehow disappeared without the grave's surface being disturbed. Obviously, the body was taken from underneath by the Silurians - but, like a lot of the elements in this episode, several minutes of screen time are spent on something which doesn't really amount to anything.

Meanwhile, the Doctor and Amy have made their way into the drilling control room and start investigating the hole in the ground. The ground attacks again, with more holes appearing in the floor; Nasreen rescues Tony, but Amy is dragged under, to the Doctor's horror. The story suddenly comes alive, with great performances from Karen Gillan of Amy's terror, and from Matt Smith of the Doctor's desperation to save her, and his helplessness as she disappears from view. He quickly discovers that a whole network of tunnels has been created below the drilling project, and that several creatures are moving up through them - they will be arriving at the surface within minutes.

Chris Chibnall's major contribution to the *Who* universe is as head writer (and writer of eight episodes) for the first two seasons of *Torchwood*. The first season had a lot of problems, but the second year was a great improvement, ending with a trilogy of episodes by Chibnall which showed off his strengths - an ability to create tense plot situations which fitted with and utilized the regular characters very well (as he also showed with a couple of excellent episodes of *Life on Mars*). Unfortunately, his work on *Doctor Who*, which requires him to create from scratch a whole setting and guest characters for the Doctor and companions to interact with, is much less strong. His previous *Doctor Who* was the 2007 episode *42*, where a mediocre script was elevated into a fast-paced thriller by brilliant direction from Graeme Harper. The guest characters were all pretty much cardboard, but that didn't matter as the plot carried the viewer along. *The Hungry Earth*, though, is the first half of a two-parter, so the pace is a lot slower and there is no plot resolution. This tends to expose Chibnall's weakness with dialogue - there are several sequences which take ages to arrive at the point, such as the one where it slowly dawns on the Doctor that he can still hear drilling even though the drill has been shut down. By the time he gets to the punchline - "While you were drilling down, somebody else has been drilling up" - we've long since got the idea and are impatient to move on.

To be fair, there are some clever points in the script, too. When the Doctor first arrived he noticed patches of bluegrass in the area, which Nasreen explains are indications of rare minerals that led them to site the drill here. This is a neat way of explaining what would otherwise be a huge coincidence, that the drill site happens to be right above the Silurians' habitation - "The bluegrass! Oh, Nasreen. Those trace minerals weren't X marking the spot, saying 'Dig here,' they were a warning - 'Stay away.'" I also liked the understated romantic feeling between Nasreen and Tony, bringing some definition to a couple of otherwise boringly standard characters. And Matt Smith does well establishing a connection between the Doctor and the boy Elliot.

As I said earlier, there's a lot of recycled moments and ideas in this episode - for instance, we have a reprise of the idea that the Doctor is what monsters have nightmares about, from *The Girl in the Fireplace*. And later, a repeat of the joke that the sonic screwdriver "doesn't do wood," as seen in *Silence in the Library*. The Silurians set up an energy barrier around the village to isolate it from the outside world - a direct homage to another Pertwee-era story, *The Daemons*.

There's plenty of stuff happening during the countdown to the reptiles' arrival, but a lot of it is irrelevant. For example, the Doctor gets everyone working to set up a network of security cameras around the village (which they somehow manage to do within a couple of minutes) - which then proves to be totally pointless, as the reptiles send out an energy pulse which disables all the electronic equipment, including all those cameras. Then the plot requires the Doctor to be distracted and allow Elliot to run off one minute before the Silurians arrive, so that he can be chased through the graveyard by a half-seen figure. These scenes are

116

agreeably suspenseful, but it's hard to ignore the idiot plotting needed to set them up. Elliot is finally caught and taken away by a Silurian, as Tony is attacked and stung by another's long venomous tongue (an unfortunately risible piece of CGI). The Doctor and Rory track the Silurians using a hitherto unseen gadget of the Doctor's - a pair of heat-detecting sunglasses. They manage to capture one of the creatures, which is apparently enough to make the others leave, removing the energy barricade.

The Doctor interrogates the captured Silurian, Alaya, in one of the best scenes of the episode. When she tries to claim to be the last of her species, he quickly replies, "No. You're really not. Because I'm the last of my species, and I know how it sits in a heart. So don't insult me." Alaya tells how they were woken by the drilling, and issues the usual Silurian threat:

Alaya: "We will wipe the vermin from the surface and reclaim our planet."

The Doctor: "Do we have to say 'vermin'? They're really very nice."

The redesign of the Silurians from their original form has come in for a certain amount of criticism from long-time fans, but I can see the reasoning behind it. Apart from the fact that they looked different in subsequent appearances in the old series anyway, the original Silurians were the epitome of "man in rubber suit" monsters, with inflexible headpieces that totally hid the person inside, so that their actors could only indicate which one was speaking by ferociously waggling their heads. Using a *Star Trek*-style facial prosthetic instead gives much more scope to the actor, allowing them to use their own eyes and mouth, but the disadvantage is that it removes a lot of the strangeness and "alien" elements from the creatures. It would have been better had the designers chosen to retain another element of the original, the third eye in the forehead which could be used to channel various psychic powers. That would have reduced their all-too-human appearance a little.

At any rate, Alaya is completely intransigent, so the Doctor decides to go below to find the rest of the tribe to talk to them. As usual in a Silurian story, only the Doctor is interested in peace between the races, and there is hostility on both sides.

Ambrose: "You're going to negotiate with these aliens?"

The Doctor: "They're not aliens! They're Earth...liens."

Matt Smith is convincing in his passion, but it's undeniably stuff that's all been done before. After a rather amusing moment when Nasreen is the only one applauding the Doctor's speech about them being "decent, brilliant people," she rather giddily demands to accompany him on his journey, and he lets her aboard the TARDIS, which the Silurians then drag down into the earth.

Meanwhile, Rory, Ambrose and Tony confront Alaya. In the manner of one who looks forward to martyrhood, she confidently tells them that one of them will kill her, thereby igniting a war. "I know which one of you will kill me. Do you?" We're left with the thought that each of the three humans has a motive to hate the Silurians - Tony has been infected by the venom from the attack earlier, which is spreading across his skin; Ambrose has seen her son and husband abducted by the creatures; and Rory has lost Amy. (Speaking of Amy, she finally reappears after being absent from most of the episode as she wakes to find herself a helpless prisoner alongside Mo, as a masked Silurian scientist comes toward her with some kind of dissecting instrument.)

The cliffhanger, frankly, took me by surprise. It's not that it's an illogical point to place it - the Doctor and Nasreen's arrival in the Silurian base and finding that it's actually an entire underground city is nicely done, and signals a major turning point in the story. It's just that so little has actually happened, storywise, that my first thought when the theme music crashed in was "Oh...is that it?" The real story of humans versus Silurians is only just getting started, and for that you'll need to come back next week.

Steven's Classic Who DVD Recommendation: Not a hard

choice, this one. Obviously, *Doctor Who and the Silurians*, starring Jon Pertwee, with Caroline John and Nicholas Courtney, is the essential Classic Series companion to this story.

Kevin's review: I wasn't a fan of Chris Chibnall's previous *Doctor Who* script *42*, and some of his *Torchwood* episodes, so I was not looking forward to this one. My impression of Chris Chibnall is that he's a kind of functional 'paint-it-by-numbers' writer, in that I can visualise him imagining what elements he should have in his stories, writing them on a list, and then ticking them off when he's realised them. I guess you could say that he's a writer you can rely on to fill in a gap in the schedule, because he does literally tick all these boxes and he very much knows what's basically required of him. However, you don't go to him if you want huge imaginative leaps and bounds and verbal trickery, as these are definitely not his strong points. Then again, the Moffats of this world are all too rare. I don't like criticising a fellow *Doctor Who* fan in this way, especially not one who's living the dream as a writer for the show, but when there are so few slots on the show for writers other than Steven Moffat, then those that do get selected must really hit the grade.

Admittedly, when I first saw the film *Sunshine* on DVD, this made me even more critical of *42*, as I thought that it was highly derivative of Danny Boyle's film. However, I've since discovered that both *42* and *Sunshine* were made and released to the public at more or less the same time, so this criticism is unfair. Although Chris Chibnall's story of sun obsession was definitely poorer than *Sunshine*, which itself was far less successful than the previous Danny Boyle/Alex Garland collaboration *28 Days Later* (which was highly derivative of John Wyndham's *The Day of the Triffids*). Yet, as my fellow reviewer Steven notes, the script for *The Hungry Earth* overran by 15 minutes, which meant that a lot of filmed material ended up being cut out of the episode, and you would have thought that, since Chris Chibnall is such an experienced writer, this should not have happened,

119

especially given that he has a whole other episode to deal with. To be fair to him though, this must have been the most difficult series of *Doctor Who* to write for thus far, since it is by far the most intricately plotted, thus making it more difficult than usual to fit all the required elements in.

The story opens with the TARDIS crew all somewhat disappointed to discover that they've landed in the small Welsh village of Cwmtaff ten years in the future, rather than Rio. Thus it would appear that the Doctor has lost control of his TARDIS again. They're soon distracted by what appears to be a couple of people waving at them from a nearby hillside. Producing a pair of binoculars, the Doctor proclaims that these people are the future Amy and Rory, and he speculates that they've come to witness past glories. Yet the image of these two people is quite indistinct, despite the fact that we get to see them through the Doctor's binoculars...

Rather than expounding upon the laws of time prohibiting any direct meeting (which may have been cut from the overrunning script), the Doctor instead proposes that they visit the nearby mining facility that he's just spotted, in no doubt due to the fact that he's already pronounced that the ground feels strange.

Another odd scene ensues, in which Rory proposes that Amy removes her engagement ring in case it gets lost. Given the perilous nature of his travels with the Doctor thus far, one can see his point, especially since the ring appears quite lavish. Rory, after all, was only ever expecting Amy to wear this ring in quiet surroundings of Leadworth. Rory's placing of the box containing the ring into a convenient cubby hole on the TARDIS console is quite a poignant moment, which is executed very well, since one does have a feeling that we will return to this scene later on...

As Rory leaves the TARDIS, a strange woman confronts him. Since we only see this woman from the back at first, I thought for a moment that she could have been Amy from the future. However, it turns out to be Ambrose, the wife and mother of the father and son who were the first to appear in this episode. Ambrose and her son, Elliot, presume that since

Rory has exited a police box, that he must be a policeman. This is despite the fact that Rory is particularly and literally clueless in these scenes where Ambrose complains about the bodies of her relatives disappearing from the churchyard in which the TARDIS has landed (not that she appears particularly upset her missing relatives). It may be that Rory's not so clueless as he appears here, and that he's not especially interested, but he still jumps into the grave, rather than following Amy and the Doctor into the mineworks. Elliot's theory is that, since the surface of the graves hasn't been disturbed, then the bodies must have been removed from below. Although obviously the grave was disturbed when the time came to bury Ambrose's Uncle Alun. Although Alun only died a few weeks ago, Ambrose and Elliot display no obvious signs of grief.

Elliot's deductive reasoning appears to be derived from his love of *Sherlock Holmes*, and it's possible that Chibnall is trying to convey that this dyslexic child is probably an idiot savant in the mould of the hero from Mark Haddon's *The Curious Incident of the Dog in the Night-time*. So dyslexic is Elliot, that he has been previously shown to be unable to read *The Gruffalo*, a picture book aimed at children much young than him. The excerpt from *The Gruffalo* that Mo, Elliot's father, read out at the beginning of this episode, was probably chosen to provide an early, negative image of the Silurians, who could easily be viewed as being just as monstrous. I'm not sure that Chris Chibnall has really set out here to educate the audience about dyslexia; it could just be that Elliot's love of audiobooks just serves to emphasise the fact that he has been kidnapped, as the earphones through which he listens to these fantastic stories are very pointedly found in the churchyard just after he has vanished.

The scene where Elliot is pursued in the graveyard is very effectively realised. This, again, is the epitome of the "dark fairytale", as we see images of spritelike beings flashing past on screen. The way the Silurians move in this incident is quite similar to that of the mysterious assailants in Chris Chibnall's *Torchwood* episode, *Countrycide* (although these disappointingly turned out to be human cannibals rather than aliens). Also very effective are the buglike masks that these Silurians wear, that almost make them look like the stereotypical 'greys' of alien abduction lore. These visors are certainly far more effective than that adopted by the main villain in *42*, since his wielding mask looks to have been a device that the production team adopted to basically make him look more monstrous than he otherwise would have been. As *Doctor Who Confidential* makes clear, these Silurian masks were the result of a decision by the production team to balance the budget in these two episodes, as it would have been far too expensive to have all the Silurians wearing facial prosthetics.

The prosthetics here are very well done, as they do allow the actors playing the main Silurians a great deal of facial expression. And, unlike the producers of *Star Trek: the Next Generation*, who used to signify an alien by just giving them, say, an unusual nasal ridge, the producers of *Doctor Who* have always been far more imaginative in the presentation of the Doctor's opponents. Obviously, one design aspect of the original Silurian costume is very much missing, as these new Silurians don't have third eyes in their foreheads. Then again, this third eye was mostly utilised in 1984's *Warriors of the Deep* to signal which one of the Silurians was talking (rather like a Dalek), as the costumes were otherwise very inexpressive. Thus I suspect that we can ultimately blame *Warriors of the Deep* for the absence of the third eye, as it would have been quite irritating for a red light to be flashing on Alaya's forehead as she was speaking. One Silurian's costume was very much marred in a scene of *Warriors of the Deep* where you saw too much of the human actor's neck; my fellow reviewer Steven has informed me that this sloppiness was due to the fact that production of this episode was rushed in order to facilitate the BBC's coverage of the snap election in 1983.

Instead of the third eye being used as a weapon, the Silurians now have a venomous tongue. I didn't think this effect was as bad as Steven thought it was. However, I did wonder why the Silurians didn't resort to it all that much in the succeeding episode when the Doctor disabled their weaponry. So, I can only conclude that Chris Chibnall utilised the tongue here to provide Tony with a motive for killing Alaya. This sets up the scene at the end where Alaya pronounces that she already knows which of the humans will kill her. Again, this is an aspect of Chris Chibnall's writing that I don't like: his obvious creation of a "cause" that leads into an equally unsubtle "effect".

The scenes where various characters are sucked into the earth are very well realised. However, this is not the first time that such scenes have appeared in *Doctor Who*: 1984's *Frontios* also featured aliens that utilised gravity to pull humans through the ground into their subterranean lair. A couple of years later, the same device featured in *Trial of a Time Lord*, where Sabalom Glitz is left holding the spats from the Doctor's shoes as he sinks into the ground, although this proved to be one of many illusions that the Doctor encountered while in the Matrix.

The Doctor doesn't display much emotion as a result of Amy's abduction, probably because he also becomes concerned about whatever is travelling up to the surface. Much of the activity that then follows is indeed a waste of time, as the Doctor instructs Ambrose's family to set up cameras all around the church, which they improbably accomplish in a couple of minutes. Again, as Steven notes, this is all to no effect, as the Silurians knock out the cameras. Amy herself doesn't have much screen time, but in one highly amusing scene, she is rightly very indignant when she's told to "Shush!" by an alien figure.

The Doctor pointedly tells Ambrose off when she gathers a collection of offensive weapons. However, the Doctor then raises the ante by setting out to assault and kidnap one of the Silurians. Thus, towards the end, we have the rather unsavoury sight of the Doctor keeping Alaya in chains. Admittedly, Alaya is very hostile, but the Doctor's usual tactic is to reason with his opponents, rather than imprison them. To make matters worse, the Doctor then pronounces that both sides have hostages! Such an offensive act flies in the face of the Doctor's previous pacifist disavowal of the use of weapons. To make matters worse, the Doctor chooses to take Nasreen down to the Silurian lair, rather than returning Alaya to them safely in exchange for Amy. Given that we've already seen humans carrying out one very beastly act with regards to the Star Whale this season, and the evidence of human antagonism to the Silurians that the Doctor has himself witnessed in previous adventures, leaving Alaya behind in the care of Ambrose and Tony is incredibly naïve of him. This is especially so after Tony has already suggested that they dissect Alaya. The only reason for this seemingly bizarre comment is so that Chris Chibnall can signal early on that the humans are just as 'bad' as the Silurians, who have indeed "dissected" Mo while he was conscious.

The Doctor's decision is made to appear more bizarre by the fact that even though chained, Alaya is still hostile and clearly aiming to provoke a war. The Doctor probably doesn't help things by immediately proclaiming that Alaya is beautiful when he removes her mask. Although his admiration of her species is genuine, it's probably not what you want to hear when you're a woman chained to a wall. Alaya then makes a strange claim that she's the last of her species, which seems to be an attempt at self-preservation that flies in the face of her more evident desire to get herself killed in order to start a war. So, this claim by Alaya is manifestly nothing more than a device for the Doctor to remind the audience that he's the last of the Time Lords. Since we really haven't heard the Eleventh Doctor spout on about this so much, one can only presume that this reminder will have more relevance in the 6th series…

Did You Know? Meera Syal is most famous for appearing in the comedy series *Goodness Gracious Me*, along with Nina Wadia (Dr. Ramsden in *The Eleventh Hour*).

9: Cold Blood

Writer: Chris Chibnall
Director: Ashley Way
Originally broadcast: 29 May 2010

Cast

The Doctor: Matt Smith
Amy Pond: Karen Gillan
Rory Williams: Arthur Darvill
Alaya: Neve McIntosh
Nasreen Chaudhry: Meera Syal
Tony Mack: Robert Pugh
Ambrose: Nia Roberts
Malohkeh: Richard Hope
Eldane: Stephen Moore
Mo: Alun Raglan
Elliot: Samuel Davies

Steven's review: *Cold Blood* completes the two-part story of the clash between the Silurians - a species of intelligent reptiles that long ago dominated the Earth - and present-day humanity, showing the two sides being unable to overcome their seemingly irreconcilable differences. For the most part, the story quite closely follows the path taken by the original Silurian story (called, oddly enough, *Doctor Who and the Silurians*) forty years ago. However, there's a real sting in the tail, courtesy of the overarching plot arc of this season, the "crack in the universe" that seems to be following the Doctor, Amy, and Rory wherever they go. Previously, the crack had been most prominent in *Flesh and Stone*, where indeed it provided the actual resolution of that story's threat; here it simply arrives as an appendix to the main story. But more of that later.

I was rather harsh toward the first episode of this story, *The Hungry Earth*, finding it somewhat lacking in meaningful plot (there was lots of action, but little of it relevant) and serving mainly as a prologue to set up the actual humans-versus-Silurians story. Its purpose was to create and isolate a small group of humans that could then, in this episode, be placed in conflict with an equally small group of Silurians. The two groups serve as proxies for their respective races, enabling the story to at least attempt to present world-spanning issues without trying to depict a full-scale inter-species conflict that would be impossible to show on the canvas of a television series. Indeed, apart from the odd CGI vista here and there to create a sense of scale, this story could more or less be told with the resources of the old *Doctor Who* series - specifically, the Jon Pertwee era, from which it draws so much inspiration.

One of the attractive attributes of the Silurians in their original story was the way they were depicted not as a horde of identical monsters, but as actual characters, with individual motives and disagreements among themselves as to the best way to deal with the humans. The writer of this story, Chris Chibnall, has reused this idea - not that this was visible last week, since we only saw one Silurian, the warrior Alaya, who was captured by the Doctor in order to give the humans a hostage to exchange for Amy and the others who had previously been taken by the reptiles. Kept under guard, Alaya proves to be totally hostile to the "apes" (as she contemptuously refers to them), taking a perverse delight in taunting Ambrose and her father Tony with the Silurians' abduction of Ambrose's husband and son, and the fact that the venom she stung Tony with earlier is slowly killing him. She aspires to martyrdom, being totally willing to die in the belief that it will ignite a war in which her people will reclaim the surface. In one of the high points of the episode, she manages to goad Ambrose into repeatedly attacking her with some kind of taser-like weapon until she gets the death she so eagerly sought. Ambrose's horrified realization that she may have destroyed the chance for a peaceful resolution, even as she defends her actions ("I just want my family back"), is very effective.

Once we get down to the Silurian city, the reptiles become

more complex. The leader of the warriors, Restac, soon captures the Doctor and Nasreen, who were drawn down to the city in the TARDIS. Her desire to revive all of her soldiers from hibernation and lead a war to reclaim the surface brings her into conflict with the scientist Malohkeh, who doesn't share her instinctive hostility to the humans. He's not exactly a warm, cuddly character, as he is quite happy to experiment on the captured humans in the interests of science, but when Restac overreaches her authority he takes action against her by reviving the ruler of the city, Eldane - whose calm, reasonable tones are provided by Stephen Moore, well known to sci-fi fans as the voice of Marvin the Paranoid Android from Douglas Adams' *Hitchhiker's Guide to the Galaxy*. The conflict between the three Silurians - the wise elder, the young firebrand, and the pragmatic scientist - is a direct reflection of the original Silurian story. Its outcome, though, is different: in the original, the youngster killed the old leader in a coup and began a direct attack on the humans, which led directly to the final disaster. Here, Restac rather vindictively has Malohkeh shot by her warriors, but Eldane has her measure, and ends up finding a way to defeat her.

Throughout this story, both humans and Silurians are always bringing out the worst in each other, ignoring the Doctor's exhortations to find common ground and rise above their conflict. Both sides have valid grievances - undeniably the Silurians attacked the humans first, but then we find out the Silurians were only awakened in the first place by the threat to their city posed by the humans' drilling. Chibnall sharpens the conflict further with the capture of family members on both sides - it turns out that Restac and Alaya are from the same "gene chain" (which of course also, conveniently, allows them both to be played by Neve McIntosh). The lack of a clear division between "good guys" and "bad guys" is the best thing about the story - both species have a valid claim to the planet and are going to have to find some way to share it.

The episode makes the interesting choice to slightly

distance itself from the viewer by starting with a voiceover narration from Eldane (which returns in the middle, and again at the end) that immediately introduces a sense of scale and importance to the proceedings. I found that one effect of the narration was to introduce an element of doubt into my mind as to how I expected the story to go. If you imagine the episode without it, even without knowing how previous Silurian stories have ended, it seems inevitable that everything will completely fall apart from the moment the Doctor tells Rory and the others to come down to the Silurian base and to bring Alaya with them, not knowing that Alaya is already dead. The opening narration, however, implied a successful resolution to the conflict, which intrigued me - not least because it would be a far-reaching change to the present-day world of the show, even more so than the way the existence of aliens seemed to become everyday knowledge during the Russell T Davies era. The Doctor's emphatic statement that this situation was *not* a fixed point in time, where the outcome could not be changed (as seen in, for example, *The Waters of Mars*), was also suggestive. In the end, the series (probably wisely) decided not to go down that path, and the final twist, with Eldane finding a way to deal with Restac and put his people back into hibernation for a thousand years, was a neat way of bringing this particular story to a close without asking us to swallow a pat resolution of the entire human/Silurian conflict.

The Doctor spends much of his time being frustrated that he can't seem to bring the two sides together, and Matt Smith gives his usual excellent performance. Interestingly, he is separated from both Amy and Rory for most of the episode; instead, Nasreen is by his side as a substitute companion, and works rather well, as she is fascinated by the Silurian city, and takes the lead in trying to work out a way for humans to share the world with the reptiles. It was a nice touch to bring back her romantic relationship with Tony (as established last week), when he needs to stay in the Silurian city due to his infection by Alaya's venom, and she decides to join him in hibernation.

The one aspect of the story I had a real problem with is the portrayal of Amy. Chibnall writes her in a shallow, very self-consciously "sassy" way - she's flippant and snappish toward Rory, and in the Silurian city she keeps making lame quips that suggest nothing so much as a failure to understand the seriousness of the situation. Indeed, in the scenes where she is supposed to be helping Nasreen negotiate with Eldane, she is rather weirdly shown as seemingly bored and half-asleep. This unsympathetic treatment of the character is a disappointment, particularly after her excellent development in earlier episodes like *Amy's Choice*. Rory, on the other hand, is very good throughout. As with last week's episode, Arthur Darvill gets lots of scenes away from the Doctor and Amy, and clearly shows Rory growing in confidence as a leader, taking charge of the group on the surface after Alaya's death and paying attention to the Doctor's instructions.

In the end, the Doctor gets everyone out of Restac's clutches thanks to his sonic screwdriver, which is unfortunately overused in this story, giving the Doctor the ability to disable the Silurians' guns with a wave of his hand. Normally I'm not that bothered about the sonic screwdriver being used to hurry the plot along, but this really was going too far. Anyway, once they've got away, Eldane manages to shut down the Silurian city with a convenient "toxic fumigation" facility that will kill any Silurians that don't return to hibernation. And now it's time for the standard "get the hell out" scene that usually ends a story like this - we're expecting the Doctor to herd his surviving allies into the TARDIS and for them to all escape with seconds to spare. Which is exactly what happens...

Except that this is where the episode takes a sharp turn, as the crack in the universe suddenly shows up in the wall of the cave next to the TARDIS - this time it's a wide, deep gash in the stone with bright light pouring out from it. The Doctor decides to examine it more closely, reaches into it and brings out something wrapped in his handkerchief. But the delay allows Restac to catch up to them. She is dying from the toxic gas, but manages to get one shot off first - and Rory leaps in front of the Doctor and is fatally hit.

This entire ending sequence is gripping, as tendrils of light from the crack take hold of Rory's body and begin to erase him from history, just as happened to the clerics in *Flesh and Stone*. The Doctor has to physically drag Amy away and into the TARDIS, and Karen Gillan's performance comes back into focus after the lapses earlier in the episode, as a distraught Amy frantically tries to hold on to the memory of Rory. But a sudden lurch of the TARDIS breaks her concentration, and it's immediately clear she's totally forgotten about him. On the floor, the Doctor sees the engagement ring which Rory left in the TARDIS last week - the only trace left of him.

Back on the surface, the tie-up with the beginning of last week's episode is completed as Amy again sees her future self waving to her from a distance - but now she's alone. Time has definitely been changed after all. It's a real gut-punch of an ending, but it does have the effect of somewhat diminishing the story that led up to it. I know I'll most likely be thinking about Rory's fate rather than the Silurians whenever I look back on this story. And that is only reinforced by the final shot, as the Doctor unwraps the piece of "shrapnel" he found in the crack - and is shocked to discover it's a piece of the TARDIS' police box exterior. Another piece (literally) of the twisted jigsaw of this season, leading to what should be a cataclysmic finale in a few weeks time. I can't wait to find out how it all fits together.

Steven's Classic Who DVD Recommendation: After you've seen *Doctor Who and the Silurians*, check out its sequel, *The Sea Devils*, starring Jon Pertwee and Katy Manning.

Kevin's review: The recap of the previous episode shows Rory placing Amy's engagement ring back in its box on the TARDIS console, so the curious scene in which he took the ring off Amy for its safekeeping is given a great deal of prominence from the start. And indeed, it turns out, contrary to the expectations of say, the casual viewer, that this scene was very important indeed…

Back to the story itself, it's not long before Alaya has provoked Ambrose to the extent that the human kills the Silurian, just as Alaya had been hoping she would. When confronted with what she's done, Ambrose babbles that she was just trying to gather information and protect her family. The use of torture to extract information is a rather subtle allusion to similar methods previously adopted by the CIA during George W. Bush's presidency. The seemingly intractable clash between Homo Reptilia and Homo Sapiens also seems to be an unsavoury reference to the similar contemporary Israeli/Palestinian dispute. This idea is only reinforced by the fact that the Silurian scientist is given a name that sounds quite Arabic (Malohkeh is quite close to a Iranian name that means "Queen", Malekeh). Ambrose herself has a quite masculine name that derives from the name of the food that gave the Greek gods immortality. By her actions, Ambrose seems destined for immortality also, but for all the wrong reasons.

One of the biggest departures from their appearance in the Classic Series is the prominence of female Silurians in this adventure. Indeed, the fact that Ayala and Restac are female very much adds to the drama, beyond the fact that they are sisters. Akin to Ambrose, Restac (and her female warriors) act like very aggressive mothers that are intent on protecting their nests. This is a very interesting concept that hasn't previously been explored on *Doctor Who*, so Chris Chibnall gets some bonus points for a spark of originality here.

At first, I didn't think this concept ultimately worked very well, as reptiles don't usually care for their young as mammals do. However, Chris Chibnall could argue that some reptiles very much do so, such as crocodiles. Indeed, there are some palaeontologists, such as Robert Bakker, who argue that dinosaurs must have been warm blooded, since their larger bodies could not have functioned if they had the cold blood that we associate with reptiles today. The

Doctor's heat detecting sunglasses in *The Hungry Earth* established that the Silurians have cold blood, hence the name of this episode (which also, of course, has associations with dispassionate slaughter). Beyond this, Robert Bakker has postulated that such dinosaurs would have had more advanced social systems that most reptiles today, and would have exhibited quite different behaviour, and some species may well have moved around in herds. Thus, advanced reptiles, such as the Silurians here, could exhibit similar behaviour to higher mammals, such as us.

However, one thing that reptiles should definitely not sport is mammary glands, as they do here. Obviously, the production team could have got around this by only casting flat-chested actresses to play the Silurian warriors, but this could have turned into something of an impractical chore. This is also not the first time that female warriors have appeared in *Doctor Who*: that distinction goes to 1965's *Galaxy 4*, which involved a similar long-lasting conflict between the Drahvins and the Rills, with the twist being that the beautiful Drahvins are the villains rather than the hideous Rills. This story also involved one of the Doctor's companions, Steven, being kept hostage by the Drahvins, so *Galaxy 4* could very well have influenced Chris Chibnall's writing of *Cold Blood*. Of course, it later emerges that the Drahvins have obviously not forgotten their encounter with the Doctor, as they are part of the alien alliance that is so eager to imprison him in *The Pandorica Opens*. And although these Silurian women have achieved warrior status, there still appears to be a glass ceiling, as their ultimate leader, Eldane, is very much male, so feminism has still got some way to go in Silurian society.

At times, I found Eldane's privileged position just as irritating as Restac does. In particular, I was quite irked at Eldane's voiceovers, as this device is usually restricted to quite important characters in *Doctor Who*: such as the Doctor himself in *The Deadly Assassin*, Rassilon in *The End of Time*, and Amy in *The Beast Below*. Now, it seems, any old Silurian duffer can do a voiceover, as long as he saves valuable time by telling us (rather than showing us) what is happening, and imparts prophetic sounding information about events that he can have no possible knowledge of due to his being in hibernation. Eldane also pops up at the end in the Silurian lab, even though Restac gave no orders to assault him, only the Doctor and the humans. And it's Eldane that provides the solution to the immediate dilemma, by forcing Restac's warriors back into hibernation or else face death in the fumigation gas (although this gas doesn't appear to affect humans - either that, or the TARDIS crew just outruns it). Admittedly, the Silurians have previously been shown to employ a different kind of gas in this story to decontaminate the humans (to the extent that it appears to clean Amy of all the mud that had clung to her during her abduction through the earth) and to incapacitate them, so this device is not completely out of the blue. Although one would have thought that the Silurians would have been capable of developing a fumigating gas that's not lethal to them.

Alaya had earlier been astonished that her venom had yet to kill Tony. The representation of this green poison flowing through Tony's veins is quite similar to that from the Jon Pertwee adventure *The Green Death*, which also featured a Welsh mine. The Cybermen also have a tendency to infect humans in this manner, as demonstrated in *The Moonbase* and *Revenge of the Cybermen*. Despite the fact that Tony looks very rough and dishevelled when he arrives in the Silurian city, he is given the role of bearing Alaya's body: it would certainly have added insult to injury if he had dropped her! The Doctor explains away Tony's survival by stating that he's mutating, rather than dying, which presumably means that he's changing into some kind of human/Silurian hybrid, and one would have thought that he therefore could have played some role in negotiating a lasting peace. However, the fact that Tony's mutating, and any consequences of this, is immediately dismissed, as the concentration is focussed on getting rid of this infection from his system. The fact that she has the hots for him, as well as a unique opportunity to study the Silurians' science, is very much a factor in Nasreen deciding to stay in the city. And thus any hopes of a reconciliation between the two species is dashed as soon as it has started, as the two most credible witnesses won't be around to prepare humanity for sharing the planet.

So, I guess Chris Chibnall here expects Elliot to do the reverse of the mouse in *The Gruffalo*, and to spread the word that these green scaly monsters are not to be feared. The Doctor tells Eldane that the Silurians should hibernate for an additional thousand years, as hopefully humanity will have evolved enough to accept them by then. However, we know from this season's *The Beast Below*, that in the generations succeeding the 29th Century, humanity is pretty much the same as it ever was. The Doctor also does not bother to tell Eldane that the surface of the Earth will still be badly affected by the solar flares by the 31st Century, but hey! There'll be hardly any humans around, so they won't exactly be standing in Homo Reptilia's way...

Admittedly, you can't expect today's production team to be restricted by events that were first mentioned in a 1975 story (*The Ark in Space*), but when these events (i.e. the solar flares) played a role in one of this season's episodes that was written by the showrunner himself, then pedants like me are entitled to ask for a little more consistency. And there's all that hogwash about 2020 not "being a fixed point in time", meaning that the humans and Silurians could have negotiated a settlement in this story if they had really wanted to: it's hogwash because no *Doctor Who* story set in the near future features the Silurians. Admittedly, *The Dalek Invasion of Earth* (set in 2164) was broadcast half a decade before the Silurians were originally devised. Then again, this is the one future tale most likely to have involved the Silurians, as they would have surely noticed the Daleks' attempt to drill to the Earth's molten core.

Malohkeh, like Alaya before him, seems curiously uninterested in the fact that the Doctor is not human, as the Time Lord is (presumably) the first extraterrestrial that the Silurians have ever encountered. Possibly this was cut from the script, as it doesn't have any direct bearing on the story itself. When Malohkeh decontaminates the Doctor, Matt Smith screams in much the same tone that Peter Davison did whenever he was suffering pain in his role as the Fifth Doctor. This is probably coincidental, but it's a nice touch if it is deliberate. Presumably it's Malohkeh who's been stealing bodies from the graveyard, and it's probably just as well, under the circumstances, that Ambrose doesn't demand the body of her uncle back, as Malohkeh has undoubtedly dissected it.

The one bit of CGI that didn't really impress me in this episode was the representation of the huge flanks of hibernating Silurians. Then again, my expectations have previously been raised by *Doctor Who*'s ability now to compete with the visual splendour presented by Hollywood productions. I was also surprised by the fact that the Silurian warriors apparently hibernate with their weapons in hand. Although I guess that this means that they are immediately ready for action upon waking. Amy accepts Mo's suggestion to purloin Silurian weapons a little too readily, given the Doctor's personal refusal to handle weapons; however, it's not long before the far more martially aware Restac disarms her. Not that the Silurians are any more competent when faced with the might of the Doctor's sonic screwdriver!

Another hole in the plot is the fact that the Doctor and Nasreen are allowed to wander around the Silurian city freely before being detected and apprehended, despite the Doctor's belief that it was the Silurians that pulled the TARDIS beneath the earth in the first place. Then again, logic has never gone hand-in-hand with the Silurians, as the Doctor repeats the assertion (from Malcolm Hulke's own novelisation of his story *Doctor Who and the Silurians*) that the reason why they went into hibernation in the first place was because they were afraid of the lump of rock that was rapidly approaching Earth, which later turned out to be the Moon. The Moon, of course, became Earth's satellite many millions of years before there was any life on the planet, and may indeed have contributed to its development, so the rationale behind the Silurians' hibernation just doesn't make any sense. Like most of the Doctor's opponents, the Silurians are also incredibly bad shooters; for instance, one incredibly badly aimed shot impacts *behind* the Silurian that's attempting to sting the Doctor as he makes his escape from the conference chamber. So bad are the Silurians at shooting their own weapons, that it makes Rory's death all the more tragic. Even more so, since it appears that the Doctor was very close to reaching his sonic screwdriver.

As my fellow reviewer Steven notes, the sonic screwdriver has never been quite so proficient at disabling alien guns before. I mean, the *Doctor Who* production team in the 80's showed the sonic screwdriver being destroyed on screen merely because it was good at getting the Doctor out of locked doors. Now, as in *The Vampires of Venice*, it seems to have morphed into a medical device, as the Doctor sweeps it over Rory as he lies dying. Admittedly, in a famous scene from *The Sea Devils*, Jon Pertwee's Doctor exploded some mines via the sonic screwdriver, but it had no effect on the Sea Devils' own weaponry (which, as *The Brilliant Book of Doctor Who 2011* states, were a direct influence on the design of the Silurian guns in this adventure - indeed, the back of the Sea Devils' heads are not too dissimilar to their Silurian cousins here).

It's interesting to note that the Doctor here seems to be immune to the crack in the universe's malign influence, as he reaches directly into the crooked smile, and is yet not swallowed whole, unlike the clerics in *Flesh and Stone* who just wandered too close to the fissure. No doubt swallowing the Doctor would have been too much of a paradox, because as we now know, the explosion of the TARDIS (which could not have happened if the Doctor had never existed) caused the crack in the universe. However, if the Doctor had been presuming that the crack in the universe was solely dependent on Amy and Rory's marriage, he (and the audience) is very much disillusioned of this notion now.

Presumably Rory is enough a temporal paradox to satisfy the crooked smile's hunger in this instance, so that it doesn't go around gobbling all the hibernating Silurians, as it did with regards to Octavian's clerics. Despite Amy's traumatic forgetting of her lover, there's still a little bit of Rory remaining in the ring that he had so pointedly placed on the console...

Unlike the clerics from *Flesh and Stone*, who Amy can still recall, she can't remember Rory (as the Doctor explains) because he was part of her personal history. When Amy is struggling to retain her memories of Rory, one of the flashbacks is when Restac shoots Rory, although, for some bizarre reason, the energy discharge from her weapon, which kills Rory, no longer appears on screen. The Doctor's status as a Time Lord would appear to provide him with some additional protection in this respect, as it's to his woe that he can still remember Rory. Yet the very fact that he can do so, and the presence of the ring, does give the viewer some hope, allied to the fact that it's only been a fortnight since Rory last "died"...

Any optimism is all rather dashed by Eldane's rather rude interruption at the end, and by the fact that the future Rory has disappeared from the hillside. What's more, the shrapnel that the Doctor has retrieved from the crack in the universe appears to have come from the shell of his own TARDIS...

Of course, when you think about it, this doom-laden scene is full of baloney, especially when you consider that the actual exterior of the TARDIS is not a wooden box. Admittedly, when the TARDIS exploded in 1968's *The Mind Robber*, the wooden hull fell apart into its requisite parts, but that was meant to look surreal. In the event of the TARDIS actually exploding, the notion that the chameleon circuit is still functioning stretches credulity somewhat... Then again, I'm a fussy pedant, who was just as blown away by this traumatic ending as the huge majority of other viewers.

Did You Know? Chris Chibnall appeared on the BBC's *Open Air* in 1986 as part of a group of *Doctor Who* fans, in which he was very critical of *Terror of the Vervoids* as being a clichéd, stereotypical story featuring the Doctor running through corridors chased by monsters. So, on the basis of this story, you could argue that not much has changed! Bizarrely enough, some of Chris's fellow fans on the show criticised the overall story arc of *The Trial of a Time Lord* as being far too complex! And that there was a danger that this would possibly alienate the casual viewer. Then again, *The Trial of Trial of a Time Lord* was hampered by the early death of Robert Holmes (who was due to write the most episodes of this series), and by the resignation of script editor Eric Saward, which meant that there was no showrunner with the expertise of Steven Moffat taking care of all the details.

10: Vincent and the Doctor

Writer: Richard Curtis
Director: Jonny Campbell
Originally broadcast: 5 June 2010

Cast

The Doctor: Matt Smith
Amy Pond: Karen Gillan
Vincent: Tony Curran
Dr Black: Bill Nighy
Maurice: Nik Howden
Mother: Chrissie Cotterill
Waitress: Sarah Counsell
School Children: Morgan Overton and Andrew Byrne

Steven's review: *Vincent and the Doctor* is one of the episodes this season that I was particularly looking forward to. It's not often that a writer as prominent as Richard Curtis gets involved with the show, and having the man behind *Blackadder* (as well as several highly successful feature films) contributing an episode was a prospect to savour. And I wasn't disappointed - the result is a complete success. While a bare plot summary - the Doctor meets Vincent Van Gogh and helps him defeat a giant chicken from outer space - might suggest a less than serious episode, *Vincent and the Doctor* is in fact a deeply felt piece of work, with a wonderfully complex portrayal of its central character and plenty to say about topics that *Doctor Who* doesn't normally touch.

We open in the Van Gogh collection in the present-day Musée d'Orsay, in Paris. A guide, Dr. Black, provides a tour group (and, of course, us) with some necessary exposition about Van Gogh - principally, how he was almost completely unappreciated during his own lifetime. It was clearly Richard Curtis's involvement that led to this character being played by an uncredited Bill Nighy (*Love*

Actually). It's a lovely cameo, and giving the part to an actor of such stature ensures that the audience pays attention to what he's saying, both here and at the end of the episode.

The Doctor and Amy enter during Dr. Black's talk, simply wandering through the back of the shot in a very nice low-key way. They come to Van Gogh's painting *The Church at Auvers*, and the Doctor spots a strange element in it - the head of an alien creature is looking out from a window of the church. The Doctor decides a trip back to 1890 is in order to talk to Vincent Van Gogh and find out what's going on. This first section of the episode is extremely straightforward; it's simply designed to get the Doctor and Amy together with Van Gogh as quickly as possible. They arrive in 1890 and almost immediately track down Vincent, in a cafe that looks exactly like another of his paintings - *The Café Terrace*. As usual with period episodes of *Doctor Who*, the BBC design, costume and makeup departments have done outstanding work. Director Jonny Campbell and his team have made just as good use of the Croatian town of Trogir here as they did in *The Vampires of Venice* a few episodes ago.

When their talk with Vincent is interrupted by an attack on a local girl by the mysterious unseen monster, the Doctor and Amy are soon inviting themselves into the artist's home. From this point, the episode is pretty much entirely a three-hander between the Doctor, Amy and Vincent. Matt Smith and Karen Gillan are both excellent this week, enjoying playing with the dialogue Curtis has written for them. The loss of Rory at the end of last week's episode is clearly weighing on the Doctor, but he has to avoid showing it because Amy has no memory of the event.

As good as they are, though, the show belongs to Tony Curran, who puts in a spectacular performance as Vincent. Given the opportunity to present this great but mentally fragile artist as a complex, fully realized human being, he seizes the chance with alacrity. He is thoroughly believable as a man who sees the world in a very different way, rising to heights of passion as he tries to communicate to the Doctor his experience of the colours of the world.

The episode doesn't shy away from Vincent's struggles with depression; indeed, without in any way forcing the parallel, a monster which is visible only to him, strikes without warning and can't be reasoned with makes an ideal metaphor for the demon within, while ensuring that the story remains accessible to the children that make up a crucial part of the show's audience. And as for his physical appearance, that's simply perfect - at one point he's holding up an actual Van Gogh self-portrait next to his face, and the resemblance is amazing. The one obvious divergence from the real Vincent - Curran's Scottish accent - is elegantly covered with a good joke implying that the TARDIS is translating him for Amy's benefit.

The actual monster-chasing plot is kept extremely simple. The creature attacks again at night outside Vincent's house; Vincent draws a picture of it so the Doctor can identify it as an alien creature called a Krafayis; they go to the church where they know it will shortly arrive; there's a brief chase and a fight, and the creature is killed. Around this straightforward plot, though, are arranged many moments of comedy, beauty, depth, and tenderness. There are some gorgeously composed images, such as in a scene on the morning after the attack, when Amy has filled Vincent's garden with sunflowers and is sitting among them.

I'm almost taking it for granted now, but Matt Smith is yet again brilliant as the Doctor. This episode lets him demonstrate that he doesn't even need anyone else on screen to play off, as he's given a great solo comedy sequence when the Doctor takes Vincent's drawing back to the TARDIS and uses its computer to attempt to identify the creature. ("This is the problem with the impressionists. Not accurate enough. This would never happen with Gainsborough, or one of those *proper* painters.") From the TARDIS' storage cupboards he digs out a hilariously clunky contraption to use as a portable monster detector, and there's another mainly comic sequence as the lumbering Krafayis pursues him back through the town. (As for the appearance of the aforesaid space poultry, it's not the greatest piece of design, and the

141

CGI is never totally convincing, but since the monster is definitely a subsidiary part of the story, and spends most of its time invisible, it does the job quite adequately.)

In contrast to this fooling around, a dramatic high point comes with a powerful scene as they are getting ready to go to the church. The Doctor finds Vincent lying on his bed, sobbing, and gently approaches him. Then, unwisely, the Doctor tries to snap Vincent out of his depression, but Vincent yells at him to get out. Shortly after, though, he rejoins the Doctor and Amy as they are about to go to the church, his black mood having dissipated. He is in his hat and coat, and picks up his brush like a gunfighter in a spaghetti western arming himself for battle. On the way to the church, there's a clever moment as Vincent realizes that Amy has her secret sadness too. He notices that she is crying without realizing it.

Vincent: "It's all right. I understand."

Amy: "I'm not sure I do."

As with the moment later when the Doctor accidentally blurts out Rory's name to Vincent, the season arc story is kept bubbling along underneath without needing to be brought into the foreground. It's been rather prominent lately (especially, of course, in last week's episode), so it's nice to have it recede again for a bit.

There's some more fun dialogue as the Doctor has no choice but to wait for the monster to appear while Vincent is painting the church - he can't stop himself making jokes about Michaelangelo and Picasso, and complaining, "Is this how time normally passes? Reeeeeally slowly. In the right order. If there's one thing I can't stand, it's an unpunctual alien attack." Eventually, to his relief, the monster arrives, and they corner it in the church. In a twist, the Doctor realises that the Krafayis is blind as well - they are just as invisible to it as it is to them. There's a struggle, which ends when Vincent, intending only to ward off the monster, accidentally kills it by impaling it on the legs of his easel.

The monster plot may have ended, but there are still ten minutes to go. The extended epilogue that follows is, in many ways, my favourite part of the episode. It starts with the Doctor, Amy, and Vincent, lying on the ground and looking up at the night sky as Vincent rhapsodizes about what he sees there. Illustrating his words, the view of the night sky morphs beautifully into Van Gogh's famous *Starry Night*. It's a moment of pure magic.

What follows is also magical, as the Doctor and Amy, rather than simply taking their leave of Vincent, decide to give him a trip in the TARDIS to the modern-day exhibition where we started. Looked at realistically, this is a very uncharacteristic thing for the Doctor to do - there's not the slightest worry expressed about affecting the course of history or anything like that. But really, this is just a wonderful bit of wish-fulfilment - given a time machine to play with, who wouldn't want to go back to visit their heroes of the past and show them how they would be famous and revered in the future? Vincent gets to experience the success he was denied in his lifetime, and is reduced to tears of joy as he overhears Dr. Black deliver a passionate encomium.

The only thing I didn't like about this sequence is the decision to use a rather saccharine ballad on the soundtrack, which tips the scene over into unwanted sentimentality. I would have preferred Murray Gold (who has been a much reduced presence this season compared to previous years) to have been given the opportunity to score this scene. Fortunately, it's not the end of the episode; there's still more to come. The Doctor and Amy deliver Vincent back to his own time, make their farewells, and return to the museum, with Amy expecting to see many more Van Gogh paintings.

But the episode finally brings us back to reality with the reminder that a condition like depression is not to be negated by one moment of joy. As Vincent said, "Doctor, my friend. We have fought monsters together, and we have won. On my own I fear I may not do as well." Amy is distressed to discover he still took his own life at age 37. After she bitterly says they didn't make a difference at all, there's a lovely bit of philosophy from the Doctor.

Murray Gold's music finally comes to the fore in an

intensely emotional ending, as Amy discovers there has been one tiny change after all. Vincent's painting of a vase of sunflowers now has a dedication - "for Amy." A final grace note in a masterpiece of an episode.

Steven's Classic Who DVD Recommendation: There's only one Classic Series story that comes close to equalling this episode's saturation in the world of art, and that's *City of Death*, starring Tom Baker and Lalla Ward; one of the best stories in the entire series. Written by Douglas Adams, it has a brilliant Steven Moffat-style time-twisting plot, lovely location filming in Paris, and any amount of great dialogue, all topped off with a surprise cameo from John Cleese. Do yourself a favour and check it out.

Kevin's review: *Vincent and the Doctor* opens with a mighty disturbance in a wheatfield, which is probably the first manifestation of the invisible monster that features in this episode, the Krafayis. Vincent Van Gogh is immediately introduced to us, painting one of his most famous pictures, *Wheatfield With Crows*. The crows are disturbed by the lumbering Krafayis, and fly up into the sky. Vincent's representation of these crows is quite similar to a certain "crooked smile" that has recently been haunting the Doctor. And this is not the only reference to the overall story arc that features in this brilliantly beautiful episode.

During a visit to the Musée d'Orsay, the Doctor spots a strange face in Van Gogh's painting *The Church at Auvers*, and immediately decides that he must speak to the artist. He therefore asks Dr. Black to give an exact date for the picture, and the art historian says that it was painted in early June, less than a year before Van Gogh died. However, in real life, this painting was completed just over a month before Van Gogh killed himself, and was actually inspired by a memory of a church from his childhood, rather than one in Auvers. Indeed, Van Gogh was actually in the care of Dr. Gachet at the time, the doctor whose portrait in the gallery alerts the Time Lord, as he initially thinks that the children talking about the painting have recognised him. The Doctor also rather conveniently stands on the left hand side of *The Church at Auvers*, so that we only snatch a brief glimpse of the woman in the picture, who was obviously not present when Vincent composed this painting in the episode. Despite the very dark blue sky in the painting, *The Church at Auvers* is actually a daytime scene, rather than a nighttime one. And although *Wheatfield With Crows* is shown at the opening of the episode, many commentators believe that it may have been Van Gogh's final painting. Added to this is the fact that by the time that the Doctor and Amy meet Van Gogh, not only is he in the care of Dr. Gachet, but he's already mutilated one of his own ears. So, the *Doctor Who* production team have taken a great many liberties with Van Gogh's timeline. However, as Steven Moffat says in *Doctor Who Confidential*, their aim was to present the legend of Van Gogh, rather than to create a wholly realistic dramatisation of his life, as this would have put paid to the Krafayis before they'd even started!

Indeed, despite the twisting of these autobiographical details, this is the episode in this run of *Doctor Who* that really does return to the show's original brief of being educational, with no bug-eyed-monsters (BEMs). Unfortunately for Sydney Newman, some BEMs called Daleks quickly trundled along in 1963 to skew his original vision for the show. And while there is a BEM in this episode, the Krafayis is invisible, and thus is barely on screen. Although my fellow reviewer Steven has criticised the Krafayis' appearance, I think it's quite fitting for a beast that ends up in a post-Impressionist painting, with its fowl-like features seeming quite reptilian and Native American at the same time.

The episode as a whole is visually stunning, as the production team really do bring Van Gogh's paintings to life. The realisation of *Starry Night* is particularly spectacular, and an inspiration to any in the audience, whether they be young or old. And of course, the subject of starry skies is one that the story arc will soon return to. The production team really excel themselves with their recreation of Van Gogh's *Café Terrace at Night*, as it looks truly authentic (*Wikipedia* notes that this 1888 Van Gogh painting was the first one in which he depicted stars). The thought passes my mind that they could have recreated this image in Arles itself, as the café that Van Gogh painted still stands there. However, the actual street is no longer cobbled, so this might have required too much set dressing, and it's become rather a tourist trap due to its association with Van Gogh. Besides, not all the Van Gogh paintings that feature in this episode are depictions of Arles, where Vincent is supposedly living when the Doctor sets out to meet him. Anyway, the *Doctor Who* production team does a truly tremendous job of realising Van Gogh's paintings in the Croatian town of Trogir. So much so, that their representation of Van Gogh's *Bedroom in Arles* is instantly recognisable and almost indistinguishable from the painting.

Of course, one of the main themes in this episode is that no one, apart from Vincent, appreciates his artwork. So there are a number of humorous scenes in which Vincent places a coffee pot on one of his paintings, and completely obliterates another while the Doctor and Amy look on in horror. I initially thought the scene where the Doctor tries to talk about Vincent's mental condition was at first misjudged and was thankful when Van Gogh silenced him. However, on second viewing, I recognised that the tone of this dialogue was pitch perfect, as it was in the rest of the episode. I believe that *Vincent and the Doctor* is the only episode of *Doctor Who* that has featured a voiceover during the closing credits suggesting that any viewers affected by issues portrayed by the programme should call the BBC Action Line for assistance, as this is a refrain that I usually associate with the ending of say, *EastEnders*. I think that *Doctor Who*'s very professional production team superbly presented Vincent's mental issues, and was another instance of the programme living up to its educational brief.

I suppose that, like Simon Nye's episode, I was expecting a few more belly laughs from such an accomplished comedy writer as Richard Curtis. However, the episode is not all doom and gloom by any means, especially that scene where Amy archly picks a whole barrel load of sunflowers and suggests that Vincent paints them. There's also a running gag concerning the fact that Vincent's straggly beard is a tad irritating to anyone he kisses, such as Dr. Black (Bill Nighy is superb when you see the art historian briefly entertain the thought that he may well have been kissed by his hero). The Doctor's encounter with Dr. Black gives him another opportunity to enthuse that "bowties are cool", a refrain that will really gain momentum during his next encounter with River Song.

When the Doctor retrieves the bizarre Perseus-mirror-type contraption, we learn that he had a two-headed godmother with bad breath! Maybe she was an Aplan? (On a pedantic note, she must have given it to him fairly recently, as the Doctor has never previously utilised it in his encounters with invisible monsters, and one would have thought the Doctor's body heat detecting sunglasses from *The Hungry Earth* would have proved far more useful here, so the Doctor must have lost them.) Vincent's romantic ovations to Amy leads to the pleasing thought that any such union would have meant the production of the most ginger of babies, an idea that should surely please even the most sensitive redhead. Although the new TARDIS is not pleasing to my eyes, it would no doubt impress Van Gogh far more, as the redesign is one that very well looks as though it was dreamt up by a post-Impressionist! It's also quite amusing that the TARDIS ends up getting covered by flyers, as this is what happens to most current day phone boxes. Thankfully the organic flyers burn away in the time vortex (which makes the Tenth Doctor's decision to allow Captain Jack to cling onto the TARDIS in the vortex during *Utopia* appear to be even more cruel). Tony Curran's portrayal of Van Gogh was also sublime, and it goes without saying that he really looked the part. So powerful was his performance that I was more than a little teary teary-eyed at the end.

Yet the poignancy of this scene is due to Amy's tragedy, as

well as Vincent's. It was only a few weeks ago in *Flesh and Stone* that the Doctor was excitedly exclaiming to himself that not only can time be rewritten, it can also be unwritten. The reason why he took Amy to the Musée d'Orsay in the first place was to cheer her up after the loss of Rory. However, Amy's perfectly happy, as she never knew Rory existed, so it seems rather that it's the Doctor who needs cheering up. The Doctor's only grief is subtly shown by the fact that he has a tendency to accidentally call other people "Rory" in this episode. Thus it's the Doctor who's rather dragging his feet at the end in response to Amy's belief that time can be rewritten, and that they will have made a huge difference to Vincent, that will be displayed by his having a much longer life, and an even more prolific output. Amy is initially sorely disappointed to find that little, if anything, has changed in the Musée d'Orsay. Yet there is some small comfort and hope when she discovers that one of his pictures of sunflowers has been dedicated to her.

Did You Know? Richard Curtis stalwarts Rowan Atkinson and Hugh Grant played the Doctor in Steven Moffat's first *Doctor Who* script, *The Curse of Fatal Death*, which was an extended sketch that he wrote for *Comic Relief* in 1999. Richard Curtis' long-time partner, the rather marvellous Emma Freud (great-granddaughter of Sigmund) was one of the script editors for *Vincent and the Doctor*.

11: The Lodger

Writer: Gareth Roberts
Director: Catherine Morshead
Originally broadcast: 12 June 2010

Cast

The Doctor: Matt Smith
Amy Pond: Karen Gillan
Craig: James Corden
Sophie: Daisy Haggard
Steven: Owen Donovan
Sean: Babatunde Aleshe
Michael: Jem Wall
Sandra: Karen Seacombe
Clubber: Kamara Bacchus

Steven's review: Over the last five seasons of *Doctor Who*, the week or two just before the big finale has tended to be where the oddball, envelope-pushing episodes turn up. Format-stretching exercises (like *Love & Monsters* and *Turn Left*), cheap budget-savers (*Fear Her*, *Boom Town*), and episodes that do without one or both of the regular cast (see *Blink* or *Midnight*) have all appeared here. *The Lodger* fits right in with this off-kilter tradition, presenting *Doctor Who* as domestic sitcom. Its setting is something of a throwback to the previous era of Russell T Davies - the sort of mundane, present-day world that formed the bedrock of those years, and which this season seems to have deliberately avoided until now.

The script is provided by Gareth Roberts, reusing the basic idea of a story he wrote for the comic strip in *Doctor Who Magazine* some years ago. That story featured David Tennant's Doctor being stranded on Earth due to a random TARDIS malfunction (in basically the same way as this episode starts), and inviting himself to stay with Mickey Smith for a few days until the problem was sorted out. To this fish-out-of-water premise, Roberts has added a strand of menace, in the form of a mysterious flat above where the Doctor is staying, a voice from which periodically lures passers-by inside, from which they never emerge.

Instead of Mickey, the Doctor's bemused flatmate for his stay on Earth is Craig Owens (James Corden, a high-profile comedy star in the UK), a thoroughly typical office worker with no real ambitions other than getting through life one day at a time. He has a mundane call centre job, and a domestic relationship that is likewise going nowhere, with his girlfriend - which, as he carefully explains to the Doctor, means "a friend who's a girl" - Sophie (a very sweet performance from Daisy Haggard). Right from their first scene it's obvious that these two are madly in love with each other, and equally obvious that they both lack the nerve to admit it. They're locked into a cycle of evenings of "pizza-booze-telly" (and ignoring the odd strange sound emanating from upstairs) and both immediately shy away from anything that might lead to them getting closer. It's a credit to the actors that watching these two dance skittishly around each other remains funny rather than frustrating - helped by the fact that once the Doctor gets involved, without even really intending to he starts pushing them both out of their comfort zone.

Sophie: "Life can seem pointless, you know, Doctor? Work, weekend, work, weekend, and there's six billion people on the planet doing pretty much the same."

The Doctor: "Six billion people... Watching you two at work, I'm starting to wonder where they all come from."

The Doctor, having been led to the flat by Craig's advertisement, quickly wins Craig over and takes up residence. He has a comms device in his ear (which we have to assume was in his pocket when he was rudely dumped out of the TARDIS at the beginning) that enables him to talk to Amy, still trapped in the TARDIS. Karen Gillan's involvement in this episode is pretty much limited to staggering around the console of the lurching TARDIS, as the ship is caught in a "materialization loop" which prevents it from landing properly. She does later get to offer the Doctor some advice about passing as an ordinary human (which he ignores), and uses the TARDIS databank to look up the plans for Craig's building, but that's about it for Amy this week.

The first half of the episode contains a long string of sitcom-style sequences - the Doctor cooks an omelette, the Doctor takes a shower, the Doctor meets Sophie while wearing only a towel, and so on. He is deliberately keeping a low profile and hiding from whatever is in the flat above until he can find out what it is, so in one sense these scenes are just padding out the episode's running time. But they're also fun in their own right, full of great dialogue:

Craig: "Where did you learn to cook?"

The Doctor: "Paris, in the 18th century. No hang on, that's not recent, is it - 17th? No, no, 20th. Sorry, I'm not used to doing them in the right order."

Later, the Doctor gets to join Craig's football team and win a match for them. Watching this sequence, I thought that it must have been included to give Matt Smith a chance to show off his skills (for those who don't know, Smith was on his way to becoming a professional footballer before a back injury curtailed that career and diverted him into acting). I was surprised to find, though, it's actually been carried over unchanged from the original comic strip story. Interestingly, Craig momentarily seems to sour on the Doctor at the way he simply takes over the game, and in a more serious episode that could have been explored more deeply, but since this is a comedy the conflict is gone again by the next scene.

That evening, the Doctor, missing the broad hint that Craig wants to be alone with Sophie, finds himself watching the pair again tie themselves in knots to avoid admitting their true feelings. In one of the best scenes of the episode, his gentle questioning leads Sophie to confess that she does have ambitions, of working in an animal sanctuary abroad.

Catherine Morshead's direction, as with *Amy's Choice* earlier in the season, is mostly straightforward and unshowy, although there is some nice creepiness as a string of people, culminating with Sophie, get lured up the mysterious staircase. When the Doctor and Craig realize that Sophie is in danger and finally approach the door of the upstairs flat, the moment of realization as Amy yells, "It's a one-story building - *there is no upstairs!*" was really well done.

Once through the strange door, the Doctor and Craig find an impressively huge space with a TARDIS-like console in the center. The entire upper floor flat is actually a crashed time ship, concealed by a handy perception filter, and the Doctor gets to make not one but two pop-culture references - to *Thunderbirds* and *Star Trek: Voyager* - as an emergency hologram appears:

The Doctor: "Right, stop! Crashed ship, let's see. Hello, I'm Captain Troy Handsome of International Rescue. Please state the nature of your emergency."

As with a couple of previous Steven Moffat stories (*The Empty Child* and *The Girl in the Fireplace*), the root of the problem is an overly literal-minded repair mechanism running out of control, rather than any particular malice or villainy. The ship has been luring people inside in an attempt to replace its crew, but it lacks the ability to realize that the process merely burns them out and destroys them. It latches onto the Doctor as a suitable replacement pilot and begins dragging him toward the console. I could have done without the unnecessary and ridiculous inflation of the threat level at this point - apparently if the Doctor's hand touches the console, "the planet doesn't blow up, the whole solar system does!" I suppose the idea was that if this machine is capable of interfering with the TARDIS to the extent we've seen, it must hold an enormous amount of power, but really there was no need for such a jarring clunker of a line.

My favourite part of the episode was the way the domestic romance plot and the sci-fi plot reflect each other and neatly come together at the end. The ship is in a similar situation to Craig and Sophie - stuck in a rut, repeating the same actions over and over, with no idea how to get out of it. The Doctor can't help the ship directly, but he inspires Sophie to want to change her life (which, ironically, is what puts her in danger

- until that point the ship had ignored both Sophie and Craig because they had no desire to be anywhere else). Craig is able to shut down the console temporarily and release the Doctor because he's "sofa man," the one who's got no ambition to go anywhere. Then the Doctor drives him to blurt out his feelings for Sophie, and as the two finally admit they're in love the emotional overload drives the ship into self-destruct. It all comes to a satisfying culmination with the Doctor's shout of "For God's sake, KISS THE GIRL!!" being echoed by Amy (and the audience) as the music swells to a comically overblown climax.

Apart from anything else, this episode was an impressive showcase for Matt Smith. With no companion to have to share centre stage with this week, he really took over the story. He is so adept at constantly finding ways to keep the viewer's attention, both physical - I laughed out loud when he took a mouthful of wine, made a face and immediately deposited it back in the glass - and verbal. I love the way this Doctor is always letting his mouth get ahead of his brain ("I'm good at fixing rot. Call me the rot-meister. No, I'm the Doctor, don't call me the rot-meister"). This was actually the last episode filmed for the season, and it shows how well Smith has grown into an assured command of the role over the year - I can't wait to see where he takes the Doctor next year.

But first, there's one more adventure to come for this season. Back in the TARDIS, the Doctor quickly ties up the loose ends of the plot with a bit of casual time-twisting, reminding himself he needs to change the will that will cause Craig's friend to come into money and move out, thereby leading Craig to advertise for a lodger in the first place, and telling Amy to write the note which directed him to that advertisement. In his jacket, Amy finds the engagement ring that is all that's left of her fiancé Rory after the events of *Cold Blood*. *Twilight Zone*-style music plays, as faint memories stir...

Steven's Classic Who DVD Recommendation: The Classic

Series never really did this sort of domestic comedy, so instead I've selected another story where the Doctor gets separated from his TARDIS and has to contrive a way of getting back to it - *Mawdryn Undead*, starring Peter Davison.

Kevin's review: *The Lodger* is another rather splendid episode full of sparkling wit and humour, and is thus a bit of a respite from the dark aspects of the previous episode, and the foreboding surrounding the succeeding series finale.

The idea of the Doctor having to spend time in contemporary domesticity is a rather good one. Of course, the Doctor has spent time as a human before, during the 2007 two-parter *Human Nature/The Family of Blood*. However, in that instance, the Doctor had only scattered memories of his life as a Time Lord that he could not comprehend, and his character as a human was somewhat subdued, which suited the much more formal environment of a pre-First World War English public school. Although the Doctor is also hiding from an alien threat in this episode, it would not have been appropriate for him to cast off his Time Lord persona in the same manner, as he needs all his wits about him to retrieve both the TARDIS and Amy. Rather like the *Family of Blood*, the villain of this piece adopts various human disguises to lure good samaritans off the street. We've often seen Steven Moffat utilise creepy electronic voices, and this is a trait that Gareth Roberts continues here, by employing the house's entry phone to achieve the same effect.

Despite having previously claimed to have been bored by the passing of ordinary time in both *Amy's Choice* and *Vincent and the Doctor*, our favourite Time Lord seems positively hyperactive here, taking delight in the most seemingly mundane of things, such as cooking and rewiring Craig's house. No doubt part of this is due to the necessity of the Doctor getting on with his new landlord, Craig. In one of the many lovely scenes in this episode, the Doctor tells Craig that he and other people refer to him as "the Doctor", although he has no idea why. There's a nice bit of continuity

154

in Craig's kitchen, as there's a postcard of one of Van Gogh's self portraits on the fridge (there's also a very disturbing portrait of a clown-like man in Craig's hallway: the Oligarch of Lammasteen, according to *The Brilliant Book of Doctor Who 2011*).

Rather like the crack in the bedroom wall, there's a strange stain on Craig's ceiling, which morphs whenever there's a disturbance upstairs. The Doctor tells Craig not to touch the stain, which Craig, of course, eventually does (although it's surprising that he hasn't done this prior to the Doctor's arrival). This turns out to be an excuse for the Doctor to fill in for Craig at work, and for the Doctor to display even more disgusting culinary skills as he cooks up a cure for the malaise that Craig develops after touching the stain. Although James Corden is a somewhat controversial personality in the UK (due mainly to the fact that his sketch show *Horne & Corden* was quite disappointing, and his public display of umbrage when a rather tipsy Patrick Stewart criticised his obesity), there is no denying that he's a master of this brand of comic acting, and his performance is pitch perfect in *The Lodger*.

The first sign of Craig's annoyance at the Doctor's stealing his thunder in the football match is very well done. As previously discussed with regards to the number on the back of Rory's stag shirt, such shirt numbers do have a variety of meanings. For instance, a number 7 shirt is most often associated with flair midfield players, such as David Beckham, so it seems that Craig visualises himself as being in the same mould. The Doctor, of course, wears the number 11 shirt, since he's the Eleventh Doctor, and happily for him (if not for Craig) this is a shirt number that's often worn by strikers. Another example of the meticulous planning that went into this season is the fact that this episode aired at the start of the 2010 World Cup: I suspect that England would have done much better if they'd had Matt Smith on their team!

The one piece of dialogue that seems a bit off key in this episode is when the Doctor asks if football is the sport "with sticks", which seems to refer to cricket. Now, while the alien Doctor can't be expected to have a great deal of knowledge concerning Terran sports, he did spend the whole of his Fifth incarnation dressed in cricket clothes, and proved to be a dab hand at this sport in 1982's *Black Orchid*. Having written that, it could be that the Doctor is referring to the goalposts.

Given Matt Smith's athleticism in this episode, it's hardly surprising that the actors portraying the Doctor are getting progressively younger, as this is very much a young man's game now. For instance, during Russell T Davies' time as showrunner, there would be one episode of each series that would not feature the Doctor and his companion so much, which would give the actors a bit of a breather. So while Karen Gillan was absent for most of this story, the Christmas special, and large parts of the Silurian adventure, Matt Smith has been hardly off screen for the whole of the series, and even popped up in the *Sarah Jane Adventures*.

It appears that the Eleventh Doctor can't help but intervene in the love affairs of others. Admittedly, he may be compensating here for the tragic end of Amy's relationship with Rory by trying to get Craig and Sophie to articulate their feelings for one another. Amy comments on the Doctor's matchmaking skills at the end of this episode, jokily asking the Doctor if he can find her "a fella". This echoes a similar comment that Sophie makes earlier on in the episode when Craig reads out his ad for a new housemate, when she says Craig's mission in life should be to find her a man. Thus this makes Amy's discovery of Rory's engagement ring at the episode encompass several meanings; as my fellow reviewer Steven writes, it could prompt her to recall her former fiancé, or equally, it could make her think that the Doctor was planning to propose to her!

Now that we've seen the preview trailer for series 6, it would appear that *The Lodger* has an additional significance for the continuing story arc, as we saw a clip of another time engine that's very much like the one that's featured in this episode, so we may well find out who built it. The rumours are that a villain last seen in 1969's *The War Games* will reappear in series 6. Now, this could either be the Gallifreyan War Chief, or the War Lords. Given that the Doctor is convinced that he's the last of his species, it's unlikely to be the War Chief, so one can only presume that the loss of Gallifrey in the Time War meant that the forcefield in which the Time Lords imprisoned the War Lords' planet is no longer active. Thus it would appear that the War Lords have utilised their knowledge of Time Lord technology to build their own time engines.

Indeed, the time engine featured here is quite similar to the TARDIS, in that it's bigger on the inside than the outside, and it has a central time rotor. In addition to this, it has a very chameleon-circuit type of perception filter. However, like the current redesign of the TARDIS, the exterior flat door is quite visible from the flight deck. Although the flat door does flicker and phase out in this episode, because it's part of the perception filter. Thus it would appear that the appearance of the police box's exterior doors on the bridge of the TARDIS is also an illusion, which would indeed metamorphose if the TARDIS chameleon circuit were to ever function again.

Yet the exterior of the time engine is quite different from actual appearance of Gallifreyan time capsules that we've seen on screen, as the ship very much looks as though it's capable of interstellar flight through ordinary space, as well via the time vortex, and that the space and time travel functions are separate parts of the same machine. This vessel also seems similar in design to Scaroth's spaceship from the 1979 adventure *City of Death*. Gareth Roberts has stated that the villain of this episode was originally going to be Meglos, a cactoid creature that featured in a far less distinguished Tom Baker story from 1980. This gives an indication of how far the scripts in this series must have morphed from their original inception.

This episode could have done with some more screen time, as some elements of the plot are confusing. For instance, it's unclear where the Doctor got the headset through which he communicates with Amy. As Steven speculates, he could have been carrying it when the TARDIS abandoned him, or it may be that he adapted some Earth technology in the 24 hours before he turned up at Craig's flat. The revelation that Amy would write a note at the end of this episode to direct the Doctor to Craig's flat is a detail that's very much lost due to everything else that's going on. Yet this could explain why the Doctor is happy to hang around, as he knows that everything's going to be OK in the end (although Rory had much the same belief with regards to the appearance of his future self in *Cold Blood*). There's also the question of why the hologram didn't pick up on the Doctor's wanderlust earlier, as it must surely be greater than any of the humans that it abducts. Then again, this could be down to the fact that the Doctor's impersonation of a human isn't that bad, although, as Craig notes, the Doctor's behaviour is still quite weird.

However, with the benefit of hindsight, the Doctor's exclamation that that the time engine wouldn't be able to cope with a complex being such as him as a pilot, and would explode, taking the entire solar system with it, does make sense in the context of the wider story arc. For this is another of several instances in this series where the motif of an exploding time machine is very much utilised. Since this is not a Gallifreyan time engine (since a link with a Time Lord pilot would cause this damaged vessel to disintegrate), the consequences of it exploding, while serious, are not as dire as if a vessel of a much higher technology (i.e. a TARDIS) were to explode... Which of course, greatly ties in with the series finale. Fortunately for the solar system, the time engine implodes rather than explodes in this instance.

Did You Know? Daisy Haggard, who charmingly plays the role of Sophie, is the great-great-grandneice of the Victorian gothic novelist H. Rider Haggard, the creator of Allan Quartermain, an Indiana Jones prototype that featured in his famous novels *She* and *King Solomon's Mines*.

12: The Pandorica Opens

Writer: Steven Moffat
Director: Toby Haynes
Originally broadcast: 19 June 2010

Cast

The Doctor: Matt Smith
Amy Pond: Karen Gillan
Rory Williams: Arthur Darvill
River Song: Alex Kingston
Vincent: Tony Curran
Bracewell: Bill Paterson
Winston Churchill: Ian McNeice
Liz Ten: Sophie Okonedo
Claudio: Marcus O'Donovan
Commander: Clive Wood
Commander Stark: Christopher Ryan
Cyber Leader: Ruari Mears
Judoon: Paul Kasey
Doctor Gachet: Howard Lee
Dalek: Barnaby Edwards
Dorium: Simon Fisher Becker
Guard: Joe Jacobs
Madame Vernet: Chrissie Cotterill
Marcellus: David Fynn

Steven's review: The last few years of *Doctor Who* have seen the season finales keep getting bigger and bigger, as former showrunner Russell T Davies seemed to thrive on creating ever more apocalyptic threats for the Doctor to face - to the Earth, to the universe, to Time itself. Eventually, you would think, a limit must be reached, beyond which no further escalation is possible. New showrunner (and writer of this episode) Steven Moffat may just have reached that limit with this two-part finale that begins with *The Pandorica Opens*. Not only does the ultimate threat outstrip anything seen before, the episode is as densely plotted as any that Moffat has written for the series, picking up threads from across the whole season, putting them through some dazzling twists, and leading up to a cliffhanger that looks absolutely impossible to get out of.

The opening sequence immediately shows off the careful planning that has gone into the construction of the whole season. We follow the journey of a painting by Vincent Van Gogh across the centuries until, in the year 5145, it finds its way into the hands of River Song. Along the way, it passes through the care of Bracewell and Winston Churchill from *Victory of the Daleks* and Liz 10 from *The Beast Below*, in scenes that were obviously shot back when those episodes were made and cleverly held over until now.

The sequence becomes another *tour de force* for River Song, along the lines of the opening teaser from *The Time of Angels*, as she escapes from her Stormcage prison cell (we learned that she had been in prison in *Flesh and Stone*) with the aid of her trusty hallucinogenic lipstick. Then she gets to play Han Solo in the *Star Wars* cantina (just the latest of many *Star Wars* riffs this season) as she negotiates with a blue-skinned merchant to obtain a vortex manipulator, "fresh off the wrist of a handsome Time Agent" (which prompted thoughts about how great an episode starring both River and Captain Jack Harkness would be). Having secured this crude but effective means of time travel, River eventually meets up with the Doctor and Amy in the camp of a Roman legion in the Britain of 102 AD. As the opening titles crash in, we finally get to see Vincent's painting - it depicts the destruction of the TARDIS in a fiery explosion, and its title is...*The Pandorica Opens*.

This two-part finale is directed by another of this season's first-time directors, Toby Haynes. Like Adam Smith, who did such a good job on the season opener and the Weeping Angels two-parter, Haynes is a real find for the show. He establishes an epic, widescreen feel with shots of our heroes on horseback, racing across the empty plains to the distant but immediately recognizable form of Stonehenge, while getting the plot exposition across with efficient cross-cutting to a continuation of the previous scene in the camp, as River explains that co-ordinates on the painting show that the legendary Pandorica ("A box, a cage, a prison…built to contain the most feared thing in all the universe") is at this time and place. As he did the last time River mentioned it, in *Flesh and Stone*, the Doctor dismisses the idea of the Pandorica as a fairytale, but eventually he comes up with the idea of checking out the nearby ancient monument on the basis that "if you buried the most dangerous thing in the universe, you'd want to remember where you put it."

The idea of revealing the purpose of Stonehenge as being to mark the position of an alien artefact is a lovely conceit, made even more so when they use some of River's handy technology to move one of the massive stones to reveal an entrance to the "Under-henge". The whole sequence as they make their way into a huge underground chamber is a standout, with cobwebs everywhere and flaming torches making the episode look like an *Indiana Jones* film - fittingly so, since the behind-the-scenes programme *Doctor Who Confidential* showed how Haynes used a playback of John Williams' evocative music from *Raiders of the Lost Ark* during the shooting of these scenes to get the proper pacing and sense of wonder as the Doctor, River and Amy make their way into the Pandorica chamber. The chamber is dominated by the Pandorica itself - an enormous, ominous black cube with intricate clockwork designs on its surface.

The Doctor: "There was a goblin, or a trickster, or a warrior. A nameless, terrible thing, soaked in the blood of a billion galaxies. The most feared being in all the cosmos. And nothing could stop it, or hold it, or reason with it. One day it would just drop out of the sky and tear down your world."

Amy: "How did it end up in there?"

The Doctor: "You know fairytales. A good wizard tricked it." *(He moves off.)*

River: "I hate good wizards in fairytales. They always turn out to be him."

161

River discovers that the multiple layers of security inside the Pandorica are being unlocked, as it slowly begins to open. (In the light of later events, we can surmise that it was the Doctor's touch on the outside of the thing that started the opening process, though that's never actually stated.) It's fairly obvious that the Doctor's description of what's inside the Pandorica is actually a description of the Doctor himself - as seen from the point of view of the enemies he fights and defeats (paying off a line put into *The Hungry Earth* about how he's not scared of monsters, monsters are scared of him). In the manner of a stage magician forcing a card on his victim, Steven Moffat keeps harping on the question of what's going to emerge from the Pandorica at the end of the episode - a future Doctor? a past Doctor? - in order to distract the viewer's attention from what he actually has in mind.

They realize that the Pandorica is signalling its opening across the whole of space and time (neatly answering in passing the question of how Vincent got the knowledge of it in the first place), and thousands of spaceships are now arriving - Daleks, Cybermen, Sontarans, and every other kind of alien the Doctor's ever faced. (I loved how Moffat slipped in references to completely obscure species like Chelonians or Drahvins for the long-time fans here.) For a moment the episode threatens to turn towards the epic freewheeling of a Russell T Davies finale, with a shot of scores of CGI ships hovering above Stonehenge, but then River is sent off to get help from the Romans and the Doctor and Amy return to the chamber, where in a marvellously intimate scene the story finally picks up the thread left dangling at the end of the previous episode, *The Lodger*.

Amy shows the Doctor the engagement ring she found in his jacket. It's actually hers, but at the end of *Cold Blood* her fiancé Rory was killed and then all her memory of him erased by one of the cracks in the universe that have been a regular presence throughout the season - the cracks that it's now obvious are caused by the explosive destruction of the TARDIS. Matt Smith has been consistently brilliant all year, but particularly so in quiet scenes like this, showing the Doctor's attempt to conceal his pain at Amy's blithe dismissal of the ring ("So, who are you proposing to?") and compellingly delivering what turns out to be the crucial speech of the whole story:

Amy: "It's weird. I feel…I don't know, something."

The Doctor: "People fall out of the world sometimes. But they always leave traces. Little things we can't quite account for. Faces in photographs, luggage, half-eaten meals. Rings. Nothing is ever forgotten, not completely. And if something can be remembered, it can come back."

The Doctor finally confesses to Amy that, contrary to what he said in *The Eleventh Hour*, he had a reason for inviting her to come away with him. But just as we're on the brink of further revelations ("Your house… It was too big. Too many empty rooms. Does it ever bother you, Amy, that your life doesn't make any sense?"), the episode radically changes gear into a dramatic action sequence. Various bits of a Cyberman that had been scattered around the place (head, arm, and so on) start attacking them. The Doctor is knocked out, and Amy is chased and trapped in a small side chamber.

Like everything else in the episode, this attack sequence is well done - the Cyber-head with its writhing tentacle-like cables that wrap around Amy's arms and legs is like something out of *The Thing*, and the head splitting open to reveal a human skull inside is another great *Indiana Jones* moment. The sequence is certainly needed, since otherwise the action of this middle section of the episode would consist entirely of a large box slowly opening, but it can't help but feel like the self-contained set piece that it is. It does, however, end with the first big twist of the episode, as the Roman help arrives and a centurion destroys the Cyberman. He removes his helmet - revealing himself to be Rory.

I had already caught a semi-spoiler about the episode beforehand, so Arthur Darvill's reappearance wasn't quite the shock it must have been to anyone who had no idea it was coming. The resurrection of Rory immediately heightens the intensity level, as befits a season finale, and gives all three of the regular actors some great material to work with. It's not all fraught with emotion, though - the Doctor's recognition of Rory is played for comedy, with him absentmindedly prattling on about missing the obvious ("Yeah, I think you probably are,") and wandering away, before there's an off-screen crash and he comes slowly back in. Then the two of them look embarrassed and can't think of anything to say - rather like two workmates accidentally meeting at the supermarket. Rory tells how he somehow ended up here after his death ("I died, and turned into a Roman. It's very distracting,") and the Doctor has no explanation.

The emotional climax of the episode, though, is the reunion of Amy and Rory. Rory is hurt when he discovers Amy has no idea who he is. He follows her up to the surface and, in a series of scenes played brilliantly by both Arthur Darvill and Karen Gillan, attempts to revive her memory of him. As in *Vincent and the Doctor*, Amy finds herself crying without knowing why; then an edge of hysteria creeps in as she laughs: "It's like I'm happy! *Why* am I happy?"

Meanwhile, River attempts to bring the TARDIS from the Roman camp to Stonehenge, but something goes wrong. A hitherto unseen force takes control of the TARDIS and sends her back to Amy's house in Leadworth on the crucial date - June 26, 2010 - the date established in *Flesh and Stone* as being when the explosion that caused the cracks in the universe takes place. It's quite strange to watch River wandering around the location familiar to us from *The Eleventh Hour*, an episode she never appeared in. She discovers signs that something has been through the house, but in Amy's bedroom, she sees all her childhood "raggedy Doctor" dolls laid out, just as she left them ("Oh Doctor, why do I let you out?" River says, cryptically). Then she makes a shocking discovery. In the second big twist of the episode, the illustrations in a book in Amy's room show the exact same Romans as are with the Doctor - and worse, the design of the Pandorica echoes the design on the cover of a book about the legend of Pandora's box. (I should note that

Moffat played fair with the audience here. Earlier, Amy said that the Roman invasion of Britain was her favourite history topic at school, and Pandora's Box was her favourite story. The Doctor noticed the coincidence, but got distracted by other things). In the book, River also finds a photo of Amy, evidently from a fancy-dress party, with Rory dressed as a centurion...

River: "It's a trap. It has to be. They used Amy to construct a scenario you'd believe. To get close to you."

The Doctor, recognizing the danger of the TARDIS being at that location, orders River to get out of there, but the strange force again takes control and prevents her from leaving - she can't even get the doors open. The second major ongoing plot thread of the season comes to the fore as an unknown voice says, "Silence will fall." We've heard of this mysterious "Silence" in *The Eleventh Hour* and again in *The Vampires of Venice*, but exactly what it means is still not apparent.

Now the plot twists come thick and fast. The Pandorica finally begins to open, as some sort of activation signal is broadcast. All of the Romans are revealed to be Autons, plastic replicas of humans with hidden guns embedded in their wrists (last seen in *Rose*, the first episode of the revived *Doctor Who* series in 2005, although they originally date from the Jon Pertwee era of the early 1970s). In particular, Rory is in fact an Auton, programmed with memories gleaned from some sort of "psychic scan" of Amy's house (although that doesn't explain how his memories go all the way up to the real Rory's death - a small but irritating hole in the plotting). Rory struggles against his conditioning, as Amy finally manages to recognize him: "Rory Williams, from Leadworth. My boyfriend." In a terrible (by which, of course, I mean beautifully constructed) bit of irony, Rory desperately yells at her to get away from him, but she refuses to leave him. Finally, he can't stop himself from succumbing to his programming, and firing at her. The whole sequence is probably Darvill and Gillan's best work of the season so far, culminating with the image of Amy reeling backwards in

165

Rory's arms.

Meanwhile, as the Doctor is held by the plastic Romans, all the aliens from the ships around the area teleport in to face him. In the final twist, the Pandorica stands open - and is revealed to be empty. It is indeed designed to hold the Doctor, but rather than emerging from it, he is being put into it. This grand alliance of species has been created because they believe that the Doctor is responsible for the cracks that threaten the whole universe, and has to be stopped. The sight of the chamber filled with the crowd of strange creatures is memorable, although the suspicion arises that the aliens we see are just those that happened to be laying around the costume department at the time. The presence of the Silurians, or the Weevils from *Torchwood*, is otherwise a little hard to explain, and there are no creatures that would require CGI to create, like the lobster-aliens from *The Vampires of Venice*. It was a nice surprise that they got Christopher Ryan from 2008's *The Sontaran Stratagem* back for a few lines, though.

Matt Smith is superb as the defeated Doctor - strapped into the Pandorica, he sounds weary and exhausted, but at the same time almost proud that all these races are working together, even if it is against him. He tries to convince them that the TARDIS, and not him, is the cause of the disaster ("Total event collapse - every sun will supernova at every moment in history!") but the Pandorica is closed again and sealed, with him shut inside.

Finally, River gets the TARDIS doors open at last, only to find the exit totally sealed off by a wall of rock. She has time only for a heartfelt "I'm sorry, my love," before the TARDIS console begins to blow up.

So, to recap: the Doctor is sealed inside an impenetrable prison by an alliance containing every enemy he's ever faced; Amy has been shot by a plastic replica of her dead fiancé; River is about to die, trapped inside the TARDIS as it explodes; and that explosion leads to the unravelling of the entire universe. In the final shot - almost an exact reverse of the opening shot of the season - we pull back from Earth as all the visible stars silently explode and disappear, leaving the Earth drifting alone through the void. Fade to black.

Now get out of that!

Classic Who Recommendation: *The Pandorica Opens* is not the first *Doctor Who* story to feature a Dalek alliance with other aliens, and the deaths of some of the Doctor's companions, as both these were facets of the 1965-1966 adventure *The Daleks' Master Plan*. Only episodes 2, 5, and 10 are currently known to survive in their original format. However, there are audio recordings of all episodes of *The Daleks' Master Plan*, which have been released by the BBC on CD.

Kevin's review: This episode begins with Vincent Van Gogh tormented by a vision of the future after his recent encounter with the Doctor. Once the painting is finally revealed onscreen, one can understand his anguish, as it's a depiction of the TARDIS exploding. However, rather than give it its obvious title, Vincent names this painting 'The Pandorica Opens'. In a nice touch, the credits reveal that the physician attending Vincent is none other than Dr. Gachet, whose portrait figured prominently at the beginning of *Vincent and the Doctor*.

This painting is smuggled out of France during the Second World War, and Bracewell recognises its significance. Winston Churchill seems very unimpressed by it, despite the fact that it shows the destruction of the TARDIS that he was so keen to get his hands on. However, it's likely that his comment is meant as an attempt at art appreciation, as the wartime prime minister dabbled a great deal in oils, although his paintings were more from the realist rather the post-Impressionist school.

Churchill rings the Doctor, but the TARDIS bypasses the call to River Song in the Stormcage prison. We learn that the year is 5145, which is presumably River Song's time period. Having utilised the hallucinogenic lipstick to once more enable her escape, River dons cat burglar gear and makes her

167

way to the Royal Collection, where she is intercepted by Liz 10, who is somehow still alive a couple of millennia after the events of *The Beast Below*. Admittedly, her metabolism had been slowed down to prevent her from ageing in that previous adventure, but one can only feel sorry for any would-be Prince Charles's hanging around, for it doesn't look as though she'll be vacating the throne any time soon! Her longevity speaks volumes about the impotency of any republican movement for these several thousand years. Despite the revelation in *The Beast Below* that the Royal Family has passed the story of the Doctor down its many generations, none of them seems to have noticed this picture of the TARDIS exploding, and Liz 10 seems genuinely surprised when she sees the picture. Then again, the Royal Collection is no doubt very large, and the Royal Family probably has many crises, such as the solar flares, to deal with over the millennia.

River then goes to the Maldovarian bar to get herself a vortex manipulator, which has apparently been taken from the wrist of a "handsome time agent"; although the suggestion is that this time agent's hand has been severed in the process. Oh well, if it's Captain Jack Harkness' hand, I'm sure that it will regenerate soon. So, it would appear that River and Captain Jack are contemporaries.

Meanwhile, the Doctor decides that it will be a lovely idea to find out what the oldest message in the universe actually means, only to be somewhat mortified that it's River's catchphrase: "Hello Sweetie!" I don't know what language it was originally in, but Amy can evidently read the TARDIS' translation. However, there is a bit of Ancient High Gallifreyan in the message (which looks like Greek) that again, Amy can't read, which turns out to be the coordinates for Wiltshire in 102 A.D. Upon arrival, the Doctor and Amy are greeted by a Roman who thinks that the Time Lord is Caesar, and that Cleopatra is waiting for him. Telltale signs of hallucinogenic lipstick are smudged around his lips, so River has evidently utilised the vortex manipulator to get to the point in time specified by Van Gogh in his painting.

Alert viewers with some historical knowledge will have noticed that this (as the Roman Commander later points out) is impossible, since Cleopatra died over a century previously. Which does make one wonder just how many Roman soldiers River had to kiss to make her story believable...

There doesn't seem to be any real danger here, as this is obviously a couple of millennia before the TARDIS is due to explode: June 26th 2010. However, the Doctor is taken aback enough by Van Gogh's painting to consider that the Pandorica is not a fairytale after all. The Doctor realizes that there's a very good hiding place for the Pandorica close by: Stonehenge! However, rather than taking the TARDIS there, our gallant heroes strangely take the decision to travel there on horseback. Perhaps the Doctor doesn't trust the TARDIS to make this short hop, yet travelling via his vessel would have indeed saved them some time, and River could have assisted with the piloting. Maybe the Doctor is wary of travelling in the TARDIS since he saw the depiction of its explosion? There's also the fact that Van Gogh's coordinates specified the Roman camp, rather than Stonehenge itself, so presumably something quite important there...

River reveals that she has no knowledge of what happens when the Pandorica opens, so this obviously occurs earlier in her time stream than the events in *The Time of Angels/Flesh and Stone*. The Doctor states throughout this episode that the Pandorica is supposed to contain the most feared being in the universe, without ever seeming to imagine (unlike many viewers) that this warrior could be himself. My fellow reviewer Steven rightfully recalls the Doctor's statement from *The Hungry Earth* that monsters are frightened of him, so he has previously viewed himself in this way. However, Moffat expertly hides the twist in another sublime script.

So much is going on in the Doctor's head that he doesn't pay too much attention to Amy's revelation that her favourite storybook as a child featured Pandora's box. This rather misogynist Greek myth cast Pandora as the woman responsible for all the evil in the world, as Zeus gave her a box and commanded her not to open it. Overcome by curiosity, Pandora of course opened the box, and let out all the evil in the world. In much the same manner, Eve got humanity expelled from the Garden of Eden by persuading Adam to eat the fruit from the Tree of Knowledge. However, there is an adjunct to the Greek tale, in which Pandora, realising what she had done, immediately shut the box, only to trap inside Hope. Thus, if the Doctor had paid more attention to Amy's revelation, then he might have realised that the box was also designed to hold some good in it... River surmises that the box appears to be unlocking from the inside, and both are impressed that anything could get past that kind of security. Although the thought occurs that a prison that can be unlocked from the inside must be a bit on the rubbish side.

However, the Doctor is a bit distracted by the fact that there are so many aliens gathering above the Wiltshire skies, and dispatches River to collect some Roman troops from the camp as some form of defence. Now that River has gone, Amy takes the opportunity to ask the Doctor about the engagement ring that she found at the end of *The Lodger*, presumably because she thinks that it might have been intended for Song. The Doctor then reveals that he did have a purpose in taking Amy away with him on the eve of her wedding, and then tells her that if something can be remembered, then it can be brought back, which immediately made me think that the mysterious soldier that volunteered to help River was Rory.

However, before we can get any more revelations, the disembodied Cyberman then attacks the Doctor and Amy. Confusingly, this appears to be one of the Cybus Industries Cybermen from the parallel Earth that featured in 2006's *Rise of the Cybermen/The Age of Steel*, although the fact that they have Cyberships tends to suggest that they are the original extraterrestrial Cybermen from the Classic Series. The Cyber head, with its writhing tentacles, looks much like an inverted Medusa, so this is probably part of the "dark fairytale" motif.

Thus we discover that the mysterious Roman soldier is indeed Rory. Meanwhile the Doctor obliviously uses the sonic screwdriver as a medical scanner again. Then again, since River has previously referred to the Doctor as a "wizard" in this episode, the sonic's new functions make a whole lot more sense, because it has effectively become a magical wand rather than just a screwdriver. Rory, disturbed at the fact that Amy doesn't recognise him, tells the Doctor how he came to be there, likening it to a kind of dream, which is another motif that runs throughout this series. My fellow reviewer Steven criticised the fact that Rory's memories of encountering the Doctor and his death are intact. However, a possible explanation could be that the Nestenes are not wholly reliant on the scan that they made of Amy's home, and that they're still gathering material from Amy's subconscious mind, which does contain a trace of Rory that she's later able to recall. This is made evident by the fact that she's unaccountably weeping at the end, just as she had done during her encounter with Van Gogh.

Yet one element of the plot that I did think was hard to swallow was the fact that Rory was an Auton. Admittedly, this does work very well on a fanboyish level, but I would have thought the majority of viewers would be more than a little lost here, as the Autons exhibit behaviour that they haven't really demonstrated since their 1970 debut *Spearhead from Space*. The Autons here are obviously more advanced, as their duplicants don't have the telltale waxy sheen that have previously been the one flaw in their design that was still evident in 2005's *Rose*. I guess the casual viewer will probably surmise that that Rory is some kind of robot, judging from the jerky movements that accompany the Nestenes' recall of them.

Meanwhile, the Doctor has instructed River to bring the TARDIS to him, as he needs some instruments from his time capsule. Thus his decision to not even consider taking the TARDIS to Stonehenge in the first place appears even stranger, especially when the TARDIS starts misbehaving when River tries to fly it. It would appear that someone or something is utilising the TARDIS and River to pass on a message to the Doctor. The pedant in me notices that River appears to be talking to the Doctor from the phone on the console, rather than the communicator that Amy utilised in *The Lodger*, and the similar device that the Doctor employed to communicate with Danny Boy in *Victory of the Daleks*.

A rather sinister voice declares in the console room that "Silence will fall", and the scanner cracks into the "crooked smile". This wizened voice almost sounds like that of the decrepit Master that featured in *The Deadly Assassin* and *The Keeper of Traken*, or possibly Davros. However, it's probably just as likely to be an incredibly irate intergalactic librarian. Like Steven, I thought that River's exclamation of "Oh Doctor, why do I let you out?" sounded quite significant as she explored Amy's house, and discovered that all the Roman soldiers at the camp were fakes. This is quite a loving, exasperated expression, and tones in well with River's final cry of "I'm sorry, my love," as the TARDIS console explodes... Which reinforces the belief that she could be the Doctor's lover... or mother!

Unfortunately, the Doctor discovers that while the TARDIS does indeed explode on 26th June 2010, it doesn't occur during Amy and Rory's wedding. The Doctor is further shaken by the revelation that the grand alliance of his enemies has come to imprison him to prevent the explosion of the TARDIS that has caused the cracks in the universe, since who else could fly (and thus cause the explosion of) the TARDIS but him? Maybe they're right, if River is a future Doctor.

Like Steven, I also thought that the presence of the Silurians at the Pandorica opening was a bit strange, as this is a couple of millennia before any of the Doctor's encounters with them. So, maybe the "crooked smile" did perform a Pacman impression, and wreaked havoc with the Silurian city that we encountered in *Cold Blood*. They then must have hitched a ride back in time with one of the other aliens present here, much like the Cybermen, who have never demonstrated any mastery of time travel.

It's a bit bizarre that this grand alliance has gone to all the trouble to bait the Doctor by including elements from Amy's childhood, as the Doctor himself dismisses Amy's 'coincidental' love of the stories of the Roman invasion of Britain and Pandora's box. They've certainly amassed a big enough alliance to contain him by force; albeit they're very wary of having to rely on such means, as it hasn't done them any favours when facing the Doctor before. No, the Doctor is more intrigued by the fables that surround the Pandorica, which are mainly related here by River, not Amy. So, it would seem that the alliance's tactic is merely to ensure that the Doctor stays around long enough for them to gather their forces against him and to ensure that they can imprison him within the Pandorica. The books about the Roman invasion and Pandora's box haven't been made prominent whenever we've seen Amy's bedroom before, so these elements from Amy's childhood are just devices that make this particular episode that much more exciting, especially with regards to her revived boyfriend.

Things are also not good with Amy and Rory. Having finally remembered Amy, Rory is unable to prevent his Auton nature from partially taking over him, as he shoots and kills Amy. So, yet another companion seemingly bites the dust, while all the other stars in the quickly blink out and disappear… The alliance obviously wasn't listening to the Doctor when he made the following pronouncement in *The Time of Angels*: "There's one thing you never put in a trap, if you're smart. If you value your continued existence. If you have any plans about seeing tomorrow, there's one thing you never ever put in a trap…"

Did You Know? Clive Wood, who plays the Roman commander in this episode, previously starred in Steven Moffat's first television hit, *Press Gang*.

13: The Big Bang

Writer: Steven Moffat
Director: Toby Haynes
Originally broadcast: 26 June 2010

Cast

The Doctor: Matt Smith
Amy Pond: Karen Gillan
Rory Williams: Arthur Darvill
River Song: Alex Kingston
Amelia: Caitlin Blackwood
Aunt Sharon: Susan Vidler
Christine: Frances Ashman
Stone Dalek: Barnaby Edwards
Dave: William Pretsell
Augustus Pond: Halcro Johnston
Tabetha Pond: Karen Westwood
Dalek voice: Nicholas Briggs

Steven's review: "Okay kid, this is where it gets complicated." Given the way things stood after last week's cliffhanger, it was obvious that *The Big Bang* would have to be quite a different kind of episode from *The Pandorica Opens*, but I doubt anyone watching would have guessed just how different it would be. Writer and showrunner Steven Moffat keeps the threat level set to "universal," but the canvas of the story radically shrinks to contain just our regular characters - the Doctor, Amy, Rory, and River Song. It's the most intimate of apocalypses - for a large part of the episode, there simply is no one else on screen. Or off it, for that matter - the rest of the universe is gone, reduced to a memory; and indeed, as I highlighted last week, memory turns out to be the crux of the story. It's also the story of the Doctor repairing the damage he caused to Amy when he first met her as a child, when he flew off in the TARDIS promising to return in five minutes, and didn't come back for twelve years. It ties up the whole season excellently - though not without leaving a couple of threads dangling, to be taken up next year - and gives us the first completely happy season ending for the new *Doctor Who*.

A montage from *The Pandorica Opens* brings us back to that tremendous cliffhanger, with the Doctor sealed away in the Pandorica by a grand alliance of all his foes, Amy having been shot dead by a plastic Auton replica of her fiancé Rory, and the TARDIS exploding with River Song inside, causing the entire universe to unravel and dissolve into nothingness. Whatever viewers were expecting to happen next, it's unlikely to have been what we actually see... a caption saying "1,894 years later." It seems like we're starting the season all over again with the opening moments of *The Eleventh Hour*, as seven-year-old Amelia Pond prays to Santa to send someone to fix the sinister crack in her bedroom wall. But now, things are different; this time, there's no TARDIS falling from the sky to crash-land in her backyard. In fact, the night sky is totally empty apart from the moon; Amelia makes paintings of stars which no one has ever seen, and her aunt Sharon worries about her growing up to join a "star cult" ("I don't trust that Richard Dawkins," she says, hilariously). But then a museum flyer carrying a handwritten message - "Come along, Pond" - is slipped through her door, leading to Amelia dragging her aunt off to the building where the huge black Pandorica cube is exhibited, looking as ominous as it did the last time we saw it when the Doctor was imprisoned within it. Amelia hides until the building is empty, then goes up to the Pandorica and touches it. In response, it slowly opens - to reveal Amy, very much alive, whose first words are the line I've quoted at the top of this recap. As the opening titles crashed in, I realised my jaw was literally hanging open - I can't remember the last time a TV show took me by surprise like that.

Who expected the end of the universe to be so much fun? The first half of the episode is a dazzling exercise in plot pyrotechnics, as the Doctor uses the vortex manipulator

175

acquired by River Song last week to zip back and forth through his timeline and set up both his escape from the Pandorica and Amy's survival and eventual reappearance in the box. This had the potential to be utterly confusing for the audience, but Steven Moffat has a genius for writing these jigsaw-puzzle plots - as he has shown not only in his *Doctor Who* work, but also in *Jekyll*, and even in some episodes of his sitcom *Coupling*. Here, the pieces may arrive in a mystifying non-chronological sequence, but it's always eventually clear how everything connects up, thanks to the use of props such as a mop and a fez to make it clear where the Doctor is in his personal timeline. Also, sequences that initially appear without context (like the Doctor's initial appearances to Rory) will be at least partially repeated once their proper place in the timeline arrives, just to make sure everyone keeps up.

Provided you accept the paradox of a circle of cause and effect, with no beginning or end (an idea Moffat also employed in *Blink*), the cliffhanger resolution - Rory releases the Doctor from the Pandorica with the sonic screwdriver, which the Doctor then goes back and gives to Rory so he can release him - works very well. Of course, there's always a danger with this sort of "cheating" that the question of why the Doctor doesn't do this all the time will arise. Moffat at least tries to address this with a line to the effect that this sort of pinpoint time-jumping is only possible now that the universe is a considerably smaller place. For in another twist, the entire alliance of aliens from the climax of the last episode turns out to be a huge red herring; the Pandorica chamber now contains only a few remnants, frozen in stone form:

The Doctor: "History has collapsed. Whole races have been deleted from existence. These are just like afterimages, echoes. Fossils in time, the footprints of the never-were... The universe literally never happened."

Rory: "So how can we be here? What's keeping us safe?"

The Doctor: "Nothing. Eye of the storm, that's all. We're just the last light to go out."

There are lots of clever, inventive moments in passing, like the Doctor realizing he doesn't have the sonic screwdriver any more, having given it to Rory back in 102 AD, so he pops back to tell Rory to put it in Amy's coat pocket after using it, returns to 1996, calmly retrieves the screwdriver from Amy's coat and moves on. In the course of joining up all the events we've already seen, there's even room for some farce-style comedy: Amelia tugs at the Doctor's sleeve and demands a drink because she's thirsty, because earlier in the day someone plucked her drink out of her hand while she was looking at the Pandorica, so the Doctor jumps back to that moment, steals her drink, returns and gives it back to her. And just as in *The Eleventh Hour*, Caitlin Blackwood gives a wonderfully natural and believable performance as Amelia; she's certainly one of the best child actors ever to have appeared in the series.

The only gripes I had with this part of the episode concerned some of the set-up for Amy's survival. The idea that the Pandorica has the ability to keep its occupant in stasis ("This box is the ultimate prison - you can't even escape by dying.") is reasonable enough, but it should have been established previously - an uncharacteristic lapse from Moffat, who is usually meticulous about setting up his plot elements in advance. More importantly, last week it seemed quite clear that Amy had been killed; now we're told that she's only "mostly dead" and that the Pandorica can hold her and use a "scan of her living DNA" (provided, of course, by Amelia's touch 1,894 years later) to restore her. The *Princess Bride* reference is cute, but doesn't make up for retconning the cliffhanger as brazenly as any old-fashioned movie serial.

Amy's story does, however, provide the central character focus for this part of the episode. Rory decides he must stay with the box and guard it through the centuries. The sight of him in his Roman garb, left silently sitting by the Pandorica as the Doctor departs for the future by the quick route, is a memorable image (as with last week's episode, Toby Haynes' direction is exemplary throughout). Moffat seems to have a fascination with exploring the concept of romance across time - see *The Girl in the Fireplace*, *Blink*, and most importantly River Song's temporally mixed up relationship with the Doctor. Here, when Amy awakes there's a lovely scene where she finds a display in the museum telling the story of the Lone Centurion and his mission to guard the Pandorica, and this proof of Rory's devotion to her results in her final commitment to them being a couple - something which the season has been working toward since *The Vampires of Venice*. When Rory meets up with her again they're immediately in a passionate lip-lock, as the Doctor looks on impatiently. ("And... breathe! Well, someone didn't get out much in two thousand years.")

Despite the impending universal oblivion, the predominant tone of the episode so far is comedic, with many funny lines and bits of business along the way. Some favourites, in no particular order: "Come along, Ponds!"; Amy figuring out what year she's in by checking her younger self's height and hair length; the Doctor trying to work out what to do with the fez he's accidentally grabbed, before just plonking it on his head; and the one that makes me laugh every time, when Amelia demands a drink while Amy and Rory are kissing in the background, and the Doctor says, "Oh, it's all mouths today, isn't it?" and shoves the fez onto her head so it comes down over her whole face. When Moffat is firing on all cylinders, as here, he seems incapable of writing a dull moment.

A certain level of menace is provided by one of the stone Daleks, which, having been hit by the "restoration field" from the open Pandorica, comes back to life and starts trundling around the museum after them, but what really brings the comic shenanigans to an end is one final time-jumping sequence. A duplicate Doctor, injured and dying, from twelve minutes in the future suddenly appears and collapses in front of them, and young Amelia silently disappears from the story, wiped from existence.

Amy: "But how can I still be here if she's not?"

The Doctor: "You're an anomaly - we all are. We're all

178

just hanging on at the eye of the storm, but the eye is closing and if we don't do something fast, reality will never have happened. Today, just dying is a result!"

The scope of the story expands again on the roof of the museum as the Doctor goes looking for his TARDIS, and finds it... in the sky. The idea that the exploding TARDIS serves in place of the sun in this alternate reality is not only a fine piece of Big Ideas storytelling, but also neatly plugs what would have been an obvious plot hole - namely, how humanity could possibly have survived if no stars ever existed in this universe. The Doctor also detects a voice coming from the "sun" - River's last line from the previous episode: "I'm sorry, my love" - and realizes that the TARDIS has protected River by sealing off the console room in a time loop. I suppose this is as arbitrary a solution to River's cliffhanger as the revival of Amy was, but as a long-term fan it's one I'm more inclined to forgive because throughout the Classic Series, the TARDIS had a long history of capabilities that got conveniently introduced to serve the plot of one story and were then rarely (or never) mentioned again.

The Doctor uses the vortex manipulator again to retrieve River. It's been interesting to observe the Doctor's increasing warmth toward River over the four episodes she's appeared in this season. Certainly the banter between them when he turns up in the TARDIS ("Hi honey, I'm home!" "And what sort of time do you call this?"), and the way they materialize arm-in-arm back on the roof, is as relaxed as they've ever been. I also loved the way she and Amy intuitively teamed up to destroy the fez ("What in the name of *sanity* have you got on your head?!"). But when the Dalek finally catches up to them and fires at the Doctor, badly injuring him, he disappears twelve minutes into the past, and River demonstrates a side of herself we haven't previously seen. Furious, she squares off against the Dalek and prepares to kill it while it's gathering power for another shot.

When she rejoins Amy and Rory and they ask what happened to the Dalek, she just says flatly, "It died." The idea of River being able to make a Dalek beg for mercy moves her several notches up the scale of awesomeness, and I'm looking forward to finding out how she got that reputation, and how it ties in to what we discovered in *Flesh and Stone* about her being in prison for killing "a good man" - who may or may not be the Doctor. But that's for later; right now, Amy and Rory discover that the "dead" Doctor's body is no longer where they left it.

Amy: "But he *was* dead."

River: "Who told you that?"

Amy: "He did."

River: "Rule One: the Doctor lies."

Cleverly, the injured Doctor was using his earlier counterpart and his companions to distract the Dalek while he got on with fixing the real problem. They find him slumped over inside the Pandorica, having wired the vortex manipulator into it in order to carry out his plan, which is to fly the Pandorica into the exploding TARDIS. The Pandorica, being the ultimate inescapable prison, carries within it a memory of the old universe, and this, together with its restoration field, will be propagated simultaneously to every point in history by the explosion, thus producing "the Big Bang, mark two" and restoring the old universe. It's a solution which kinda, sorta, *maybe* makes sense if you squint and resolutely refrain from examining it closely, but the amount of handwaving involved may surprise some viewers, who might have been expecting something from Moffat with more science-fictional rigor. This season finale resolution is very much of the same type as those we've seen previously from Russell T Davies, where the real significance lies not in how the particular plot problem is solved, but in the effect of that solution on the Doctor and his companions. *In Journey's End*, for instance, the threat of Davros and the Daleks is dealt with quite perfunctorily, but the consequences of the events (especially for Donna) are profound.

Over and over again in interviews, Moffat and his fellow executive producers used the phrase "dark fairytale" to describe what they were attempting to achieve in this season. Indeed, this final story is the best example of *Doctor Who* moving away from science fiction and into a realm of Terry Pratchett-like fantasy. Events on Pratchett's Discworld are heavily influenced by "narrativium" - the shape of a story can force things to happen, rather than the other way around. Here, the power of memory is able to restore to reality things and people that have been lost to the cracks in the universe. (Amusingly, Terry Pratchett wrote a column for *SFX* in May 2010, where he praised the series for its entertainment value, but bemoaned the fact that it is still generally considered science fiction. Naturally, one British newspaper couldn't resist spinning this into PRATCHETT ATTACKS 'LUDICROUS' DOCTOR WHO, considerably overstating the case.)

The Doctor's final scene with Amy before he puts his plan into action is an emotional high point, brilliantly played by both Matt Smith and Karen Gillan as well as being beautifully directed. With the greenish light from the Pandorica interior making even his youthful features look haggard and wan, the Doctor resumes the conversation they were having last episode before they were interrupted by the Cyber-attack:

The Doctor: "Amy Pond. The girl who waited. All night, in your garden. Was it worth it?"

Amy: "Shut up. Of course it was."

The Doctor: "You asked me why I was taking you with me, and I said: no reason. I was lying."

Amy: "It's not important."

The Doctor: "It's the most important thing left in the universe. It's why I'm doing this. Amy, your house was too big. That big, empty house. Just you."

With the gentleness that seems to have become a central facet of this Doctor's character, he steers Amy to the realization that the crack in time in the wall of her bedroom has been eating away at her life for years, removing even the memory of her parents. But the upcoming "big bang" will give her the chance to restore them, just as her memories effectively restored Rory after they were used as the basis for constructing his Auton duplicate.

The Doctor: "Just remember, and they'll be there."

Amy: "You won't."

The Doctor: "You'll have your family back. You won't need your imaginary friend any more."

With a last message of GERONIMO, the Doctor launches the Pandorica into the explosion. The huge cataclysm reverses itself as the universe gets back on track, and the cracks start closing. But now the Doctor no longer belongs in this universe, and his timeline is unravelling. He starts to rewind through his recent adventures - after a brief stop in the TARDIS, he finds himself back in a suburban street just after the events of *The Lodger*. He sees Amy and calls out to her, and realizes that she can hear but not see him. This leads to his ingenious, last-ditch plan to save himself, and the most cunning of all Moffat's connections between this episode and the earlier ones. When *Flesh and Stone* aired, I (and many others) noticed an anomalous scene in the forest, where after the Doctor has left Amy behind to go off with River and Father Octavian, he suddenly turns up again and talks to Amy with an entirely different demeanour. Now we finally get the context for that scene - it's *this* Doctor, travelling backwards through his timeline, speaking to Amy, taking advantage of the fact that Amy has to keep her eyes closed (to avoid activating the Weeping Angel which is within her at this point). It was a particularly clever trick of Moffat that the Doctor so emphatically tells Amy she has to remember what he told her when she was seven, which led to much speculation about what precisely we had seen in the Doctor's interaction with Amelia in the first episode that could be so significant. We had no way of knowing then that deducing the significant thing was impossible, because we hadn't actually seen it yet; the crucial thing the Doctor wants Amy to remember is what we are about to see him tell her.

The unravelling continues, and finally delivers the Doctor to Amelia's house on the fateful night in *The Eleventh Hour*. Out in the yard, little Amelia has fallen asleep on her suitcase, having waited in vain for her friend to return after five minutes as he promised. Gently, the Doctor picks her up and takes her back to her bed. And now, a moment of pure magic, as the Doctor simply sits down and addresses the sleeping girl with a valedictory speech that is both brilliantly written and superbly delivered:

The Doctor: "It's funny… I thought if you could hear me I could hang on somehow. Silly me. Silly old Doctor… When you wake up, you'll have a mum and dad, and you won't even remember me. Well, you'll remember me a little. I'll be a story in your head. That's okay. We're all stories in the end. Just make it a good one, eh? 'Cause it was, you know. It was the best. A daft old man, who stole a magic box, and ran away. Did I ever tell you I stole it? Well, I borrowed it - I was always going to take it back. Oh, that box. Amy, you'll dream about that box. It'll never leave you. Big, and little, at the same time. Brand new and ancient, and the bluest blue ever."

In moments like this it's incredibly hard to comprehend that Matt Smith was not yet 28 when he recorded this series. His control of his performance is such that he can perfectly evoke this old, old man who has experienced hundreds of years, and now knows his time has run out. (And, of course, it's typical of Moffat's - and the Doctor's - cleverness that hidden within this emotional climax are the key words that will trigger the Doctor's return.)

Deciding that there's no point in holding out any longer ("I think I'll skip the rest of the rewind. I hate repeats"), the Doctor finally accepts his fate, and walks toward the crack in the wall. As he disappears, so does the crack, and the music (which has been wonderfully effective throughout this episode, but particularly in the second half) underscores a lovely transition from a view of the night sky - showing that the stars are back - into morning, the morning of Amy's wedding.

Karen Gillan subtly indicates how Amy is different in this new, restored timeline. She is still a strong personality, but the brittleness and tendency to flare up at the slightest provocation are gone. The momentary disorientation she experiences when she wakes up to discover that her parents have been restored to her life would have caused the old Amy to be instantly suspicious, and probably snap at Rory on the phone, instead of bantering with him. Amy truly has now been healed of the damage accidentally inflicted by the Doctor all those years ago.

We cut to the wedding reception, where Amy's happiness at listening to her father bumble through giving his speech is cut short by the sight of River Song - dressed in mourning black - walking past outside. She has left her diary for Amy, and the sight of the book - its pages now all blank - triggers her memories.

Amy: "I remember! I brought the others back, I can bring you home too. Raggedy man, I remember you and you are late for my wedding!!"

(Glasses rattle as a wind starts up. The chandelier starts to swing.)

Amy: "I found you in words, like you knew I would. That's why you told me the story - the brand new, ancient blue box. Oh, clever, very clever."

Rory: "Amy? What is it?"

Amy: "Something old. Something new. Something borrowed. And something blue."

What a punch-the-air moment. I'd almost be prepared to believe that the realization - that the old traditional wedding rhyme was also a perfect description of the TARDIS - came to Steven Moffat first, and he then worked out the rest of the season to lead up to this moment. At any rate, the TARDIS materializes, and the Doctor steps out, cutting a dashing figure in his white-tie wedding finery. From this point on it's all celebration as the Doctor enthusiastically joins in the dancing (remarkably badly) and contemplates the happy couple ("Two thousand years; the boy who waited. Good on you, mate"). The sight of a relaxed Amy laying back in her new husband's arms and laughing at the Doctor's dancing is a fitting conclusion to the emotional journey that she and Rory have taken through this season.

Things only turn serious again when the Doctor heads back to the TARDIS. River is there, and he gives her back the diary ("The writing's all back, but I didn't peek") and the vortex manipulator. They share a teasing exchange, full of implications for the future:

The Doctor: "Did you think I was asking you to marry me, or asking if you were married?"

River: "Yes."

The Doctor: "No, but was that yes, or... yes?"

River: "*Yes...*"

The Doctor: "River... who are you?"

River: "You're going to find out very soon now. And I'm sorry, but that's when everything changes." *(She disappears.)*

Alex Kingston and Matt Smith have shown such great chemistry this season that I almost don't want their relationship to change, but it seems that the Doctor's growing ease around River will soon be shaken up. *Doctor Who* has never really done multi-season arcs before, but the true identity of River Song is one thread that is being explicitly held over until next year. The other one is the question of what's going on with the Silence - the mysterious disembodied voice that proclaimed, "Silence will fall." As the Doctor says, "The TARDIS exploded for a reason. Something drew the TARDIS to this particular date and blew it up. Why? And why now?" Back in *The Eleventh Hour*, Prisoner Zero told the Doctor: "The universe is cracked. The Pandorica will open. Silence will fall." The first two of those have now been dealt with, and apparently the third will be the big bad for next season.

But for the moment, we end on a note of happiness, with the cracks in the universe repaired, and the Doctor and his newlywed companions taking off on a journey that we'll rejoin at Christmas. For the first time since the new *Doctor Who* series started, there are no cast members departing at the end of the season. Overall, despite a few humdrum episodes (mainly in the first half), it's been a very successful year, for Steven Moffat and especially for Matt Smith, who quickly moved out of the shadow of David Tennant and established his own interpretation of the Doctor. You don't see many people worrying about him being too young for the role any more. I can't wait to see where these guys take us next.

Steven's Classic Who DVD Recommendation: *Pyramids of Mars*, starring Tom Baker and Elisabeth Sladen. If pressed to nominate one favourite story from the Classic Series, I'd pick this one. It's drenched in period atmosphere, and the acting from the whole cast, especially the regulars, is top class. And it's also one of the few *Doctor Who* stories to feature a fez. Fezzes are cool.

Kevin's review: *The Big Bang* is a rather excellent series finale, albeit with a few holes in the plot. Once the Pandorica's doors closed, everything in the Universe was erased. All that's left is the Earth and the Moon, which obviously, once you think about it, can't have existed without the rest of the Universe. However, the Doctor explains this away by saying that the Earth is in the eye of the storm, and thus remains intact (for a while). Conveniently, for the sake of the plot, duplicate Auton Rory still survives, despite not having been born twice, as he himself points out. So, there's obviously something more happening here, otherwise it's quite improbable that Rory could have survived the never-existence of the Nestenes. The thought that occurs to me is that the TARDIS must somehow be protecting its crew, just as it's later shown to save River in a time loop. Indeed, the very fact that the TARDIS took River back to Amy's childhood home in the previous episode is an indication that the Doctor's vessel has been implicitly trying to save him, no doubt because it knows that only he can ultimately save the day. Interestingly, the TARDIS has been shown to act in this manner before, during the 1964 adventure *The Edge of Destruction*. Coincidentally (or not) the TARDIS' actions then were aimed at preventing its destruction due a faulty control that had the ship spiralling back to the original Big Bang.

Although the Pandorica is supposedly the most secure prison ever constructed, Rory is able to open it using only the sonic screwdriver. So, perhaps the alliance would have been better advised to have constructed the Pandorica from wood, as this is the one material we know the sonic doesn't work on! As Steven noted in his review, it would appear that the Pandorica is responsive to the touch of whomever it is supposed to be imprisoning at the time, as it responds to Amelia's handling of it, just as it had to the Doctor's in the previous episode.

So, the alliance thought that they were putting all the evil in the Universe into the Pandorica, whereas we thought that they were actually imprisoning the only Hope that was left, just like the original Pandora's box myth. Fortunately enough, the Pandorica contains enough of the original Universe within it (both good and bad) to allow the Doctor to create another Big Bang that will "reboot" it. So, just as with a computer, it would seem that nothing is ever truly erased.

Thus the Doctor makes explicit the reason why he has always been so fascinated with Amy Pond: because she lived seemingly all alone in her big, empty childhood home. Amy reveals in this episode that she really doesn't know what happened to her parents. One can only presume that they were swallowed up by the crack in her bedroom wall, their existence erased for all time. And yet the Doctor firmly believes that Amy can bring her parents back. Indeed, the fact that Amy can clearly remember something about her parents was revealed in *The Eleventh Hour*, when Amelia gives the Doctor an apple that she has carved a happy face onto, in the same manner that her mother used to do for her (although the resulting "crooked smile" is just as creepy as the crack on Amy's bedroom wall, in my opinion). Although the TARDIS was undergoing major trauma at the beginning of *The Eleventh Hour*, the very fact that it deposited the Doctor in Amelia Pond's garden, was probably due to its own ongoing mission to save the Doctor from its explosion at the end of the series. It seems that the TARDIS knew that this mysterious child would intrigue the Doctor, and that this would be the eventual key to saving everyone's day.

Thus, after the Dalek in the museum has shot him, the Doctor comes to the conclusion that the only way that he can save the Universe is by sacrificing himself, despite his reluctance to do the same at the conclusion of *Flesh and Stone* (although it's debateable whether the "crooked smile" would have swallowed him then, as doing so would have prevented the TARDIS from exploding!). Incidentally, I must say that the new Daleks look far more threatening when they're covered in crud. The Doctor's last message of "Geronimo!" is a nice touch, as the Doctor had previously used this expression when first embarking on this series' very rocky adventure! Indeed, during the dramatic denouement of *The Lodger*, just before the time engine imploded, Craig also used this expression, which he had appropriately derived from his telepathic headbanging with the Doctor.

Although I was surprised to see Amy in the Pandorica at the beginning of this episode, the very fact that she was still alive wasn't all that startling, especially when one considers that Rory has "died" at least twice before during this series. The fact that Amy is also able to bring the Doctor back did strike me at first as being very much a cheat. For instance, I got very fed up with the final couple of series of *Buffy the Vampire Slayer*, because several characters suffered similar life-threatening injuries during episodes, only for them to appear to be totally fine in the succeeding weeks. So, I do think that you have to be very careful when you play the "Death card", because each time you employ it (especially with regards to the same character) it gradually diminishes in effect and power.

If audiences know that the main characters will always survive, then they will attach less significance to each time the protagonists subsequently face danger, to the extent that they may even care less for the characters concerned. This is a tricky one for the *Doctor Who* production team to balance, because, they of course want the drama that results from the placing of their characters in jeopardy. And I don't think Steven Moffat has got the balance quite right here, since the survival of the Doctor and the TARDIS at the end could be dismissed by some casual viewers as being the stereotypical "it was just a dream" scenario to get everything back to normal. Moffat could undoubtedly argue that in "dark fairytales", such fantastical things do happen. However, I would counter this by arguing that most heroes that die in "dark fairytales" stay dead. Although in Classical myth, such heroes would still exist in the Underworld after death, and could be consulted with, this was the full extent of their role, and they could never come back to life. Orpheus famously got permission to retrieve his wife from the Underworld, but unfortunately he ignored the explicit instructions not to look back, with the result that his wife forever vanished from existence.

Fortunately for the Doctor, he is allowed to look back on his immediate timeline as the Pandorica seminally crashes into the exploding TARDIS (thus creating the second Big Bang). Perhaps this is also a reflection of the interlude that the Tenth Doctor was allowed to revisit his companions as he faced up to his "death" during *The End of Time* in 2009. Indeed, one can't be too critical about Steven Moffat cheating with regards to the Doctor's "death" in this episode, as regeneration is the epitome of the get-out card, which the *Doctor Who* production team have frequently employed throughout the show's history. And yet each regeneration is a "death" in its way, as obviously the Doctor is never the same afterwards!

Steven Moffat does have a tendency of allowing great characters to live on in some way in his stories, most notably demonstrated at the end of *Forest of the Dead*, as the Doctor's quick thinking enabled the consciousness of his "wife", River Song, to live on in a virtual reality environment. It was also apparently Moffat's idea that Jenny survives at the end of *The Doctor's Daughter* in 2008 (albeit the decision to kill her off was bizarre in the first place). As an aside, I've sometimes wondered if "River Song" is a moniker that Jenny has adopted in later life... In addition to this, Steven Moffat's first story for the revived series was notable for the fact that no characters died during it, which was understandable when you consider that it was juxtaposed by the preceding *New Adventures* series of *Doctor Who* novels, which tended to have a very high body count.

Steven Moffat's saving grace in this series is that he provides a very well thought out rationale for the death and revival of each of the main characters. So, their "deaths" are not cheap ones without any consequences, but are quite integral to a most satisfyingly complex plot. Indeed, one could argue that Moffat is merely utilising a device beloved of all the classical storytellers: repetition.

Sometimes such repetition is subtle, such as the ongoing motif of exploding time machines that has been deployed throughout this series. Repetition is often employed for comic effect, as the mantra that "bowties are cool" humorously morphs into the far less acceptable "fezzes are cool". Sometimes the effect is simultaneously comic and sombre, especially with regards to the Doctor's last message of "Geronimo!" See how the Doctor stumbles at the end as he tries to comprehend who River is: when he asks whether River is married, the words used are almost exactly the same as the scene in *The Time of Angels* where Amy asks the Doctor if River is his wife; only this time, the Doctor's in Amy's subordinate place, while River is in the omniscient role that the Doctor himself usually occupies. And one would have thought that, having saved the Universe with a second Big Bang, the Doctor would be omniscient in a godlike manner, and yet it's the beguiling River who has the power to bring him back down to Earth.

The focus on Van Gogh's painting *Starry Night* in *Vincent and the Doctor* becomes more far more pointed here, where there's a distinct lack of stars in the night sky. Some *Doctor Who* fans have pointed out that several characters throughout the series have shouted that "time's running out". However, the Doctor doesn't make a big deal of this refrain in this episode in which time is literally running out. Most viewers wouldn't have noticed the repetition of this phrase anyway, since "time's running out" is a cliché in such dramatic series, and thus suffers from being repeated too much.

You can't really understand this series unless you've watched each episode at least twice, and all the episodes back to back. Otherwise you'll miss the significance of the scene where Rory notices Amy crying at the wedding, as similar scenes featured in both *Vincent and the Doctor*, and *The Pandorica Opens*. Like the previous scenes in which this occurred, Amy is crying, but she doesn't know why she's feeling sad. And, of course, it's a moment of pure genius that allows Steven Moffat to steal and adopt as his own that old marriage mantra of "Something old. Something new. Something borrowed. Something blue." Since many avid viewers would have expected the explosion of the TARDIS to occur on Amy and Rory's wedding day, many would have been disappointed in the manner that this occurred, as there was not a nuptial in sight. However, the wily old Doctor and his TARDIS were smarter than that, as Amy and Rory's wedding is indeed a far more fitting occasion for the restoration of the TARDIS. Although some might view the Doctor's dancing to be akin of that of an embarrassing uncle (I thought it was quite good myself). Given that both of them have recently died, Amy and Rory are still very keen to join the Doctor on his troubles, although the latter is probably worried about what would happen if he left his new wife with the Doctor for too long, given her provocative demands for a kiss in the shrubbery with the Doctor…

There are several satisfying loose threads that will have many viewers (like me) gnashing at the teeth in eager anticipation of the 6th series. Firstly, there's the question of who or what the Silence is, why they caused the TARDIS to explode, and whether they were satisfied with the resulting momentary silence (probably not). There are some rumours going around that the aliens behind the Silence are called the

Silents, appropriately enough. The Doctor did say in this episode that as a result of the TARDIS exploding, "reality will never have happened", and the last time we saw Davros, he was none too keen on reality…

There's also the much more pleasurable question of exactly who River is, and why she can remember him despite his obliteration from history (although apparently it's only Amy who can restore the Doctor). And why, unlike most of the Doctor's companions, River's prepared to gun a Dalek down in cold blood. Then again, when it comes down to the Daleks, we've also seen the Doctor coming very close to doing the same thing (such as in 2005's *Dalek*)… Although River uses the vortex manipulator to leave at the end, the chronology of this series dictates that she is due to be incarcerated in the Stormcage containment facility again, as the events of *The Time of Angels* occurred (from her point of view) after *The Big Bang*. It's also quite intriguing that she regards her book of spoilers to be so sacrosanct that she didn't even give anything away about the destruction of the universe during the Doctor's previous encounter with her… And yet, time has manifestly been rewritten when River's entries reappear in the book… So it would appear that River has a higher regard than the Doctor now has for the Laws of Time, for it's his growing belief that Time can be both rewritten and unwritten, something that he will very much utilise during his next adventure.

Did You Know? Richard Dawkins, the famed scientist mentioned in this episode, is married to Lalla Ward, who played the Doctor's Time Lady companion Romana from 1979-1981. Richard Dawkins isn't Lalla Ward's first husband, as she was previously married to Tom Baker, her co-star on *Doctor Who*. Indeed, Lalla was introduced to Richard Dawkins by legendary *Doctor Who* script editor Douglas Adams.

A Christmas Carol

Writer: Steven Moffat
Director: Toby Haynes
Originally broadcast: 25 December 2010

Cast

The Doctor: Matt Smith
Amy Pond: Karen Gillan
Rory Williams: Arthur Darvill
Abigail Pettigrew: Katherine Jenkins
Kazran/Elliot Sardick: Michael Gambon
Co-pilot: Micah Balfour
Captain: Pooky Quesnel
Pilot: Leo Bill
Young Kazran: Laurence Belcher
Boy and Benjamin: Bailey Pepper
Old Benjamin: Steve North
Isabella: Laura Rogers
Old Isabella: Meg Wynn-Owen
Teenage Kazran: Danny Horn
Eric: Nick Malinowski
Servant: Tim Plester

Steven's review: At long last, BBC America has bowed to the reality of the internet and broadcast the *Doctor Who* Christmas special within hours of its UK premiere. It's particularly fortunate that as many viewers as possible got to see this episode at the correct time of year, rather than weeks or months later, as *A Christmas Carol* is definitely the most Christmassy of all the Christmas specials so far. Previous specials have seen various trappings of Christmas given a *Doctor Who* twist (killer Christmas trees, robot Santas, and so on), but this is the first time the Christmas episode draws inspiration from one of the classic works of Christmas literature. Despite the title, though, this is not simply an adaptation of the famous original; such a thing would make no sense, since we already know that Charles Dickens exists in the Doctor's universe (*The Unquiet Dead*). Instead, writer Steven Moffat neatly engineers a situation where the Doctor deliberately chooses to act in a way that follows the basic structure of *A Christmas Carol* - just with time-travel, rather than ghosts.

The teaser dumps us straight into the action: a spaceship is in trouble, its engines failing, plummeting into the atmosphere of a planet covered with dense white clouds. On board are four thousand people, including our honeymooning companions, Amy and Rory. They manage to send a distress signal that brings the TARDIS flying to the rescue, but it can't simply lock on and tow the ship to safety - and the clouds make any sort of controlled landing impossible. With admirable efficiency, the main threat driving the plot has been set up in under two minutes, with several gags along the way referencing everything from *Star Trek* (the design of the ship's bridge, especially the viewscreen, and the navigator with an artificial-eyesight device on his face) to *Red Dwarf* ("The light's stopped flashing... Does this mean he's on his way, or do I have to change the bulb?"). Amy and Rory are wearing their policewoman/kissogram and Roman outfits from previous stories, which I'm sure was done not only to hint that they were engaging in a bit of roleplaying in the honeymoon suite, but to mislead fans who saw the publicity photos into thinking that Moffat, with his penchant for time-twisting plotting, might be revisiting the events of the last year (as if they weren't tangled enough already). Surprisingly, it turns out that there is plenty of 'timey-wimey' trickery to come, but Amy and Rory are barely involved in the story - they'll remain trapped on board the USS *MacGuffin* for the duration.

Below the cloud layer, we find a different world altogether. One of the things that struck me forcefully about this episode is simply how *good* it looked. New production designer Michael Pickwoad presents a positively cinematic setting that initially looks like a picture-postcard Victorian

Christmas. But a closer look reveals electric lighting, loudspeakers on the lampposts, and costumes that incorporate helmets and goggles reminiscent of early aircraft pilots. It's the sort of thing which was being attempted in *The Beast Below* - to create a setting based firmly on British iconography, with a surreal twist - but this episode is on a bigger scale, and much more successful. This Victorian-ish human colony is more or less superimposed onto a sort of bizarre undersea world - the clouds and fog are actually home to flying fish of all sizes up to and including man-sized sharks. There are some vague attempts at providing justifications for all this, with the Doctor mumbling about "crystalline fog" and so on, but they're unlikely to satisfy those who prefer their *Doctor Who* to be more science fiction than fantasy, and it's probably best to view this environment as simply continuing the style of storytelling which informed much of the last season. Besides, the image of schools of small fish swimming through the air, circling around street lamps, is wonderfully beguiling.

The ruler of this town, Kazran Sardick, is a thoroughly unpleasant person who seems to derive his pleasures from being as petty and mean as possible to anyone and everyone. A Scrooge-like moneylender who takes family members as collateral for loans and stores them in cryogenic stasis caskets, we see him refusing a poor family's request for their frozen relative - a beautiful young woman - to be let out for just one day; to let them have Christmas Day together. He sneers at the family to go home and "pray for a miracle," when suddenly there's a disturbance at the chimney. In a shower of soot and sparks, the Doctor makes a spectacular entrance ("Christmas Eve on a rooftop, saw a chimney, my whole brain just went, *What the hell*!"). He's here because Kazran is the owner of a device that can control the clouds of this planet, and is the only hope for the crippled spaceship to land safely. When he tries to operate the controls himself he finds they are "isomorphic," and will respond only to Kazran (for long-time fans, an in-joke referring to the Tom Baker story *Pyramids of Mars*, in which the Doctor used a bluff about the TARDIS controls being isomorphic).

The producers scored a considerable coup by getting Michael Gambon for the part of Kazran. He will be most familiar to a lot of the audience (particularly the children) as Dumbledore, but for me he is indelibly linked not to Harry but to Dennis Potter. His unforgettable central performance in *The Singing Detective* (the 1986 version, that is, not the inferior 2003 remake) is a large part of why that production is one of the greatest dramatic works ever created for television. I was greatly looking forward to seeing him in this episode, and he didn't disappoint. As we find out over the course of the story, Kazran is a man whose emotional makeup was greatly influenced by his brutal, domineering father Elliot Sardick - whose brief appearances in flashback scenes are also portrayed by Gambon. His own childhood interests were crushed, as he grew up to follow his father in the "family business" - the atmospheric control system that now gives him power and influence over the whole planet. Something I particularly enjoyed about Gambon's performance here is the way, whenever Kazran is being especially unpleasant, his voice takes on some of the characteristics of the coarser, more thuggish voice Gambon provides for Elliot. It's as if he can't help himself becoming the embodiment of his own father.

Meanwhile, Matt Smith continues to show all the brilliance that I've come to expect after the last series. The only things I didn't care for in the portrayal of the Doctor in this episode (and the writing is perhaps more to blame than the performance here) were a couple of particularly hyperactive moments that would have fit perfectly into the little pantomime skit Moffat wrote for Smith's live performance at the *Doctor Who* Prom concert (which was shown on BBC America a few hours before this episode). "Big flashy lighty thing. Big flashy lighty things have got me written all over them. Well, not actually… give me time. And a crayon." At least Kazran does get to mock him about it ("Was that a sort of threat-y thing?"), but I find this sort of superficial wackiness tends to detract from the Doctor's presence without adding anything interesting in return.

Apart from those little glitches, though, Smith and Gambon work excellently together. Their first, long confrontation scene is a treat. When the Doctor asks who the frozen woman is and Kazran says she is "nobody important," his quiet reply - "D'you know, in nine hundred years of time and space I've never met anyone who wasn't important before" - manages to slip in a disconcerting amount of menace underneath the last few words. Even after he discovers that only Kazran can operate the controls, he still can't stop himself trading barbs ("I'm Kazran Sardick. How could you possibly not know who I am?" "Well... just easily bored, I suppose"). He tries cajoling, then veiled threats; nothing works against Kazran's determined intransigence. But when he sees Kazran raise his hand against the little boy from the poor family - but be unable to make himself complete the action of hitting him - the Doctor begins to realize that there might be a way to change Kazran's mind after all.

As I said earlier, this is not a straight adaptation of *A Christmas Carol*, but rather an independent story incorporating some of its motifs. The social commentary from the original is not used here (although Kazran does make a couple of snide remarks about "surplus population"), and there is no allegorical reveal of two children named Ignorance and Want. Instead, Moffat makes use of an idea that formed the basis of his first-ever piece of *Doctor Who* fiction, a highly regarded short story published in 1996 called *Continuity Errors* - the Doctor reforms Kazran in the present by changing his past.

Kazran is sleeping in his chair when he is jolted awake by the ghost of Christmas Past - a video image projected onto his wall by the Doctor. It's a recording he made as a boy, showing his twelve-year-old self wanting to make a film about the fish that fascinate him, but being berated by his father who slaps him - something the grown-up Kazran was unable to do to the boy earlier.

He tells the Doctor to get out; in response, the Doctor

simply tells him he'll be back... *way* back. The moment where the sound of the TARDIS leaving becomes the sound of the TARDIS arriving, and in the recording the boy Kazran looks up and sees the Doctor at his window, is a simply magical transition. Director Toby Haynes, having successfully coped with Moffat's time-jumping plotting in last season's finale, is equally adept here at finding ways to ensure that the viewer is kept up to speed with Kazran's shifting timeline. As the Doctor interacts with the boy Kazran, the adult version finds himself with memories of those events - but in addition to, not instead of, his previous memories, in much the same way as Amy and Rory found themselves with memories of multiple timelines at the end of the last series.

I do wonder whether Steven Moffat is to some extent playing with fire here. Something *Doctor Who* has always shied away from is using the TARDIS as a means of solving story problems, especially by going back in time. The chief narrative function of the TARDIS has always been to deposit the Doctor and his companions at the start of an adventure and take them away at the end. In the Classic Series, of course, its navigation was generally too unreliable to do anything else. And even when the Doctor did later manage to gain more control over his journeys, there was always technobabble available to "explain" why established events could not be interfered with. Even in recent stories that have featured manipulation of timelines, the TARDIS has generally not been involved. By using the TARDIS in this fashion here, Moffat's fascination with the possibilities of time travel (and his undoubted ability to exploit those possibilities) may have opened up a can of worms and created a situation where it's hard to avoid asking why the Doctor can't fix every problem he encounters by just going back in time.

Anyway, be that as it may, the Doctor now spends some time getting to know Kazran as a boy. Matt Smith has already shown several times how well he can work with child actors, and this episode provides another example.

Laurence Belcher gives a very natural and believable performance, establishing a real rapport with Smith just as the intelligent, likeable young Kazran does with the Doctor. This section also contains my favourite joke of the episode:

Young Kazran: "Are you really a babysitter?"

The Doctor: *(presents his psychic paper)* "I think you'll find I'm universally recognised as a mature and responsible adult."

Young Kazran: "It's just a lot of wavy lines."

The Doctor: *(examines it)* "Shorted out. Finally, a lie too big."

The Doctor sets up his sonic screwdriver to attract one of the fish; unfortunately it ends up attracting one rather bigger than he was expecting, and young Kazran finds himself facing a full-sized shark floating in his bedroom. (Amusingly, in the accompanying *Confidential* episode, Moffat reveals that the shark-in-the-bedroom image comes straight from his own childhood nightmares.) The shark bites the Doctor's sonic screwdriver in half, but leaving the cloud layer means it's dying. The boy asks the Doctor to take the shark back to the clouds, but that will require borrowing one of the cryogenic caskets. He picks the one containing the young woman we saw earlier, who he knows shares his fascination with the fish, which leads to the introduction of the episode's other guest star.

The role of Abigail was the first acting role for Welsh mezzo-soprano Katherine Jenkins, and she made a great job of it. Not only is she visually stunning, but as the episode progresses she has to carry more and more emotional weight, and proves more than capable of it. Her singing voice is also put to good use; here she sings *In the Bleak Midwinter* to calm the shark - in typical Moffat fashion, combining an arresting image with the laying in of plot points for later, as the Doctor talks about how the sound of her voice resonates with the ice crystals making up the clouds.

The release of the shark back into the clouds, with Abigail and young Kazran standing in the TARDIS doorway and looking on delightedly, kicks off a section lasting nearly fifteen minutes where the Doctor and Kazran spend a multitude of Christmas Eves with Abigail. The Doctor of course journeys straight from one Christmas Eve to the next, and Abigail is frozen in her casket for the rest of the year, so only Kazran ages, changing from a boy into a young adult. As they journey to famous places on Earth, enjoy a ride through the clouds on a rickshaw pulled by their now-tame shark, or drop in on Abigail's family for a happy Christmas dinner (a scene drawing directly on the merrymaking at the Cratchits' house in the original *Christmas Carol*), Kazran and Abigail gradually fall in love. Periodically, we cut back to the old Kazran, sitting on the floor of his study, looking at the photographs of what are simultaneously both old memories and new experiences for him. And the portrait now watching over him is no longer his father - it's been replaced by a picture of Abigail. Despite my reservations above about the possible misuse of the TARDIS, the sheer joy of this sequence is hard to resist. Apart from anything else, there are some more great comedy lines from Moffat:

Kazran: "Now? I kiss her *now*?"

The Doctor: "Kazran, trust me. It's either this, or go to your room and design a new kind of screwdriver. Don't make my mistakes. Now, go!"

However, tragedy strikes when Abigail lets Kazran in on a big secret she's been keeping to herself. Unfortunately, the story requires the Doctor to be kept in the dark at this point, and Moffat resorts to a serious case of idiot plotting to accomplish this. Earlier the Doctor had pointed out a numerical readout on the front of Abigail's casket, and Abigail had confirmed that it pertained to her, and mentioned something about doctors ("Are you one of mine?"). But the story contrived to distract the Doctor before he could probe further. Then, each time Abigail is released for Christmas Eve, the direction makes a point of showing us the number on the front of her casket counting down. It's very obvious that something bad is going to happen when the count reaches zero, but we're supposed to believe the Doctor never notices the decreasing number right in front of him - even though earlier he gave an impressive demonstration of his observational skills with his deductions about Kazran's father (presented in the rapid-fire style of Moffat's other hit show of 2010, *Sherlock*).

Abigail finally tells Kazran at a party on Earth where the Doctor accidentally gets engaged to Marilyn Monroe. In a very funny scene, the Doctor wants to make a quick getaway, while the two lovers ignore him, their kissing hiding their tear-streaked faces. Back in the vault, a clearly bitter Kazran seals Abigail away before telling the Doctor he won't be going on any more Christmas Eve trips - in fact, he won't be needing the Doctor any more at all. The Doctor is left puzzled, responding to Kazran's "Times change," with "Not as much as I'd hoped." It's nice to have the audience ahead of the Doctor just for once, but it goes on way too long, and the way it's presented makes the Doctor look absurdly slow-witted.

Back in the 'present day,' the old Kazran is once again being watched over by the portrait of his father. Having originally become a misanthrope through loneliness and lack of love, he is now embittered by the pain of having loved and lost, and still refuses to help the ship land safely ("As a very old friend of mine once took a very long time to explain, life isn't fair!"). Even when Amy gets into the action, appearing to Kazran in a holographic projection as "the ghost of Christmas Present," she is no more successful than the Doctor was earlier. Finally Kazran reveals the secret that everyone in the audience had already guessed - Abigail is dying, and has only one day left to live. "So tell me, ghost of Christmas Present. How do I choose which day?"

Gambon and Smith shine again in the final confrontation between the Doctor and Kazran. Having criticized Moffat's plotting earlier, it's only fair that I give him due credit for the climax of the Doctor's manipulation of Kazran - the ghost of Christmas Yet to Come. After Kazran challenges him to show him his future, the twist occurs, which I never saw coming. The Doctor simply replies, "I am showing it to you; I'm showing it to you right now." Standing behind

Kazran is his twelve-year-old self, who looks at him, appalled. Eventually, he says simply: "*Dad?*" That one word finally penetrates the hard carapace Kazran has built up around himself. His *Christmas Carol* therapy is completed as he rejects his father's harshness and ends up quite literally embracing his inner child.

Now at last Kazran is willing to save the ship, but Moffat manages to fit in one more clever twist. The Doctor has now changed Kazran to such an extent that the isomorphic controls no longer recognize him. Instead, the Doctor has to cobble together a solution using Abigail's voice transmitted through the two halves of his sonic screwdriver - one retained by Kazran over the years, the other still in that shark flying through the clouds. This of course means that Abigail must be released from her casket - for the last time. It's a beautifully written scene as she gently chides Kazran for "hoarding my days like an old miser," before concluding: "We've had so many Christmas Eves, Kazran. I think it's time for Christmas Day."

Once again, Katherine Jenkins' marvellous voice is showcased as Abigail sings a new Murray Gold number. The melody had actually been heard earlier, forming the basis of the joyful accompaniment to the rickshaw sequence. Here, though, it is presented in a pure, unadorned version that provides a suitably moving climax as the clouds are finally "unlocked," snow falls on the town, and the ship at last lands safely.

Amy: "It'll be their last day together, won't it?"

The Doctor: "Everything's got to end some time. Otherwise nothing would ever get started."

In place of the unambiguously happy ending of the Dickensian original, this episode comes to a more bittersweet conclusion. Kazran's change of heart is rewarded with just a single day of grace, but we can be confident that he will be able to move on past the loss of Abigail, rather than remaining forever poised, in Moffat's memorable phrase, "halfway out of the dark." The Doctor's somewhat ominous words, combined with the trailer for the next season released after this episode, also remind us that *A Christmas Carol* itself is actually an interlude within a larger story. The threads left hanging at the end of last season - the truth about River Song, and the mysterious "Silence" - will be taken up again soon. But for now, we end with the sight of Kazran and Abigail dashing through the clouds in a one-shark open sleigh (well, rickshaw), enjoying their first - and last - Christmas Day together.

Classic Who DVD Recommendation: Again, Christmas is something that the Classic Series never really did (although the First Doctor did wish viewers a Merry Christmas during a seasonal episode of *The Daleks' Master Plan*). However, if you go back to the *Key to Time* series of *Doctor Who* that Steven previously recommended, you'll find that the first story, *The Ribos Operation*, conveys a similarly retro future on a snowbound planet with a ravenous beast that can be tamed (albeit with doped meat). The Fourth Doctor was given a locator to help him find the segments of the Key to Time in this story, although no doubt the Eleventh Doctor would just rely on the omnipotent sonic screwdriver to do the same nowadays!

Kevin's review: *A Christmas Carol* is certainly the most Christmassy *Doctor Who* special ever, which makes me think that Steven Moffat will find it very difficult to write an even more seasonal missive in 2011. I must admit that I cringed a bit when the episode title was first announced, as obviously, it's not particularly original. However, Moffat has certainly utilised the full meaning of the title by making Christmas carols an integral part of the plot. Although in our multi-cultural, secular society, it does sound a bit off to hear people singing the "Christ the Saviour is born" line from *Silent Night*, no matter how ironically this was intentioned. So, Steven Moffat is very much putting the Christ back into Christmas here!

As you'll know from my review of *The Beast Below*, I'm not a great fan of some presentations of a retrograde future in this series of *Doctor Who*. However, it's difficult to escape such Victoriana during the festive season, as many of our Christmas traditions derive from this era. The Doctor himself has traditionally been depicted wearing Victorian costume, as a kind of symbolism of Imperialist virtue and heroism in our post-Imperialist age. Although it's more than a little bizarre to discover that the machine that controls the skies very much resembles a traditional church organ. Admittedly, an ultra-modern gizmo would have looked very much out of place in Kazran's home, and the clouds are modulated by sonic waves, so a church organ would be an ideal way with which to manage them. This also allows the sonic screwdriver to play an integral part in the plot.

Michael Gambon plays the Scrooge-like Kazran Sardick to perfection, with the timbre of great voice utilised to powerful effect when displaying his guttural, snarling sardonic nature. Like Steven, I'm a huge fan of his starring role in Dennis Potter's fantastic *The Singing Detective*, which also featured his character confronting childhood demons via vivid flashbacks as he battled psoriasis. Michael Gambon went a bit off the boil after this seminal role, but he's really returned to the limelight during the last decade, and so it's a real coup to get an actor of his calibre and gravitas in *Doctor Who*.

I was less impressed with Katherine Jenkins, as she seemed a bit wooden at times. However, she has the good looks that make her a very believable love interest for the teenage Kazran (the moment when she greets Kazran with delight and admiration when he has reached maturity one Christmas Eve is very well done, although Kazran has done an unbelievable amount of growing in one year). Obviously, Katherine Jenkins was also cast for her fantastic voice; so much so, that the *Doctor Who* production team would really have been stymied if she had turned the role down. Although *In The Bleak Midwinter* is a carol that I like, albeit for its atypical melancholy, I didn't recognise the arrangement that she sang, which was simply beautiful. Also noteworthy is the carol that she sings at the end, which, according to *Doctor Who* Confidential, was hurriedly composed by Murray Gold.

Overall, I thought Toby Haynes' direction was very good, although I did struggle to make out what the protagonists on the space liner bridge were saying at the beginning, which meant that some of Steven Moffat's splendid dialogue was lost in all the confusion. No doubt most people would have been watching this episode with all their family, with lots of distractions going on with kids playing with new toys etc., so it was a good idea for Moffat to avoid including any vital pieces to the jigsaw puzzle that comprises the overall story arc of his tenure thus far. (Although it was great to hear Amy and Rory ask whether the Doctor was lying, as this was River Song's "Rule No.1" from *The Big Bang*.) So, we ended up with a very traditional, fluffy kind of a seasonal episode, in which one almost expected to see Natasha Kaplinsky dancing in a chorus line, much as Angela Rippon did in a *Morecambe and Wise* Christmas special in the 70's.

Over 11 million viewers for this episode rewarded the *Doctor Who* production team for their hard work, and it was also the joint second most watched programme on the day. This was especially welcoming after some silly news reports during the summer that the 2010 series had lost over a million viewers from the 2008 one. These news reports didn't take into account that viewing habits have very much changed since the development of the BBC iPlayer and Sky Plus, which now allow viewers to watch their favourite programmes at a time that suits them.

The CGI in this episode came across really well, and the shark was quite convincing. According to *Doctor Who Confidential*, the shark was given the nickname of "Clive" to avoid the public catching on that such a monstrosity would feature in the Christmas episode. However, any suspense that was intended to accompany the shark's explosive appearance was somewhat dashed by the fact that most of the episode's pre-publicity interviews explicitly stated that there would be a flying shark in the story. Perhaps Murray Gold should have nicked some of John Williams' distinctive chords to make the shark even more disturbing!

One of my pedantic gripes during this series has been the

lack of consistency when it comes down to the communicators that the Doctor employs when speaking to companions that are elsewhere. And the communicator that the Doctor utilises in this episode is again different from that he adopted in *The Lodger*. Admittedly, Amy isn't using one of the TARDIS' communicators this time; instead she has a rather bulky walkie-talkie like affair that can signal the Doctor, so probably derives from the TARDIS also. Perhaps such TARDIS communicators have inbuilt chameleon circuits or perception filters, so that they change in appearance depending on the environment? I guess one way the production team could create some consistency (and save some props) is by utilising the sonic as a communicator, as it develops yet another new function by becoming a microphone at the end of this episode!

It's while the Doctor's talking to Amy on this communicator that she overhears some music from the tannoy, which leads her to ask if it's a Christmas carol. This gives the Doctor the inspiration to adapt the famous tale by his old buddy Charles Dickens to resolve this tricky situation. A more practical and cynical man may have come to the conclusion that a more immediate route to the heart of a miser would have come in the form of money. Certainly, the space liner and its inhabitants look far richer than the deprived people on the planet below, and could have certainly summoned up enough resources to pay off Kazran. However, this resolution, as unsavoury as it may be, does not occur to the alien Doctor. Instead, he verily delights in his mission to reform the miser.

Yet the first tactic he adopts is the very unDoctorly suggestion that Kazran might be the 4004th victim that night (although the Doctor's meaning is unclear in this very contradictory piece of dialogue). Although the Doctor rightfully admonishes Kazran for saying that Abigail in her cryogenic coffin is unimportant, the Doctor at no point expresses outrage at the monstrous Sardick policy of keeping family members of debtors as security. When we see the holograms of the space liner passengers in the cryogenic chamber, the first impression is that these may be the frozen prisoners haunting Kazran. Indeed, with the exception of Abigail, we never see the release of these human beings held as collateral in this episode. Given that the Doctor has already excessively interfered with Kazran's life, one would have thought that he would have ensured their release. Instead, it's left to the viewer's imagination that once the very healthy looking Abigail has finally conked out on Christmas day, that Kazran will find it within his heart to liberate them.

As Steven and other reviewers of this episode, such as Mark Davison (1), have pointed out, it is more than a little bizarre that the Sardicks require a countdown on each cryogenic coffin that marks how many days its occupants have yet to live. Unless, of course, it's the norm to give up your terminally ill relatives to creditors in this society, although one would have thought that the Sardicks would prefer to take hostage the most beloved family members (if not, of course, the breadwinner, or else they'd never get their money back). It's also quite incredible that the exact day of death is known. Then again, the science of genetics would have undoubtedly advanced by this time, which could possibly explain such an accurate biological clock.

Yet again, there's no respite for the wonderful Matt Smith, as he spends a great deal of time on screen in this episode, with Amy and Rory very much on the sidelines. Perhaps Steven Moffat loves writing for the Eleventh Doctor so much that his companions find it difficult to get a word in edgeways? Despite some clunkers in the script (such as the improbable length of time that the space liner spends in its tumultuous descent), there are still many Moffat signature moments. As Steven mentions in his review, the scene at the end where the Doctor reveals Kazran's future to his younger self is splendidly done, and is a really nice magical twist. The Doctor's awkwardness during Kazran's and Abigail love scenes is brilliantly scripted and acted. Moffat also utilises Michael Gambon's wide range to magnificent effect in his awesome dialogue. There are not one, but two child actors in this episode, as per the showrunner's penchant for including children. However, Moffat has overcome my fears that there would be too many children on screen during this series by writing so well for the huge majority of them, so that they never become irritants.

As Steven notes, there is a danger that Moffat is bending the rules here by allowing the Doctor to employ the TARDIS as a means to directly change the past, although it is wonderful to see Kazran gain newly beloved memories on screen. This may indeed cause problems for the future, especially as Steven Moffat is particularly loath to kill off characters. Then again, the Doctor's realization that time can be rewritten (and unwritten) is something that only occurred this series. It could be that when the Time Lords were around, the Doctor really could not break their Laws of Time (especially since he had an unreliable TARDIS). However, now that the Time Lords have gone, it would appear that the Doctor has new powers. Indeed, he is now the only Lord of Time, something that will certainly come in handy in his fight against the mysterious Silence. Thus the Doctor begins to embark on the journey that will he see him become the omnipotent Doctor that River Song knows and loves. After all, we've already seen him create the second Big Bang, and you can't get more godlike than that. Hopefully the Doctor will retain a degree of fallibility. Otherwise, River Song may well just have to kill him...

Despite the overall Christmas brashness, there are also some elements of subtlety here, as some fans on online forums have observed that the carol that Abigail sings at the end does appear to pertain to the overall story arc: "When you're alone, silence is all you know. When you're alone, silence is all you see. When you're alone, silence is all you'll be." So, my guess is that, despite the ongoing roles of Amy and Rory, the Doctor may be facing some unwanted solitude in series 6. So, more screen time for Matt Smith then, what a shame!

Did You Know? Pooky Quesnel, who plays the starliner

captain in this episode, is most famous for portraying *Doctor Who* uberfan Bradley Branning's mother in *EastEnders*.

1).http://thecollectivereview.com/mark-davison/doctor-who-a-christmas-carol-a-review.html?fmt=news

Appendix

The Sarah Jane Adventures: Series 4, Episodes 5 & 6: Death of the Doctor

Writer: Russell T Davies
Director: Ashley Way
Originally broadcast: 25 and 26 October 2010

Cast

Sarah Jane Smith: Elisabeth Sladen
Clyde Langer: Daniel Anthony
Rani Chandra: Anjli Mohindra
Mr Smith: Alexander Armstrong
Luke Smith: Tommy Knight
The Doctor: Matt Smith
Jo Jones: Katy Manning
Santiago Jones: Finn Jones
Colonel Karim: Laila Rouass
Haresh Chandra: Ace Bhatti
Groske: Jimmy Vee
Groske voice: Phillip Hurd-Wood
Shansheeth voice: David Bradley
Additional Shansheeth voices: Jon Glover
Shansheeth: Paul Kasey, Ruari Mears, and Ben Ashley

Steven's review: Even after Russell T Davies handed over the showrunner role on *Doctor Who* to Steven Moffat, he continued to oversee the two spinoff shows he had created: *Torchwood* and *The Sarah Jane Adventures*. The pressure of work on the parent show had prevented him from writing for *Sarah Jane* since the pilot episode, but now in its fourth year he was finally able to contribute a story. The 'special event' status of this story was cemented by it not only marking Davies' return to the series, but the fact that it would also feature a guest appearance by a popular star from Classic *Doctor Who* - Jo Jones, née Grant, who was companion to

210

Jon Pertwee's Doctor for three years in the early 1970s - plus a visit from the Doctor himself. The chance to see Davies' take on the Eleventh Doctor was an intriguing prospect; on *Doctor Who* he had been adamant that the new Doctor would be entirely Steven Moffat's creation, going so far as to effectively relinquish his executive producer's chair one minute before the end of *The End of Time*, to allow Moffat to oversee not only the writing but also the production of Matt Smith's era right from his very first scene.

When the show tried a similar guest spot the previous year for David Tennant (*The Wedding of Sarah Jane Smith*), the Tenth Doctor was in the course of his long, angst-filled final journey towards his regeneration, and it was a little incongruous seeing him bouncing around having an adventure with Sarah Jane and her young friends. By contrast, the new Doctor fits in very well here. The absence of Amy and Rory is quickly explained by their being off on a honeymoon planet ("Which isn't what you think; it's not a planet for a honeymoon, it's a planet *on* a honeymoon - it married an asteroid..."), and Davies has managed to capture the quirky essence of Matt Smith's Doctor extremely well. He has also, whether deliberately or not, tapped into the theme running through the whole of Steven Moffat's first *Doctor Who* season - the importance and power of memory.

With a title like *Death of the Doctor*, it's pretty obvious from the start that there must be some kind of trickery involved, and yet the first half of Part 1 manages to get a surprising amount of tension and emotion out of the idea that the Doctor has really and truly died. The fact that we're drawn into the story and not just marking time until the guest stars show up is due to a top-notch performance from Elisabeth Sladen. When a force of UNIT cars pulls up outside her front door and one Colonel Karim solemnly informs her that the Doctor is dead, his remains brought back to Earth by a race of galactic undertakers called the Shansheeth, Sarah immediately reacts with blank denial. She refuses even for a moment to consider that the Doctor might be dead, and tells her son Luke that she is absolutely certain

211

that something else is going on:

Sarah: "I always thought, if ever the Doctor dies, I'll know. Somehow, I'll just feel it. Wherever he is, if he's far away on some distant star, or lost in the depths of dark ages, I'll know... But I didn't. I didn't feel a thing."

Luke's two friends, Clyde and Rani, have to awkwardly humour Sarah as she maintains a facade of brittle cheerfulness while they are all whisked off to a secret base under Mount Snowdon (with a welcome reuse of Murray Gold's driving, forceful UNIT theme as heard in *Doctor Who*'s *The Christmas Invasion* and *The Sontaran Stratagem*). Soon they find themselves in the funeral chamber facing a huge coffin, while the Shansheeth conduct a ceremony of remembrance that prompts the first of many flashback clips in this story - incorporating moments from *Sarah Jane* and from *Doctor Who*, both old and new series. The Shansheeth themselves are pretty unconvincing-looking aliens - vulture-headed, man-sized creatures that are all too obviously large puppets - but they are helped considerably by the voice provided by David Bradley which gives them a wise, calming, benevolent air that turns later on to menacing, larger-than-life villainy.

The quiet, contemplative atmosphere is shattered, literally, by a vase of flowers dropping to the ground as Jo makes her entrance - the very same kind of accident-prone introduction she had back in 1971. It may be nearly four decades since we last saw her, but Katy Manning is instantly the embodiment of the character again, helped by the fact that Davies has carefully followed the line of development suggested by her memorable departure in *The Green Death* - Jo is married, with a large family, and has spent the years since leaving the Doctor travelling around the world and getting involved in numerous activist causes. Sarah - just as she did originally, in the 70's - forms a contrast to Jo, having been rather casually dumped out the TARDIS and left alone and at a loose end until the Doctor eventually re-entered her life many years later and she took up freelance alien-fighting. The two women bond over their shared experiences (I loved

212

it when they realised that the Doctor had taken both of them to the planet Peladon), with Sarah envying Jo's seven children and twelve grandchildren, and Jo rueful that the Doctor never came back to visit *her* - as she comments wistfully, "He must have *really* liked you."

Because *The Sarah Jane Adventures* is a show aimed primarily at young children, it would be wrong to expect the same complexity of plotting as in *Doctor Who* itself. And so to get to the next stage of the story, Davies has the Shansheeth conveniently boasting of their plans for no particular reason where Clyde can overhear them - the whole funeral scenario was of course a trap; they need the two women's memories of the Doctor, after which they will kill them. On the other hand, I did like the way Davies made use of a loose end from the Doctor's visit last year, carefully taking time to explain for viewers who didn't see that episode how Clyde became "infected" with artron energy by touching the TARDIS. This allows the Doctor to finally make his appearance at the end of Part 1, by somehow locking on to Clyde and swapping places with him via a nifty morphing effect.

Rani: "That's the Doctor?"

Jo: "What Doctor? *The* Doctor, my Doctor?"

Sarah: "Well, you know he can change his face."

Jo: "Well I know, but into a baby's?"

The Doctor: "Oi, imagine it from my point of view! Last time I saw you, Jo Grant, you were, what - 21, 22? It's like someone baked you..."

In Part 2, the Doctor soon swaps places with Clyde again, this time taking Sarah and Jo with him to the alien world where he had been left stranded by the Shansheeth after they stole the TARDIS. Now the plot takes a back seat for a while, as a crucial conversation scene between the Doctor, Sarah and Jo takes place. For long-time *Doctor Who* fans like myself, this is the part we were most looking forward to - where Matt Smith faced the challenge of showing his Doctor forging a connection with these two women and having them accept him, despite the totally reversed age difference, as the same man they knew in the past. Of course, the same challenge had previously been faced by David Tennant when his Doctor first encountered Sarah again, but he at least had childhood memories of watching Elisabeth Sladen to help him - indeed, in *School Reunion*, part of the Doctor's delight at seeing Sarah again is so clearly Tennant's own fannish glee. By contrast, Sladen and Manning's stints in *Doctor Who* were over several years before Matt Smith was even born. However, after his brilliant performances over the course of this year, it was no surprise that Smith overcame the challenge easily. After Sarah inquires about his latest regeneration, and whether it hurt ("It always hurts," he curtly replies), Jo picks up on the Doctor's description of Amy and Rory:

Jo: "So you've got a married couple in the TARDIS?"

The Doctor: "Mr. and Mrs. Pond."

Jo: "I only left you because I got married..."

After a moment, she quietly asks, "Did you think I was stupid?" It's a moment strikingly similar to Sarah's pained line when she met the Doctor again in *School Reunion* ("Did I do something wrong?"), and the Doctor immediately drops what he's doing and goes over to listen as she opens up about how she called him a few months into her travels, only to find he had left UNIT and never came back - here Davies makes excellent use of what actually happened in the Classic Series after the Doctor and Jo parted. The combination of Katy Manning's monologue - not bitter, but heartfelt - and Matt Smith's reactions make this a magical moment. We see the Doctor accepting the rebuke, then turning it around and making Jo laugh with a blunt statement of "Oh, but you're an idiot!" before pointing out all the things she's done over the last forty years.

Jo: "So you've been... watching me? All this time?"

The Doctor: "No. Because you're right, I don't look back. I can't." *(beat)* "But the last time I was dying I looked back on all of you, every single one. And I was so proud."

Matt Smith even puts a hint of Jon Pertwee into his "Hello..." as Jo finally accepts that yes, he really is her

Doctor. I would have been happy to listen to them simply conversing for the rest of the episode, but at this point Sarah calls them back to the story. As I noted earlier, Davies is not particularly concerned with complex plotting here (which is something he could often be accused of on *Who*, as well), and the shortcuts are obvious as Sarah's sonic lipstick and the contents of Jo's bag turn out to be exactly what the Doctor needs to get his "space-swapping doodah" working properly so that they can return to Earth. Later, the sonic lipstick will happen to be inconveniently drained at a critical point where Sarah and Jo have to be trapped behind a locked door, and there's even what looks like an odd continuity error where the Doctor tells Sarah early in Part 2 that the Shansheeth took his sonic screwdriver, but later says it's in the TARDIS.

Meanwhile, Clyde, Rani, and Jo's grandson Santiago are pinned down in the base's ventilation tunnels, and Col. Karim - who, unsurprisingly, is revealed as the chief villain - demonstrates some cunning when she uses them to divert the Doctor's attention so that the Shansheeth can capture Sarah and Jo. Karim is a character type that Davies has used before, notably with Lance, Donna's husband in *The Runaway Bride* - she has been seduced by the idea of leaving Earth and going out into the universe. With his typical deft characterisation, Davies gets across a whole backstory with a simple statement, which will probably go over the heads of younger children while inviting adults to imagine any amount of unpleasantness: "The Shansheeth can take me to the stars, because there's nothing left for me here on Earth - not anymore."

The Doctor rescues the kids, in the course of which Davies has a mischievous dig at the supposed limit of twelve regenerations for Time Lords - a piece of lore from the Classic Series which, despite never having been referred to since *Doctor Who* was revived in 2005, has been latched on to by many people and led to much speculation, since we're already up to the eleventh incarnation of the Doctor. Of course the BBC will never end *Doctor Who* just because of a bit of decades-old continuity, and whichever production team is in charge when the Thirteenth Doctor decides to leave will simply come up with a way for him to keep on regenerating. Personally I find it a very uninteresting subject for debate, and I only wish the exchange here ("Is there a limit? I mean, how many times can you change?" "Five hundred and seven!") would end the matter. But, as Davies himself ruefully admitted in a recent interview, it'll never stick - that twelve-regeneration idea seems to be just too well established.

In order to gain access to the TARDIS, the Shansheeth place Sarah and Jo in a machine that give memories physical form, and attempt to force them to produce the TARDIS key. It's a neat reveal that makes sense of the Shansheeth's earlier focus on memories in the funeral scene, and also recalls how important memories have been in *Doctor Who* this year - most notably, of course, when Amy saved the Doctor himself by remembering him back into existence in *The Big Bang*. But perhaps the cleverest aspect of this story is the way Davies has managed to justify the presence of long-running companions like Sarah and Jo rather than simply having them there as a gimmick - the plot reaches a satisfying conclusion as the Doctor yells at them through the locked door to release *all* of their memories of him into the machine. Amid another fan-pleasing blizzard of flashback clips, the machine overloads and self-destructs. And in a final twist, the coffin that the Shansheeth created to fake the Doctor's funeral serves to protect Sarah and Jo from the explosion that destroys the villains. ("The coffin was the trap; the coffin was the solution. That's so neat, I could write a thesis.")

In the aftermath, Jo gets a brief look inside the new TARDIS; there's a lovely moment where she innocently refers to the Doctor "getting into trouble with the Time Lords," and Matt Smith expertly shows the Doctor's discomfort at the accidental reminder of the loss of his people. I also liked the reference back to Sarah's line in Part 1 about how she would know if the Doctor ever died: the

Doctor gravely says, "Between you and me, if that day ever comes... I think the whole universe might just shiver..." - and then gives a "gotcha!" laugh.

After the TARDIS has left, it's time for Jo to depart too. The ending was a little too sentimental for me, with its drawn-out goodbyes and Sarah's somewhat contrived name-dropping of a whole bunch of other former companions of the Doctor. But on the whole, this was a very successful story, making use of *Doctor Who*'s rich heritage without simply being a case of nostalgia for its own sake. Katy Manning presented a very believable version of Jo so many years after we last saw her, and both Elisabeth Sladen and Matt Smith were excellent. All three were given great material to work with by Davies, who ends this little coda to his *Doctor Who* tenure with a line that, while too on-the-nose for *Who* itself, fits perfectly for *The Sarah Jane Adventures*: "Echoes of the Doctor, all over the world. With friends like us, he's never going to die, is he?" Amen to that.

Classic Who DVD Recommendation: The Classic Series of *Doctor Who* didn't do tearjerkers that often, although one notable exception is the final episode of *The Green Death* in 1973, when Jo Grant and the Doctor went their separate ways. *The Green Death* also featured a sentient supercomputer, much like Sarah Jane's Mr. Smith, although the so-called 'BOSS' is of a rather more villainous nature. In addition to this, like *Death of the Doctor*, *The Green Death* is set in Wales, and also features larger than life animals, with giant maggots and a fly, rather than this story's alien vultures.

Kevin's review: I don't tend to watch *The Sarah Jane Adventures* much, despite the fact that it's set in my current neck of the woods (Ealing), as I'm not in its target audience. And, as Steven writes, the plots are not as involving as *Doctor Who* proper. However, from time to time, *The Sarah Jane Adventures* does put on a bit on a show, such as the Tenth Doctor's recent appearance. *Death of the Doctor* goes one further by not only featuring the Eleventh Doctor, but also by reintroducing Jo Grant after a near 40-year absence.

Sarah Jane's palpable disbelief in the news that the Doctor is dead is very well handled, and we can very much understand that, from her perspective, she would instinctively know if he had died. It's interesting to see that Sarah doesn't allow any military on her property, despite the fact that Colonel Karim and her men are from UNIT. Having written that, UNIT were none too helpful during *Enemy of the Bane*, the 2008 *Sarah Jane* adventure that starred the legendary Brigadier Lethbridge-Stewart, so Sarah's reaction is understandable here. The teenagers that assist Sarah Jane in her adventures seemed to have quite matured since 2009's *The Wedding of Sarah Jane Smith*, with Rani in particular prepared to talk sense to Sarah (even though, she is, of course, wrong in her belief in the death of the Doctor).

Russell T Davies has a tendency of rather lazily basing alien creatures on familiar ones from Earth, such as the Rhino-like Judoon, and the feline Sisters of Plenitude. The Shansheeth are clearly based on vultures; however, rather than being carnivorous scavengers, they are intergalactic undertakers. So, they still hover over the dead, but in a nice way. However, Russell T Davies does cleverly make use of the white ring around their necks to create the impression that they are akin to human vicars. Indeed, the holographic Shansheeth that pronounces the Doctor's death is rather sombre and very similar in tone to a vicar.

It's rather surprising to discover that UNIT has a secret bunker beneath Mount Snowdon, as one would have thought that it would have been spotted by the many tourists that visit the National Park. Not only that, but committed environmentalist Jo Jones must be so consumed by her grief for the Doctor that she doesn't really take in her monstrous surroundings. One can only think that UNIT operate an alien perception filter there. The first thing that should really start alarm bells ringing amongst Sarah's friends is that the Shansheeth plan to blast the Doctor's body into space via a vast rocket. If this send off was good enough for James

Doohan, then it's certainly a very fitting end for the Doctor. As long as no one notices this huge rocket blasting off a fair bit of Mount Snowdon in the process. (UNIT must have the most super duper perception filter ever!)

Fortunately enough, Clyde's body had absorbed some artron energy from the TARDIS during *The Wedding of Sarah Jane Smith*, which allows the Doctor to swap places with him via some sort of vortex manipulator type thingy. Clyde's horror as he discovers that he's suddenly developed a white hand is play to great comic effect before the Doctor is able to fully swap places with him. Thus the Eleventh Doctor makes his appearance, and it's not long before he's making deprecating remarks about Jo Grant's decrepit appearance. Despite this insult, and his new countenance, the Doctor's former companions are very happy to accept that he is indeed the Doctor, especially as this means that he is still alive.

I didn't think that Russell T Davies was able to bring out the Eleventh Doctor's usual exuberance here, which is bizarre, as Davies' Tenth Doctor was just as hyperactive. However, it's hard to have too many zany characters on screen, and the focus in this story is mainly on Jo Grant, after her forty-year absence from the official *Doctor Who* canon. The Doctor makes explicit that, during the last time he was "dying", he looked over the lives of all his previous companions, not just the ones that he had encountered in his tenth incarnation. It's probably good here that he doesn't reveal the real reason why he hardly ever goes back to see his companions, as *Amy's Choice* conveyed that he would have been very bored had he done so. Still, Jo Grant's had a more exciting life than most (Sarah Jane later reveals that most of the Doctor's previous companions have subsequently led very virtuous lives).

Like most of the Doctor's enemies, the Shansheeth are very casual about being overheard when discussing their nefarious schemes, and it's not long before we discover that their main aim is to utilise Sarah and Jo's memories to manufacture a new TARDIS key. Which then rewards long time *Doctor Who* fans by providing an opportunity to show clips from the past. However, the Shansheeth's downfall comes about due to their plans being rather too complex. Simple solutions are always the best, and Russell T Davies follows in Steven Moffat's footsteps by providing the basic solution that saves Sarah and Jo's lives when the Shansheeth's machinery explodes. Albeit that the door that the sonicless Doctor has been trying to break down, and which Karim had stated to be impervious to anything but loads of dynamite, is actually as fragile as it had originally looked. In a very nice touch on Davies' part, the Groske comments that it smells like "burnt chicken" when he enters the room, as the Shansheeth have literally been fried. One suspects that the Shansheeth would have been better off just removing the TARDIS key from the Doctor via force when they originally encountered him, rather than devising such an elaborate trap. However, many like the alliance that imprisoned the Doctor within the Pandorica, the Shansheeth are probably aware that violence usually never works when faced with the Doctor.

The Doctor's remark that he has 507 regenerations does come very much out of the blue, and is stated in a such a nonchalant way that it's very hard to take it seriously. However, it's very difficult to get rid of the original 13 regenerations idea, as it was stated far more than once or twice in the original series. For instance, much of the Master's motivation from 1976's *The Deadly Assassin* and beyond was to prolong his life after he'd reached his 13th regeneration. It also contributed a great deal to the plot of *Mawdryn Undead*. Then again, the Blinovitch Limitation Effect also played a big role in this 1983 story, which involved the Doctor trying to prevent the Brigadier's older and younger selves from meeting, as physical contact between them would (and did) result in a catastrophic explosion. However, Amy's able to touch her younger self in *The Big Bang*, and Kazran hugs his younger self in *A Christmas Carol*, with no ill effects. Although the 2 sonics did spark when they touched in *The Big Bang*, probably because this sonic was generated by the TARDIS.

Moreover, the Master did manage to extend his life on several occasions. One can only presume that the Blinovitch Limitation Effect and 13 regenerations were Time Laws set down by the Time Lords, which no longer apply following their demise. After all, the incarnations of most Time Lords last considerably longer than the Doctor's, as the huge majority of them were averse to placing themselves in the same amount of peril that the Doctor usually faces on his adventures. So, it could be that the Time Lords placed an artificial limit on the number of regenerations, as their society would only have stagnated even further if there were too many 10,000-year-olds hanging around.

Colonel Karim, like a great many people in the revived series of *Doctor Who*, seems to have the most incredible wanderlust to see the stars at first hand as to make her completely reckless. Sarah and Jo are mortified when they hear that the Shansheeth's plan is to utilise the TARDIS to prevent heroes being killed on intergalactic battlefields in the first place, rather than merely caring for their bodies after death. As Steven writes, *Death of the Doctor* utilises the recurring theme during this series of *Doctor Who* with regards to the power of memories to bring people back from the dead, let alone objects. However, another running theme is the Doctor's realization that time can be rewritten and unwritten. So, there's very little to divide the Shansheeth's motivations from that of the Doctor in say, *A Christmas Carol*, when he explicitly employs the TARDIS to change a man's history in order to mould his character. The similarity in theme could be coincidental here, but it does very much suggest that the Eleventh Doctor is treading upon some very dangerous ground indeed...

Did You Know? David Bradley, the actor who voices the lead Shansheeth, is best known for portraying Argus Filch in the *Harry Potter* films.

Steven Cooper's reviews (Copyright © Steven Cooper 2010) were originally published on *Slant Magazine*'s *House Next Door* blog, whose editors have kindly granted permission for them to be reprinted within this book.

http://www.slantmagazine.com/house/

http://www.slantmagazine.com

Printed in Great Britain
by Amazon

37191022R00135